PeopleSoft Integration Tools

Stewart S. Miller

McGraw-Hill

New York • San Francisco • Washington, D.C. • Auckland • Bogotá • Caracas
Lisbon • London • Madrid • Mexico City • Milan • Montreal • New Delhi
San Juan • Singapore • Sydney • Tokyo • Toronto

Library of Congress Cataloging-in-Publication Data

Miller, Stewart S.
    PeopleSoft integration tools / Stewart S. Miller.
        p.   cm.
    ISBN 0-07-135477-8
    1. PeopleSoft software.   I. Title.
    QA76.754.M547   1999
    650'.0285'574—dc21   99-42384
                                                          CIP

McGraw-Hill
A Division of The McGraw-Hill Companies

1 2 3 4 5 6 7 8 9 0   AGM/AGM   9 0 4 3 2 1 0 9

ISBN 0-07-135477-8

*The sponsoring editor for this book was Simon Yates and the production
supervisor was Clare Stanley. It was set in Sabon by D&G Limited, LLC.*

Printed and bound by Quebecor/Martinsburg.

This book is dedicated to ALL the members of my family whom I love MOST dearly!

Contents

03   Message Agent   75

Preface

In my experience, implementing your PeopleSoft ERP platform is only the beginning of your software solution. It is important to employ integration tools that automate your business processes by using specific integration tools as well as third-party products into your ERP environment. This book will demonstrate what each PeopleSoft tool does and how to effectively use and gain the most functionality from each one.

I have been actively consulting many organizations and publishing books, articles, and detailed technical reports about ERP solutions for over 10 years in all information technology industry sectors. I have worked extensively with PeopleSoft, SAP, Baan, and J.D. Edwards. In every situation in which I've consulted, there is always the need to integrate systems effectively so that these powerful software systems can perform extensive functionality with respect to workflow applications, database integration, and messaging integration (e-mail, Internet, intranet, extranet, and kiosks).

I've written hundreds of feature articles for all of the major trade magazines, published several books that focus on ERP solutions, and have consulted for major organizations including IBM and Ernst & Young with respect to ERP systems integration.

The most challenging tasks that I've worked on involved adding functionality to an ERP implementation through the use of third-party tools. Combining technologies from different vendors always has its pitfalls, but such integration can greatly extend the boundaries of your current software.

As the Internet has grown, new functionality in commerce, mail, databases, security, and other ERP applications has evolved. Integrating new features into your ERP system and making them work (without conflict) in your selected operating system (usually Unix or Windows NT) has been my specialty. My work with ERP vendors including PeopleSoft will allow me to use this text to help you improve your enterprise resource planning solution by offering you solutions you can use in practice based on my experience and close relationship with PeopleSoft.

It is my desire to make this book a complete reference based on my experience and knowledge that will help you effectively and efficiently learn and use integration tools for your PeopleSoft ERP solution.

Introduction

Few books detail what PeopleSoft is all about. I have been integrally involved in the ERP field for several years. The success of my *Accelerated SAP: Implementation at the Speed of Business* and my *SAP R/3 Certification Exam Guide* led me to believe that many similarities exist between these two ERP platforms. It is important for me to provide my readers and clients with an insight into PeopleSoft directly and examine how several of their PeopleTools and integration tools can benefit you.

This book examines several types of clients who depend on integrating third-party e-mail systems into their primary ERP system. I make it a point to examine the PeopleSoft toolset in the introductory Chapter 1, "Introduction to PeopleSoft," and Chapter 2, "Integration Tool Background," that will ultimately be explained throughout the following chapters. The goal is to primarily give you an overview of PeopleSoft Integration tools and to conclude the text by examining how they fit directly into financials, PeopleSoft HRMS, PeopleSoft Manufacturing, PeopleSoft Distribution, and PeopleSoft for Higher Education.

I follow the introductory material with a detailed discussion of the PeopleTools platform and its toolset. I make it a point to discuss exactly what PeopleTools offers and these integration tools form the cornerstone for creating and maintaining an effective ERP solution. I discuss how this toolset allows several users (system analysts and functional users) to utilize PeopleSoft applications for very specific business needs.

Tools are important. PeopleSoft provides development tools with respect to rapid design and custom modifications. They offer administration and upgrade tools designed to refine implementation, operation, and upgrades for PeopleSoft applications. Finally, they offer reporting and analysis tools for the purpose of accessing, summarizing, and analyzing information.

Integration tools are the focus of this entire text. Everything in this book relates in one way or another to integrating with your system operations. The goal is to design a way in which PeopleTools can automate business processes. Integration tools help you integrate third-party products into your workflow design and create an open network of applications, electronic forms, interactive voice response, and self-service kiosks.

TOOLS!

Every business process depends on a PeopleSoft integration tools. They all work together to produce a more effective communication environment.

The PeopleSoft Message Agent processes messages transmitted to PeopleSoft by external systems including an interactive voice responsive (IVR), email, Internet, intranet, extranet, and kiosks. This also offers an application program Interface (API) that enables third-party systems to integrate with PeopleSoft in real-time.

The EDI Manager tool is used to define the data mappings for an electronic data interchange (EDI). You can also use it as a general data migration tool between PeopleSoft and files or batches of data.

You will find that the Workflow Processor is really a collection of online agents that run and control the workflow in your business processes. When these business processes are defined, agents are created to perform the business process tasks.

In order to move around the system, I discuss how you can correctly use the included PeopleSoft Navigator tools. These tools provide an intuitive graphical browser that displays a graphical map of the business processes they participate in. In addition, these tools allow you to navigate or select application panels by clicking on activities they need to perform.

The heart and soul of any integration tool book really rests in how well you can integrate your database into your ERP environment. In all honesty, what is an ERP solution if you cannot effectively deal with your database from any workstation? Useless really. This is why the meat of this book examines the Database Agent and how it monitors the PeopleSoft database to identify items that need to enter workflow for processing.

PeopleSoft applications can then use Forms API to direct forms to an electronic forms package as part of an integrated workflow solution.

Then your PeopleSoft environment will rely on Worklists, which are ordered lists of work a person or department has to process, whereas the list is sent to the proper person in priority order as defined using the PeopleSoft Business Process Designer.

The latter portion of this book explains how all of the PeopleSoft tools fit together and what you can do to make the most out of your investment into the PeopleSoft solution.

The Workflow Administrator is the actual section of your solution that provides you with the capability to access, monitor, analyze, and control workflow applications.

Finally, you can see specifically how all of the PeopleSoft tools integrate in your specific type of organizational structure. In the last chapters of this book, I explain how PeopleSoft integrates tools with ERP applications, including human resources and financials.

In addition, we also look at the integration of Web interfaces for PeopleSoft applications and determine how they are integrated into their existing toolset.

I end the book by examining how PeopleSoft will continue to design specific tools that not only act as a present-day solution, but also will provide you with a future. You will see how PeopleSoft satisfies both its clients and end-users with an up-to-date solution. Ultimately, you will see what future directions PeopleSoft is taking and what new tools are in development.

I enjoy helping my clients with their ERP solutions. As an active consultant on the cutting edge of this technology, I encourage you to contact me should you require help on a specific project or consulting on your ERP solution.

Thank you and best of luck!

Stewart S. Miller
President/CEO
Executive Information Services
E-Mail: miller@ITMaven.com

Introduction to PeopleSoft

This chapter looks into PeopleSoft and the types of clients who use their ERP solutions. This chapter sets the stage for the PeopleSoft toolset that will ultimately be explained throughout the following chapters. This section delves into an overview of PeopleSoft Financials, PeopleSoft HRMS, PeopleSoft Manufacturing, PeopleSoft Distribution, and PeopleSoft for Higher Education.

This first section of this chapter discusses the PeopleTools platform and its toolset. This section discusses how People-Tools offers the cornerstone for creating and maintaining an effective ERP solution. We discuss how this toolset allows several users (system analysts and functional users) to utilize PeopleSoft applications for specific business needs.

The concluding section of this introductory chapter looks at the following tools:

- Development tools with respect to rapid design and custom modifications.

- Administration and upgrade tools designed to refine implementation, operation, and upgrades for PeopleSoft applications.

- Reporting and analysis tools for the purpose of accessing, summarizing, and analyzing information.

Who Is PeopleSoft?

PeopleSoft was first established in 1987, offering software solutions for global enterprises. PeopleSoft creates, markets, and supports enterprise software solutions that support core business functions that include the following:

- Human resources management

- Project management

- Treasury management

- Performance measurement

- Accounting and control

- Supply-chain management for service and product organizations

They offer industry-specific enterprise solutions for select markets that include

- Communications

- Financial services

- Healthcare

- Manufacturing

- Higher education

- Public sector

- Services

- Retailing

- Transportation

- U.S. Federal Government

- Utilities

PeopleSoft Select is their package solution that includes

- Hardware

- Software

- Services

These elements all fit together to support medium-tier organizations that need to effectively manage their enterprise.

PeopleSoft has several thousand global customers and offers a high level of customer service. The company is growing quickly and supports new areas of ERP implementations. This chapter will focus on how PeopleSoft is concentrating on important implementation issues. PeopleSoft markets a comprehensive suite of software with built-in integration tools. This book can help you make sense of these integration tools and how you can effectively use them with your own PeopleSoft implementation.

Introduction

It is important to know that PeopleSoft offers an enterprise
suite of business applications, but you still need other
applications in order to facilitate your PeopleSoft
implementation. PeopleSoft applications must fit into your
computing environment as well as work with other
applications within an integrated approach.

Integration tools are important because they define
several methods in which you can connect PeopleSoft
applications and third-party applications together. They
give you a reference for application programming interfaces
(APIs) available from PeopleSoft.

Getting the Right Integration Tools for Your Needs

The average enterprise requires software that can meet
your needs and can adapt to your requirements as times
change. This is not always easy, as organizations go
through several cycles of development. You must deal with
integrating several different kinds of data into your
enterprise and some software solutions are too inflexible
to keep up with your changing needs.

The main idea behind PeopleSoft integration tools is to
provide a solution that will provide simple and easy access
to your mission-critical business information. It has been
created to support your operations regardless of the
changes your organization goes through and to continually
provide you with a flexible platform.

PeopleSoft created "PeopleTools" in order to meet your
changing business needs. These tools can be combined with
your PeopleSoft application and have been created
specifically to give you a simple and easy-to-use toolset
that would permit your system to change with your
organizational requirements. This would effectively give
you greater control over your entire business process.

The goal here is to tie together enterprise-application functionality within the body of your PeopleTools so that you can effectively cope with new and emerging technologies. PeopleSoft strives to give you a long-term solution that will provide the flexibility your enterprise needs that will result in an increase in your performance, productivity, and financial net worth. PeopleSoft also intends that their application functionality and technology provide a flexible integration solution. It has been designed so that its solutions will be specifically engineered to the unique needs of your organization. Its objective is to increase efficiency and enhance customer response.

PeopleSoft's flexibility is best demonstrated through their enterprise-wide solutions that satisfy ever-changing business requirements. PeopleSoft offers integrated and modular systems for several functions, including the following:

- Materials management

- Accounting applications

- Distribution

All these functions combine to support your business operations. In addition, PeopleSoft provides industry-specific solutions if you are in a select market.

PeopleTools

This is the heart and soul of this book. This section was created specifically to discuss how PeopleTools offers an effective integration to your enterprise's resource planning deployment.

PeopleTools is included with all the PeopleSoft applications. It enables you to adapt your system quickly to new business requirements. PeopleTools gives you the ability to provide support for several items including

- Multiple languages

- Currencies

- Country requirements

- Centralizing/decentralizing business functions in a
  geographically diversified environment

PeopleSoft is committed to providing a computing
solution that will deliver a great deal of performance and
can support all of your data-intensive processing needs.
PeopleTools has been created specifically to give you three-
tier transaction processing support for an enhanced
performance on wide area networks.

In most three-tier client server environments, the
majority of the application process occurs on the
application server, thereby decreasing your transaction
time. The idea here is that PeopleSoft can support several
concurrent users while it gives you a very powerful load-
balancing and fail-over capability so that you can continue
all of your business operations.

It is also possible for you to deploy your three-tier client
server environment using Windows or a convenient World
Wide Web (WWW) browser. In addition, there is a support
provider for the classic two-tier processing environments
for any PeopleSoft customer who uses local area networks.
This gives you a decent choice between environment and
solution profiles to fit your needs.

Improving Worker Efficiency

PeopleSoft helps you keep your business running as
effectively as possible by providing your users with an
information technology that allows them to work more
efficiently. This information technology includes powerful
reporting capabilities so that you can both extract and
analyze business information and make more effective
decisions.

PeopleTools enables you to add a decent level of
automation to your reporting and analysis tools, which will

provide your users with instantaneous access to database information. In addition, it also acts to integrate with the following productivity tools:

- Word processors

- Spreadsheets

- E-mail

- Fax systems

PeopleTools also adds support for online analytical processing (OLAP). This allows your users to cope with complex data. They can view or manipulate information multi-dimensionally.

PeopleSoft also offers Web-based applications that enhance your information and functionality for a variety of internal and external users. This gives your personnel the ability to execute self-service administrative functions that are pertinent for individual requirements in an efficient manner.

PeopleTools also succeeds in refining your implementation process and project management strategies. It provides you with a means of implementing your system in a small amount of time and by using a segmented method. PeopleSoft helps you kill any inefficient processes and performs your implementation in various stages. The benefit here is that you need not reengineer your entire organizational complexity at one moment. In effect, PeopleTools gives you a flexible and customizable system that can be easily migrated into your individual hardware and software platform. It results in curtailing expensive problems and reducing the learning curve for your personnel.

PeopleTools Defined

PeopleTools offers a great deal of features and functions. This is the essential foundation for PeopleSoft's technology.

It is a simple GUI toolset that allows for several concurrent users to be able to create, deploy, and support both a flexible and comprehensive business solution.

PeopleTools provides a great deal of business solution functionality. It provides its customers with specialized applications that satisfy their individual business requirements. Inside PeopleTools is the integrated development environment of the Application Designer. This tool can make the application development process simpler. The Application Designer provides a project view of your development actions. It gives you a detailed object inventory that comprises the following application items:

- Records

- Panels

- Tables

- Fields

- Menus

The Application Designer allows your users to create and edit all of the same object types by using the same simplified tools. In addition, you can make your applications more current very rapidly through the Application Designer's upgrade functions. In addition, it benefits from the simple Windows-type interface, because it offers a simple interactive environment and allows the users to customize the environment more efficiently.

Your applications can be invented, opened, and upgraded through the Application Designer. This tool allows you to create and edit several elements from your application. This effectively allows you to connect them together through your development project. You can also create your entire application through one single tool. You do not need to be familiar with programming or code to accomplish your task. You also have the option of using

PeopleCode if you need to program some very specific or complex business rules in your environment. PeopleCode is an integral component of the Application Designer.

Breaking Down the Application

You can further examine your application elements you created with the Application Designer. These components help you know your working environment better.

Records are the design elements that help you resolve your application data table structure. You can also determine what edit checks will be executed on your table data.

Fields are defined and are seen throughout several record definitions. In addition, the Application Designer sees these fields as individual reusable objects.

Panels are the same as data entry forms. They offer a familiar user interface that is used for both capturing and displaying data. Whenever you create a panel definition, you can designate exactly how the panel will appear and how the system will validate the information that users input into the system. The Application Designer allows you to rapidly design and test panels online at any time.

Panel groups and grouped sets of panels either depict business transactions or logical work units. Note that the Application Designer sees these panel groups as individual reusable objects that can be simply added to menus.

When you establish menu definitions, you are effectively designating the functional windows and menus that refine your system operations, allowing users to move from one panel group to another.

Business processes are used when the Application Designer allows you to establish graphical maps that assist you in navigating users to a panel for completing a transaction. Maps are useful visual representations that give the user an idea of what steps are involved, providing users with a definite method of moving through panels in a logical manner. In addition, business process definitions allow you to create a workflow in your PeopleSoft applications by allowing you to define rules, roles, and routings.

Application Designer

The Application Designer offers one centralized integrated development environment. This product allows you to simply create and customize applications that were meant to be used for your business processes. The Application Designer is integrated into PeopleSoft's upgrade functionality and allows you to get applications into production. It also exists within the Windows-type Explorer so you can organize your object definitions into your project workspace:

• Business applications

• Business processes

• Fields

• Menus

• Panels

• Records

Every object-type definition will be displayed in its window with the project workspace through multiple document interfaces.

Administration and Upgrade Tools

PeopleSoft gives you several tools that assist you in managing your workstation and your application information.

Development tools simplify the process of building and customizing applications. Both the administration and upgrade tools refine maintaining and upgrading your PeopleSoft applications. You can update your application function as well as large data sets. In addition, these tools make workstation installation, mass updates, and information archiving and migrating to different database platforms simpler.

It doesn't matter if you are upgrading to a new PeopleSoft product or making a transition to provide new test system functionality. The Application Designer enables you to upgrade tasks easier. In addition, the security tools make certain you have control over user access to specific data and applications.

The Application Designer refines the merging of your database objects (records, panels, and PeopleCode) between database products. The intricacies of the Application Designer development environment incorporate the capability to change control so you can track, document, and get a handle of any customization changes.

PeopleSoft Tools

PeopleSoft's Data Mover provides you with a means of transporting your data from one operating system and database platform to another. It provides you with a good way of archiving databases, records, and an easy way of executing SQL statements within any database.

The Security Administrator provides sign-on and functionality security. This is one of the two security tools that deals with information access in your database. Object security allows you to maintain control over who can access and update the PeopleTools objects that define your application.

The Import Manager allows you to import data one row at a time. You can then validate your field values against your field edits as well as the PeopleCode designated in your application.

The Process Scheduler allows your application users to execute online or background processes from the client workstation. These functions will operate on either the server or the local workstation. You can also schedule processes to operate in the background without any user intervention.

The Configuration Manager allows you to access your PeopleSoft configuration information. The benefit is that you can accomplish this task by using the standard type of Windows GUI.

Reporting and Analysis Tools

PeopleSoft gives you productivity tools that allow you to support all of your query and reporting demands. This gives you an increase in information access so that you can be better prepared to make more effective decisions and gain more from your PeopleSoft implementation.

These reporting options allow your application users to extract information whenever it is needed. You can also customize output regardless of whether you export information from your database or import into Microsoft Excel. You can compare data online or create any business document you need.

The Tree Manager will give you a GUI interface so that you can present and view information on a hierarchical menu. PeopleSoft provides you with a dating feature that will allow you to both track and maintain data-dependent information. In addition to production reporting, OLAP, with its integration tools, allows you to analyze your data through an interactive method.

The Cube Manager allows your users to define their own individual OLAP rules though the PeopleSoft metadata components. These reporting and analysis tools allow your users to enhance their decision-making processes. The Cube Manager also provides an important connection from your PeopleSoft data to your OLAP tools. These tools may include Cognos PowerPlay and Hyperion Essbase. The Cube manager will allow your users to designate specific OLAP rules through the PeopleSoft metadata components.

PS/nVision allows you to acquire data from your database and import the information into your Excel spreadsheet. The benefit is that the data is not just raw data but is summarized into neat packets that can be analyzed for specific information.

When you work with Microsoft Excel, you can make a report layout that designates what kinds of data you need to acquire as well as the format of the report you need. In addition, you can create a layout library and choose whatever format you need. PS/nVision is an important tool for creating business reports as it allows you to import current information straight from your database into your spreadsheet. The advantage is that you can use standard MS Excel commands to format and analyze in great detail.

The Tree Manager provides an excellent means of examining your business tree structure through a graphic layout that you can expand, collapse, and analyze into whatever level of detail you require. These types of trees are used a great deal within reporting tools that include PS/nVision (described above) and PeopleSoft's Code Manager.

The PeopleSoft Query assists you in both creating and executing database queries. The benefit, however, is that you need not know how to write complex SQL statements to achieve this goal. The program takes care of it for you. This is just another method that details how PeopleSoft can integrate functionality without complexity.

The Open Query API gives you the ability to access PeopleSoft data by permitting users to run queries that are created with PeopleSoft Query via the Microsoft ODBC. This is advantageous because you can use the familiar Microsoft tools to achieve your objectives.

Integration Tools

This section describes how PeopleSoft's integration tools can assist you. These tools work to support your workflow and can accommodate external systems. In many cases, you will want to automate your business processes, but this is often difficult because they are beyond the reach of most of your PeopleSoft applications. Integration tools assist you in integrating third-party products into your workflow design. You can also create an open network that includes:

- Applications

- Electronic forms

- Interactive voice response

- Self-service kiosks

All of these features combine to allow you to acquire important information, but the benefit is that you need not include PeopleSoft applications on every user's workstation. Each user has the ability to send an address change across your network without direct access to your mission-critical PeopleSoft application.

You can support your electronic data interchange with PeopleSoft because it enables you to exchange electronic transactions with other organizations, which leads to a more paperless office. In short, these interfaces function together as one entity to give you the ability to support your users and your systems and to refine any electronic commerce or ERP applications.

Integration Tools Defined

The Message Agent is a very important integration tool because it processes messages that are transmitted from external applications into your PeopleSoft deployment. This information will end up in one of the following areas:

- E-mail

- Interactive voice response systems

- Kiosks

- Workflow systems

- Internet

Each of these external applications has the power to reuse your business logic that is actually integrated into your PeopleSoft panel groups.

The Workflow Administrator gives you some important tools for maintaining your workflow while you simultaneously define and assign files. You can establish the following items in this program:

- Assign roles

- Set workflow defaults

- Schedule agents

- Monitor system workflow

The Forms API allows your applications to move forms to your electronic forms package. This is all part of your integrated workflow solution and allows you to maintain a high degree of integration throughout your PeopleSoft PeopleTools environment.

The EDI Manager allows you to use the tools you require to manage your e-commerce transactions with your trading partners. It helps you designate the EDI agent data mappings that you need to use to transfer data from transaction files and tables into your database.

PeopleTools Applications

In order to enhance worker productivity, PeopleSoft offers self-service applications that provide your personnel with easy information access and a broad range of functionality that specially meets their needs. These self-service applications help companies save money while extending functionality through

your enterprise using inexpensive Internet connections. This
type of software has an easy-to-use interactive interface created
specifically to work with the PeopleSoft Web client. These
types of applications allow access to everyone including

- Customers

- Suppliers

- Occasional users

- Employees

All of these people can execute self-service administrative functions. In addition, these applications are
connected to PeopleSoft's other products that include

- Human resources management

- Treasury management

- Performance measurement

- Accounting and control

- Supply-chain planning

These tasks can be created using the PeopleTools in
combination with standard Windows client applications.
This is beneficial because all the edits, business logic, and
workflow processes are centrally offered. Functionality is
not wasted on the use of more than one tool for one job.

These self-service applications have been created with
the purpose of using the PeopleSoft Web client. This client
is actually a collection of Java applets that can be easily
downloaded at any time, so they can be integrated with
your Web browser. This complete-Java platform has an
open architecture and offers a simple administration for
providing your enterprise solution to several people within
your organization. It is not necessary to install an
application on each and every person's workstation since
all functionality is accessed through the client browser.

The Web client is made to connect users with job-specific functionality and provides each user with pertinent information. This client can support self-service applications, and the Web Client has a worklist and query interface to assist occasional users navigate through business processes and to enhance information access.

All the information and data sent between the Web client and the application server observes stringent security measures. All the data is encrypted so that the Web client can benefit from PeopleTools without fear of being intercepted as it travels across your network.

Self-service applications can be implemented throughout the Internet through your existing corporate intranet and can include the following benefits:

- Business rules

- Workflow logic

- Security features

The PeopleSoft Web client was created specifically to interface with your current corporate intranet and it passes on the same intuitive feel of your corporate computer environment. It provides seamless integration with your system so you can continue doing work in a familiar environment.

Transaction Processing

PeopleSoft gives you complete support for three-tier transaction processing. This is where most of your application logic will run on your application server instead of your client. The application server was created specifically to ease the client processing needs away from processing work-intensive SQL transactions and more towards complex business rules. The result would decrease congestion on your local area network and increase performance across your wide area network.

This type of three-tier environment allows you to gain scalability to deal with high volumes of concurrent users as you support a consistent level of performance through your business operations.

PeopleSoft also supports two-tier architecture and enables you to configure a client to connect to either a two- or three-tier environment. This permits your users to choose a specific connection that best meets their needs.

Since PeopleSoft applications can be deployed on Windows and Web clients, you have a more intuitive environment with enhanced flexibility for providing functionality to your personnel. You will note that transactions are created with the same types of tools and will allow you to reuse business logic and databases designed with various client types. You can integrate this information in various methods to assist you in finding the best solution for your needs.

OLAP

It is important for your users to quickly receive and analyze information and, as a professional, you need information to make decisions quickly. OLAP also gives you the means to interactively analyze your data online. PeopleSoft integrates OLAP tools that includes Cognos PowerPlay and Hyperion Essbase. These tools allow you to get multi-dimensional data that is recorded in geographically diverse locations. The Cube Manager (described above) helps you define data and place acquired information in an OLAP cube. This enables users to quickly look at information from various angles, test conclusions, and determine what would happen if certain situations were to occur. You can then compare any alternative plans and find out which is best for you.

Multi-dimensional information is given to you in simple document formats so you can react quickly to any threats from your competition and can determine if any problems are causing any inefficiencies in your organization. In essence, you are inserting intelligence into your business operations.

Workflow

When you make integrated workflow part of your enterprise, you will experience a combination of information, applications, and users. PeopleTools is important in helping you define your workflow abilities. When you know what your abilities are, you can refine your business processes and determine the exact level of information you need to pass on to your coworkers at the best time.

Workflow helps increase your existing computer systems' efficiency. You can bring several elements of information together and create new avenues of opportunity that will help improve your business processes. It also works to enhance your range of tasks and can add automation to your system, which can assist you in managing your operations with database agents. These agents can tell you if specific conditions warrant immediate action in various business processes.

You can create specific workflow solutions that will meet your needs and satisfy the way you do business. You can use PeopleSoft's Application Designer and Navigator to help you accomplish these goals. These tools will assist you in the following methods:

- Automation

- Streamlining your business processes

- Navigating through business processes

- Controlling the flow of information across your network

PeopleSoft's navigator comes in handy when you require an easy-to-read graphical map of your workflow processes.

You can provide a simple method of displaying a menu and a means of navigating your PeopleSoft system. You need only click on a highlighted icon that depicts the task that must be completed. You are then guided through business processes and the activities that you need to execute. This form of navigation allows you to move through the system and is useful for any level user.

Open Architectures

PeopleSoft also makes it possible for you to use software from different sources. The idea is to eliminate conflicts and function correctly on several different

- Hardware products

- Operating systems

- Database platforms

These platforms all work together to increase the life of your system, while PeopleTools allows you to move between environments seamlessly. This means that you can scale up your hardware, switch database platforms, and make all your applications function in a familiar manner.

PeopleSoft Products

PeopleSoft builds important products that will help you achieve your ERP goal. PeopleSoft is very good at listening to their customers, determining your needs, and creating products that will satisfy your business requirements. They create their products with the capability of adapting to your needs. Their applications are industry-specific and they offer a high level of performance so you can reduce your costs and create an efficient computing environment.

PeopleSoft supports major alliances across the following formats:

- Hardware

- Database

- Service

- Software

These alliances are important in establishing PeopleSoft solutions and work to provide you with products and services that will assist your specific industry applications.

PeopleSoft provides you with business management solutions that create the cornerstone of your core business functionality for your geographically diversified enterprise. This helps you determine how you can achieve the best business management solution for the following entities:

- Human resources management

- Accounting and control

- Treasury management

- Performance management

- Project management

You can then move on to building and enhancing your supply chain. PeopleSoft provides you with integration tools that specifically help you manage your world-wide resources for both the supply and demand of your enterprise's products and services.

You can also create the next evolution of your enterprise platform by creating valuable industry solutions. In this phase, you create important elements designed for your specific industry that include

- Applications

- Services

- Support

You can then institute these factors into the following industry sectors that either you or your trading partners need to deal with:

- Financial services

- Manufacturing

- Communications

- Transportation

- Utilities

- Healthcare

- Service industries

- Retail

- Higher education

- U.S. Federal Government

- Public sector

Once you have a firm base, you can then institute industry functionality. These functions provide you with specialized processes and functions that are designed specifically for your individual business needs. This level of intricacy is integrated into your own industry-specific applications.

Finally, all of these products culminate in a foundation that strengthens the efficiency of your organization. This foundation relies heavily on PeopleTools, PeopleSoft's application development toolset that allows you to refine your solutions to satisfy your own individual enterprise business requirements. It can help you create applications and the business functionality meant for your organization alone. There is no cut-and-paste operation; that is why integrating PeopleSoft into the specifics of your organization is so important. You need a solution that is ultimately designed for your needs alone.

What Makes PeopleSoft So Special?

PeopleSoft is working to maintain a good reputation for all its customers. They are trying to create a long-term relationship in which customers keep coming back for the life of their business. They try to stay current and provide you with a high level of support that will maintain your business operations and help you through any difficulties you might have with their software implementation. They are also trying to create a high degree of quality within their products and provide an exceptional level of customer service.

PeopleSoft provides the following elements that complement and enhance your solution. Examine each of these carefully to determine how integrating the PeopleSoft solution within your organization is not only helpful, but advantageous to your ERP needs.

PeopleSoft Professional Services

PeopleSoft's professional services provide you with a high level of technical support for your complete software solution. They work with you from day one to include

- Sales process assistance

- Implementation

- Integration

- Upgrades

The professional services unit gives you fast feedback regarding product development and how they can best support your implementation providers. This unit also provides you with their best practice models and Web-based information for busy professionals, who do not always have the time to sit in class and learn the newest specifics about the PeopleSoft products. They provide several focus groups as well as constant support for new product developments in trade shows and industry conferences.

Alliance Partners

PeopleSoft strives to form alliances with implementation partners that include ranges of services that satisfy small to large domestic and international consulting organizations. These services offer additional help whenever your project team needs a boost to solve a specific problem.

Account Manager

PeopleSoft assigns you an account manager as one central contact point. This person can specialize in your implementation guidance and can also function as a go-between for you and PeopleSoft.

Education Services

PeopleSoft provides an education service that provides your project team, executives, and users with specialized training that makes certain your software solution is refined and returning your investment.

Global Support

Global support is an important PeopleSoft element because it provides you with dedicated help to solve daily problems with your PeopleSoft implementation. They provide support via telephone and the Internet to satisfy your needs.

PeopleSoft strives to maintain a strong connection with their customers. They offer a self-service Web site that offers 24-hour documentation assistance so you can update and troubleshoot your problems. The site provides product support, Usenet-type newsgroups for users to relay problems and solutions, and other help documents. This site also allows people to register for training seminars as well as access any other pertinent information they need to optimize their implementation.

PeopleSoft also provides customer relations that offer

- Support

- Satisfaction surveys

- Annual conferences

- International customer advisory board

- Regional user groups

- Special interest groups

Conclusion

Now that we have an idea as to what PeopleSoft tools are all about, we can use the information to start delving into the background of each tool. In the following chapters, we'll present you with an overview of what these tools are about and how they can fit into your organization. Knowing what PeopleTools is all about is the best prerequisite to understanding individual tools and learning how they can best meet your corporate and business needs.

02

Integration Tool Background

This chapter covers integration tools and how they can help you integrate third-party products into your workflow design. Using these tools gives you the ability to create an open network of applications, electronic forms, interactive voice responses, and self-service kiosks.

Process Scheduler

PeopleSoft's Process Scheduler is essentially one central tool that permits access to the following people:

- System administrators

- Application developers

- Application users

  These people can manage batch processes including

- Creating jobs (process groups)

- Scheduling processes

- Scheduling process requests to function on a given date during schedules that best meet your business requirements

- Submitting jobs to execute several processes as well as running subsequent processes that are created as a result of former jobs

PeopleSoft's Process Scheduler supports your application environment. In combination with your applications, the Process Scheduler has specific processes that include

- Programs

- Batch programs

- Reports

You can perform each of these processes as background tasks on your online system. You can execute reports or use benefit enrollment forms as examples of what you can do independently of your application environment.

You can essentially refine your business processes because you are benefiting from a distributed computing environment. In essence, you can schedule performance jobs on your server during the time that your online system is being used by your users. In addition, you can schedule locally run processes on your client workstation or on a remote client database server. The benefit is that you need not exit from your system.

When your schedule processes start, the Process Scheduler permits you to manage all of your batch processes centrally. This means you are running programs from the place where reports are printed and where you can issue command-line parameters to any programs with which the Process Scheduler works.

Benefits

The Process Scheduler can improve your system efficiency because data-intensive tasks operate close to the data run on the server. Any non-data-intensive task can be run on the client workstation or even on a remote server.

You will experience very few costs regarding administration. Note that server-based user accounts are not needed. In addition, users need not input other high-level passwords just to run specific processes.

Your user productivity is greatly increased because whenever a process is successfully completed, users have the ability to transfer to specific application panels directly from the Process Scheduler's monitoring utility. Workstations are also included so that users can perform other tasks as the process operates in the background on the server. They can execute tasks on the client and view output from the Process Monitor. In addition, users have the benefit of not needing to know the intricacies of running a given process.

Components

The PeopleSoft Process Scheduler is an important tool and it isn't a one-time-use product. This tool can work with all your system's elements as well as several user access types. This means that the Process Scheduler is made up of several elements that function together in the background processes. The Process Scheduler interacts with PeopleTools, request dialogs, the Process Monitor, and the Server Agent.

Process Monitor

The Process Monitor is a central utility that allows you to monitor the process requests that you send to it. It displays several logged requests that are waiting in the queue to be processed on the server or the client. However, your security authorization dictates whether you can obtain more detailed information on process requests and end-update requests manually if the need arises.

Should you need to check into a job designation, you can either cancel or hold a request that is waiting in the queue. Then you can put these requests back in the queue after you've put them on hold. This means that whenever a process is completed, the Process Monitor will explain how many tasks it has completed so you can determine its output and acquire any information that is relevant to your business objectives.

Server Agent

The Server Agent polls the Process Request table whenever process requests are sent by the client workstation to appear in your queue once you have sent them. This means that the Server Agent is itself a process that executes on the database server or on the application server.

Whenever it sees process requests in the Process Request table, the Server Agent sends requests to run as background processes in the necessary location and in the time you need to set in your process definition.

The Process Scheduler Server Agent must be started and stopped manually through the server administrator. This means that even when the program is operational it does not mean it is running. You can cut down on system resource usage when the Process Scheduler Server Agent enters sleep mode. You can then set the Server Agent to wake up and poll for any inbound process requests you need to run.

End User

When you are setting up an integration between your PeopleSoft applications and your users, you must use the Process Scheduler from the online system and your applications to execute background processes on the workstation or the remote server. The goal is to demonstrate how necessary your workstation environment is for transmitting process requests, using process requests effectively, and using the Process Monitor. Note that any batch applications need to be configured to work in your environment correctly before you can even use the Process Scheduler. This means that if components are not correctly set up on your sites and file server, then your local workstation will not function correctly when it is called by the Process Scheduler to run.

Whenever you learn about the integration of the Process Scheduler into your Windows 98 or Windows NT environment, you must remember that the Process Scheduler uses values established in the Configuration Manager to locate information it requires to execute several types of batch requests. The Workstation Administrator runs the Client Setup program and establishes a specific level of information for your ERP environment. Should you need to verify or modify the Process Scheduler settings or configuration, you can use the Configuration Manager to support or establish PeopleSoft registry settings in your workstation environment.

When you install PeopleSoft, the Client Setup program that executes on each workstation is responsible for running your applications. The Client Setup will correctly configure your workstation for use with the Process

Scheduler. This means you can use other programs that include Microsoft Word.

The Process Scheduler will run your complete requests on these other third-party programs. However, if you don't think your workstation is correctly configured to run the Process Scheduler, you will need to check to see if your application environment is set up to use the Configuration Manager the right way. You may need to have your system manger change the settings or verify with a consultant that this program is integrated efficiently with your system.

The Process Monitor is an important tool that will examine the operations of schedule processes operating on your system. This tool allows you to look at all of the processes to determine their status in the queue and define how processes will be working.

The Process Monitor can examine the status of your process requests. It has the power to kill any process requests that have been started or are currently in operation. You may choose to hold process requests that have already been placed in the queue as well as any process requests that you have taken out of the queue and have placed on hold. You can choose to erase any complete process requests from the queue or can display output for any processes that the client runs. Finally, you can transfer information from a completed process request to a specific panel you are working on.

Once these processes are transmitted into your system, you must start the Process Monitor to determine if the current processes are in operation. You can learn to filter Process Request views by using the Qualify Process List. This parameter allows you to only display processes that have specific elements. This means that you can curtail the number of rows you scan in a your Process Request view. You can filter these elements by using the Operator ID. This allows you to view only the processes sent by a given Operator ID. This means you can see your own Operator ID and then you can view any processes you are allowed to see.

You can use the server to look at processes that are queued on a specific process server. You can use the Process Class to view processes or select the Run Status to choose to view criteria by a status of successful completion or early error termination.

Process Detail Parameters

You will have to deal with some very specific parameters when working with the Process Scheduler. This means you have to be familiar with several different elements to speed up your understanding of this intricate yet powerful platform.

When viewing parameters, the Operator section will allow you to see the Operator ID that is used when you make a request, instance, operating system, database type, or server name that you can display.

Data and Time Stamps allow you to see requests that are submitted and are chosen to be run through the Run Control dialog sections. You will note that it will show you the actual processes, when they begin, and when they end. Should your request fail when it starts, these begin and end times won't even show.

The request parameter determines exactly when the request first appears on a given table. The run parameter determines when a user chooses the File and Run application options. The begin time will display the date and time that this request was first chosen and run.

When dealing with server requests, there is often a large time delay between the Request and Begin settings because the Process Scheduler Server Agent may be in sleep mode or busy with other processing functions.

Finally, the End parameter determines exactly when a process status is updated. This means, hopefully, you will have a successful update showing that your process has achieved its outlined objective.

One important problem may result during this procedure. Whenever you send in a server request, you must make certain that the internal client clock is set to the same time as that in the server. If not, you may see problems that cause erroneous data in the Process Monitor reports from your system.

The Update Process relies explicitly on your operator authorizations as well as the request status. This means that the update process is only available to you if your operator ID is permitted to update that request. However, if the section is disabled, you may not be able to modify your current status. If you are authorized, however, you will be able to deal with hold, queue, cancel, delete, and restart requests.

Run Parameter

The run parameter can display the following items:

- Run location

- Control ID

- Return Code

This means that all requests have to return a specific code value that started at 0 when the request was executed. This means that whenever the process starts to run, return codes are established by the run process through the application programming interfaces (API) given for each type of process.

When you deal with all types of processes that are completed correctly, you will expect the return codes to be 0; however, you may have processes that update the return code value when there have not actually been any processing errors. When you get a value other than 0, this may mean that the message number for a given message or other value will determine why the process has failed or caused a problem.

Request Parameters

You will find that the request parameters section will give you more information regarding your process parameters.

The process section will give you the same type of information regarding processes, while the parameters give you information about the command line, working directory, and your parameter lists. This means that your runtime definition settings are displayed for both the client and server requests. This information can help you resolve any configuration problems by determining which values are incorrect within the configuration manger.

Run Recurrence

At any time when you send a process request or a job using the Run location of the server, you can determine a run recurrent value. Should you send a process request, you will have to choose "once" as the Run Recurrence so that the process requests and jobs you operate regularly (such as payroll inventory) will run correctly. When dealing with these types of regular process requests or jobs, you will need to establish a Run Recurrence that will illustrate the needs of your systems and your users. This means that if you run your accounting program every month, you will need to set the Run Recurrence to match your needs every time that process is run.

The run recurrent will make certain that your important process requests and your job are run regularly and will always run automatically in the background without user intervention. This prevents any chance of someone forgettting to submit a process request or making an incorrect process request. Therefore, when you determine a Run Recurrence, the process request must continue to function until you stop it yourself.

End users will not have to alter any Run Recurrences on a job or process request. In most cases, your application developers will be the only ones who will need to determine when a Run Recurrence will occur. As a result, you will need to choose your existing run recurrent and send your process request when you need to.

Defining Process Scheduler Information

You cannot start any process running in the Process Scheduler until you have designated some very important preliminary information. The Process Scheduler must have certain information before it can execute any independent processes. The Process Scheduler is provided with a complete set of

- Process definitions

- Process-type definitions and server definitions

These elements are given for all processes provided with each of your PeopleSoft applications.

A set of job definitions is given for some of the six types of jobs. However, you may need to customize various table definitions to meet your individual needs. These processes may not be set up to run instantly so you may have to refine these definitions to meet your particular business objectives. As a result, you may have to map out process types you wish to schedule and then collect the parameter information on each process you need to run prior to beginning your work.

The Process Scheduler employs process types and process definitions to effectively designate the types of processes you would normally run. All of the process definitions are collected through a given process type. This means that most reports are defined within the PeopleSoft system as a given report process type that has a specific global setting that applies to all of the process definitions under that given type. When dealing with each process type, you must designate a specific process definition that you will need to execute on a normal or sporadic time frame.

It is also possible to define specific servers for which you need to execute specific process types or to use a base server definition that PeopleSoft provides with the Process

Scheduler. It is important to determine which processes you will need to schedule and put them in a logical grouping. This grouping will provide you with greater server resources and make user procedures much simpler. This means you may wish to create new process types and group your reports with all of the same types of process-type parameters. This allows them to be executed on a dedicated report server. In addition, all of these options can be accessed via the Process Scheduler definition. This means that either you or your system administrator will have to create Process Scheduler definitions only once.

You must also take into account several other important ideas when you integrate the Process Scheduler into your applications, such as API support for Crystal or COBOL. This means you will need to know exactly which types of PeopleCode exists so you can effectively program specific information into the Process Scheduler. The idea is to utilize your application development information that can be used with PeopleTools and integrate the Process Scheduler into your applications, as well as use its interface effectively in your business operations.

Process-Type Information

It is important for you to become familiar with process-type definitions so that you can designate specific items throughout your PeopleSoft implementation, such as the following:

- Parameters list

- Command line

- Working directory

- PeopleSoft parameters

The benefit of the Process Scheduler is that it has the capability to support various operating systems and database environments. Unfortunately, several operating systems and database environment combinations do not support every single process type. This means that process types of the Database Agent are only supported on the Windows-type operating systems.

It is important to note that each definition type is founded on a generic process type of definition. This means that each process definition is based on a specific process type of definition. To further illustrate this concept, there are four primary generic process types:

1. SQR reports, processes, and upgrade reports

2. COBOL

3. Crystal (Online/Report)

4 Microsoft Word for Windows

Other elements include the Message Agent API, Database Agent, nVision report books, and Visio.

Parameter Options

Specific fields each offer several flexible options for defining specific processes that include the following:

- Parameter list

- Command line

- Working directory

Each of the associated field values can incorporate client and server environment strings, predefined meta-strings, and inline bind variables. The predefined meta-strings are used to offer runtime values for definition variables. They also support data management that includes passwords that are not recorded within the database. Passwords, for example, are encrypted for privacy. These passwords are decrypted by the Process Server Agent and can send that information to the application so that the user can sign on to server operations or the database.

Specific client variable strings are part of one single set of percent signs (such as %TEMP%). Also, some server variable strings need to be placed within a set of double percent signs, such as %%TEMP%%. During runtime operations, the Process Scheduler must first examine all of the double percent variables to see if they depict a predefined meta-string value. Since the meta-string values are predefined, they can resolve variable information upon startup of each request.

Should variables not be defined within meta-strings, then the Process Scheduler will try to resolve all the Windows variables. It does this by first examining the values determined by the Process Scheduler information in the Configuration Manager. When dealing with the server, if you see a variable that is not defined as a meta-string, then the Process Scheduler attempts to acquire the value from the configuration file or the server.

When you deal with meta-strings that are within a set of double percent signs, you will realize that when the Process Scheduler processes a request and comes across a string inside the double percent signs, it will first try to compare the variable name to an internal list of its predefined meta-strings. Should that variable name not be found, then it automatically assigns it a name from a server environment.

Restart Enabled

Some options are very useful, but are restricted in functionality. One such example is the restart-enabled option that is useful for only the application engine processes. In order to enable a process request to be restarted from the Process Monitor, you must use the Restart Enabler option in the process-type definition.

While this option is only permitted for the Application Engineer process types that work with a status of "unsuccessful," you will find that there are also restrictions about its capability to restart a process pertaining to the user's security profile. Restart is only permissible when the operator of the "operator class" can update a request to cancel or delete at that moment. The parameters list of failed requests must be altered to append the current process instance before you can designate a new instance and resend the request to the queue.

After Process Requests

Once you have sent your process request, you will need to use the Process Monitor to see the status of submitted requests. The Process Monitor shows you how a process has been completed correctly and can assist you in proceeding directly from the Process Monitor to the correct panel within your PeopleSoft application. In this way, you can see the completed process results.

You can allow your users to proceed directly to a given panel from the Process Monitor; you need only define the proper values in the Panel Transfers panel. Your users only have to choose the Action and Panel Transfer to benefit from the values you have designated on the appropriate panel.

Defining Elements in the Process Server

In the majority of situations in your network environment, you will be able to determine how specific servers can execute processes to better support your system workload. This means that when you define processes, it is important to schedule everything through the Process Scheduler. You will then be able to identify servers that need to run specific types of processes.

The Process Scheduler also gives you the opportunity to organize specific processes into jobs. At least one of these processes is organized as a job and is scheduled to execute as one group.

When dealing with the Process Scheduler, both process and job have two different meanings. You need to keep a

separation between these terms when you create a process
and a job definition. While a process is a single task,
program, or routine, it can run on either the client or the
server. Jobs are made up of at least one process that has
either the same or different types that can function either
in series or in parallel when they are executed. You must
remember that jobs are not supported only on the client; in
fact, jobs require scheduling support that only a server can
provide. In addition, API processes are also allowed to be
job definitions. This means that all processes inside a job
request can tell the server about the Run status when
operations are complete. This is effectively how a decision
is made to continue with additional job processes.

As we have already-defined jobs, we can proceed to
process run control definitions. These types of definitions
allow you to designate parameters that will be supported in
a future process request during runtime.

Whenever you design an application run control, then
the run parameters you define are recorded in a run control
record of specific applications. Every application will
support its own run control record.

The Process Scheduler has specific run control record
information that specifies the output type and the output
definition affiliate with the request that is stored in the
PeopleTools run control record field. The Process Scheduler
can benefit from this type of data and will offer default run
control information at a specific time. It can also allow
operators to override parameters as they need to run a
request.

Remember that process run control information is only
associated with the PeopleTools run control record. The
run control record is not necessarily synchronized with the
application run control record. This means than any run
control you define within your application is not specially
composed for the PeopleTools process run control record.

Should you delete a PeopleTools run control via the Edit
Run Controls box, then the run control is also deleted from

the PeopleTools run control record. In addition, should an application run control record exist with the same name, it will *not* be erased from your application's run control record, so you need to be careful about name duplication so that problems do not arise from two processes with the same name.

Recurring Jobs

You can define a job request so that it can run as often as you like. This can be accomplished prior to your operational runtime or at runtime. You can also determine the run recurrent on the Process Scheduler request, which is done by modifying create, edit, or delete actions for a Run Recurrence definition. In order to accomplish this, you will need to send your job or process request so that the Run Recurrence can control it.

Run recurrences are only pertinent for server-initiated requests. You can choose the Run location of your server so that you can allow Run Recurrent options to take place. Users are not allowed to update Run Recurrences, however, because of their process profiles' authorizations that are designated within the Security Administrator. Starting and stopping the Process Server Agent does not harm the Run Recurrence, but if the server is non-functional when the request is set to recur, then problems will occur. You can only fix such problems by restarting the server or by altering the time during which the request will take place.

When you set the parameters for your Run Recurrence instances, note that whenever a process does occur it takes place from the selected options. This allows you to choose how often you need a process request of a specific job to take place. In addition, the calendar function is useful after you have chosen the "OCCURS" value. You can use the calendar window in the appropriate PeopleSoft panel to determine the days on which the job should occur. In fact, your options are dictated by the actual selection you choose within the (when an action) "OCCURS" group.

Process Security

One of the main problems when you initiate any automated process scheduling is that of maintaining security. It is often very difficult to determine how specifically authorized users can start processes online without compromising your security. The Security Administrator allows you to establish operator IDs as well as operator classes that will determine exactly what user class can access certain sensitive windows, menus, and panels in your PeopleSoft environment.

It is possible for you to limit process activities by giving access only to process-scheduling panels for certain operators. Figure 2.1 shows the new activity dialog box. One of the ways you can obtain process security is to use the Process Scheduler to establish process security groups that allow your group to process as one unit where everyone in the group has the same security privileges. However, you can define a security administrator that has the power to grant and revoke process security groups to specific operators or operator classes.

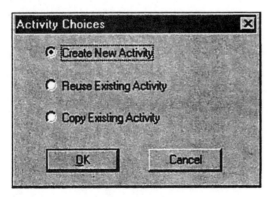

Figure 2.1 *New activity dialog box.*

Maintaining security is often difficult, but you have to keep in mind who will be responsible for certain access whenever you create process security groups. Whenever you define process definitions you can designate how each process will be assigned to one or more process security groups. As a result, you can define specific process security groups to designate at least one operator or operator class.

When you define process security groups, you can use the Security Administrator within your organization to specifically determine which operators and operator classes will be authorized to execute processes affiliated with a process security group. The Process Scheduler will inspect this table before it can display the Process Scheduler request or process any type of PeopleCode request. This is done so it can verify that the operator has signed on and is really authorized to execute a given process.

Scheduling Processes with PeopleCode

PeopleSoft application developers can make specific tasks much easier by scheduling processes through the ScheduleProcess function using PeopleCode. PeopleSoft application developers can make this function work by separating processes into specific elements. These elements involve processes that you need to have started by a given action. This may mean doing some calculations or marking a specific setting. This could potentially involve a given report that is affiliated with a specific function or set of tasks. Finally, this could also mean a recurrent process that was told to run at a specific time.

Both ScheduleProcess and PeopleCode function together to make certain that user input and row writes to the Process Request table are valid. These tools will inform the system of everything by just performing specific processes automatically without needing the user.

The process request is illustrative of the queue inside the Process Server Agent so it can define exactly which jobs must be performed. In addition, you can schedule any jobs or processes to run right away or at some defined time.

Dealing with COBOL

Whenever you deal with variables in COBOL applications, you need to remember that a process is part of the job definition. It is important to make certain the next process request will run even if the Run status established by the current request is unavailable. Under standard circumstances, job requests will only be chosen to run if the prior request has successfully completed.

For example, a Process Scheduler API-aware COBOL program needs to update its Run status with a processing request when it successfully connects. This means it must be able to update its Run status to either succeed or fail when the process is complete. Should the process function as part of the multi-process job, only then can you establish a parameter to prevent the next process from starting even if the status of the current request is successful or has caused an error. This protects you because if one process fails you won't lose the work from your whole job. You can then make certain that none of these jobs depends on the previous job's success or failure.

Administering The Process Scheduler

If you are a database, workstation, or application server administrator, you will need to know how to use the PSADMIN to both configure and administer the Process Scheduler Server Agent (see Figure 2.2). You can also use several tuning and maintenance procedures that will assist you in increasing your Process Scheduler performance abilities. Figure 2.3 shows application server components and services.

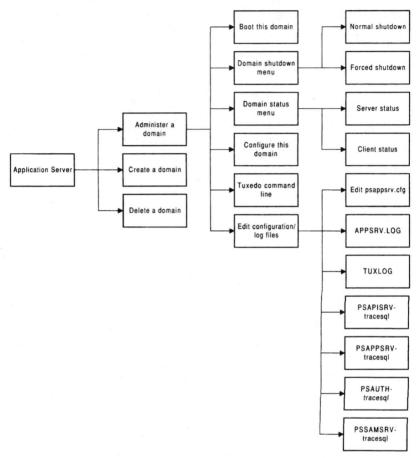

Figure 2.2 *PSADMIN.*

If you are at all responsible for any administrative tasks at your organization, you will need to understand how the Process Scheduler can be administrated in your Windows NT environment. This means that all the elements to process schedule administration must apply to both your operation system as well as the PeopleSoft-supported system.

When dealing with the Process Scheduler Server Agent, you must determine how it exists on the server and how it can execute specific processes. When these processes are started, they can run constantly in the background, but

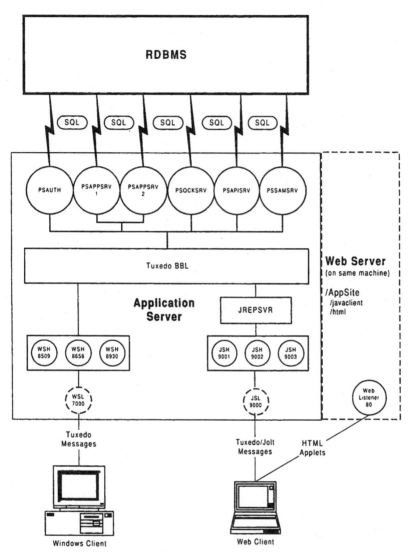

Figure 2.3 *Application Server Components and Services.*

they need no user interaction until it is required to shut a task down.

The Process Server Agent will query the Process Request table during normal intervals to determine if any process request has been sent toward the server. If they are directed towards the server, then it must imitate the proper process with respect to specific run times.

When the Process Scheduler Server Agent starts, it must connect to your database and query the Process Request table to look for any requests or processes in the queue. Should the Process Server Agent locate any processes, it will collect the data that defines the process and then start at the appropriate time. Then the Process Scheduler Server Agent can go into sleep mode for a duration of time so that it need not use any unnecessary server resources. It can then stay in sleep mode until the database administrator shuts it down.

Working with Clients and Servers

When you are working on the PeopleSoft client workstation, as a user, you can send a process request from a specific application in the Process Scheduler. Once a process request is sent, you can monitor the request status through the Process Monitor. The monitor allows you to determine if a process request is currently being processed or if it has been completed. You can then check to see if the proper server is functional.

When dealing with servers, the Process Server Agent can look for inbound process requests. When it finds one, it uses the Process Server Agent to start the associated process. Only then can the Process Server Agent start the process at the appropriate time. When it starts a process, it can update the Status column if it is API-aware.

Logging

The Process Scheduler has a logging system that enables you to alter the level of log file detail. This process relies on both the detail level and the "fence," which filters out messages that request greater detail for a specific installation process. Whenever messages are given a detail-level value, that value can determine the level of event importance. This means that the level can start the message in either the operation or the program. The programs started by such operations can be anything from simple progress messages that are highly detailed to error messages when the program is aborted.

You can imagine that a good message has the capability to go over a fence to be displayed, but a lower number indicates a higher fence, keeping an element of information from being displayed. When the fence is set to a value of three, only a message that has a detail level of less than three is shown. However, any level-zero messages that are not shown in the standard message format will not be able to be filtered out.

The Three-Tier Process Scheduler

Whenever you deal with a three-tier configuration, your ERP environment is far more complex. This complexity can cause component and software rules to be misinterpreted.

The Process Scheduler is difficult in a two-tier environment; therefore, you must really understand how each element of the Process Scheduler works in a three-tier environment.

When using the PeopleSoft workstation in a three-tier environment, any connection will start the process requests just as with any two-tier workstation. However, there are several differences in the message that the workstation produces when the user initiates a process request.

In the two-tier environment, the workstation transmits a SQL request to the database server so it can add a row to the Process Request table. However, in a three-tier connection, whenever a user initiates a process request, the workstation creates a Tuxedo message that is sent to the application server that inserts a row into the Process

Request table. Whenever a user sends a client request within a three-tier connection, the application server can insert the row in the Process Request Table, yet the process will function on the client. In the server, a row is inserted in the Process Request table while the Process Scheduler Server Agent starts the request itself.

Similiar to the two-tier workstation function, once a user initiates a process request, he can use the Process Monitor to check the status of it at any time.

The application server runs SQL on the database to add a row for any process request. You will note that the Process Monitor also uses the Tuxedo message to trigger the application server to obtain the process status from the Process Request table.

When you have the Process Schedule server within a three-tier environment, you must remember that the Process Scheduler server is a totally separate component and process from the PeopleSoft Application server and its processes. This means that even though the Process Scheduler server functions on the application server, it can also function on any supported database or batch server too. Please note that application server means the actual machine on which the application server can run.

The Process server can function independently and does not rely on the PeopleSoft Application server. It can support its own database server connection regardless of whether you are working in a two- or three-tier environment. The Process Schedule server can function in any environment and will maintain its database server connection. In addition, any process requests that are operated on the server can operate through the Process Schedule server, but a client request need not be run through it.

Database Server

The database server also has several pertinent functions that relate to a request that include command-line parameters and process status, regardless of whether it is situated in a two- or three-tier environment.

Fixing Problems

As with any ERP implementation, you are faced with some very daunting tasks if the system returns error messages. You must be prepared to handle several common problems that often result from incorrectly entered data or improperly configured systems.

If the system tells you that you are not authorized to run certain processes, you need to first examine what the cause may be. You should start by looking in the Process Security Group within the Process definition of what you are working on. Check to see if the specific process is not in the list of valid process groups within the security administrator. Correcting this problem requires that you add the Process Security Group for the specific process definition to either the operator or operator class within the security administrator.

If you get an error that says you do not have a valid type of definition, you must examine the cause of the error, as it most probably is caused when the default operating system is set to an invalid choice for your database. In addition, the server name that the Process Scheduler Request has chosen could be "any," so the process may be running on any server that has your default operating system. You need only modify the default operating system in the Process System panel to correct this type of problem.

If you get an error that says your process is not valid for your three-tier client, it could be because the Run location in the Process Definition is set to "Client." The Run location on the Process Scheduler Request dialog could also be set to "Server." These configurations are *not* valid for any three-tier environment. You can easily resolve this problem by changing the Run location in the Process Definition or setting the Run location on the Process Scheduler Request to "Client."

If you see a message that says you have an invalid output definition for a given process type, you need to check that the client destination and server destination boxes are selected. You can also fix this problem by noting that the Process Scheduler must first look at specified tables for a certain Run Control ID to obtain the output destination. Should it not locate the correct information, it will look at the operator profile to get the default output destination for a given Run location. Therefore, you must provide a default client and server output destination for the operator or operator class via the Security Administrator settings.

Should you see an error message that says that only PeopleTools are associated with your initial sign on, you may be logged on to several databases simultaneously. You are only allowed to schedule processes from a PeopleTool that is logged into the first database to which you are connected. To resolve this problem, you must schedule processes from a PeopleTool that is logged into the current database. Then log out from all the PeopleTools and databases and then relog on to the database you need.

If you are working in Windows NT and receive an error saying you are not able to start the Process Scheduler on Windows NT and that the DOS Windows is hidden, you have an incorrect entry within the startup section of your Windows/DOS configuration files. You must trace the problem using tools that include the following:

- TraceSQL

- LogFence

You can then examine the Process Scheduler as well as your config.sys and other Windows configuration files to see where the problem lies. There may be an incorrect operator ID or a system call for a tool that was uninstalled from your system.

If you have a problem where a given process is run on the client instead of the server or on the server instead of the client, you must examine the following:

- Server name

- Run location

- Recurrence name

- Data from the Process Definition panel

Any of these can potentially obscure any values that the Process Scheduler Request has set in the SchedulePrcess PeopleCode. This type of error often takes place on the Process Definition panel when the Run location is set to "Server" and the Server name is not filled in. If can also happen on the Process System Panel when the default operating system is set to "Client," as in the above example.

If you receive an error that says you can't run COBOL or SQL from the Unix command line, then you must determine if you are using the proper shell script for SQR or COBOL as this may cause the process to stop responding. You can fix this problem by making certain your PeopleSoft Server Configuration values are set properly.

If you have an error whereby processes stay in the server queue, you may have to see if the Process Scheduler is running, determine if the process type of a given process is defined correctly on the server, or check the max API setting for the Process Schedule server to see if it is correct for the maximum number of process requests that have been started.

You can solve these problems respectively by making certain that the Process Scheduler Server Agent is running on the server and determine if its status is correct from the Process Monitor and the server. Examine the process classes for the Process Scheduler Server, and if it is not there, you will have to add the Process Class from the Process Scheduler and the Process Server panel. Finally, you may have to deal with the max API problem by setting its value to a value that is correct or wait until the Process Request is complete. To resolve this final problem, you may

have to cancel process requests and then restart them if
they have crashed.

If you see processes that appear to be stuck once they
have started or are currently processing, then you may have
an implementation of incorrect API routines within your
processes. You must resolve this problem by making certain
that the Process Scheduler sets each Process Request to
have a Run status that starts in the Process Request table
whenever a given command file is started or before it is
run by a specific process. This means that if the process
executes on the Run status of the process, API codes will
update it.

Working with Jolt Internet Relays

You can use the Jolt Internet Relay (JRLY) with your Web
client connections to your application server. However, this
should only be done in cases where you have a Web server
with HTML or applets on individual machines that are
different from the application server.

Should the Web server run on the same machine as the
application server, then JRLY is not required and only then.
In addition, PeopleSoft permits Web server and application
server configurations that are the same, even though they
exist on different machines.

The JRLY is composed of two primary elements:

1. Jolt Relay

2. Jolt Relay Adapter

The Jolt Relay is composed of an individual program
and a configuration that function on the same physical
machine as the Web server. The Jolt Relay receives Jolt
messages from the Web client and then routes those
messages to the Jolt Relay Adapter on the application
server. The Jolt Relay (Front-End Relay) then receives Jolt
messages through the LISTEN port and connects to the
JRAD through the CONNECT port.

The Jolt Relay Adapter is the second component that functions on the same physical machine as the application server. This component is configured automatically on the application server domain and is part of the PSADMIN domain configuration procedure.

JRAD (Back-End Relay) actually "listens" to the Jolt Relay messages on its listener port. When it receives these messages, it sends them to the JSL or JSH.

The relationship between the components and their associated port numbers is most evident when you are configuring the JRLY system. It is important to ascertain that you can determine the best port number to be used through each component that receives messages and which port number that messages are sent to. Note that any inconsistencies cause transactions to fail.

Port Numbers

Whenever you have to work with JRLY numbers, you need to begin with the concept that the Web server and application server are on two individual machines. When your web client connects to a URL, both HTML and Java applets are downloaded to the browser. Inside the HTML you will find the specified port number required to connect to Jolt. Once you have downloaded the HTML, the Web client can then connect to the specified Web server port for the JRLY listen. The JRLY listener can then send Java messages to the JRLY connect process.

In order to maintain security, the Web client needs to reconnect to the same machines from which it downloaded the HTML. Note that the Web client only reconnects to the same machine, but that is not the same machine where the Web server processes take place.

The JRLY Connect process can use the machine's IP address and port number to connect to the Jolt Relay Adapter process on the application server. Then JRAD sends that request onto the Jolt Station Listener responsible for starting the transactions. Return messages are then sent to the client following the same procedure.

When you institute the JRLY, the JRLY listener must have the same port number determined in the downloaded HTML. This means that the Jolt listener port on your application server can either match or be different from the port number determined in the HTML.

JSL could be set to any valid port number, or if the Web and application server are on the same machines (and JRLY is not needed), then JSL (on the application server) must match the same port number determined in the downloaded HTML.

You must remember that if you have to maintain Web clients that connect via JRLY and Web clients, you will be working with components that are connecting directly to JSL on the application server and the JRLY Listening port is equivalent to the JSL port.

Working with the Web Client

The standard Windows client uses binaries created with C++ that are stored on the server and are also created using Java applets. They work as Java class files that function the same as EXE and DLL files.

All these class files are recorded on the Web server in a compressed format that can be downloaded to the client browser when the user connects to the Web site. Although applets can be very big, they are also recorded on the Web server in compressed format using JAR or CAB compression techniques that the browser can decompress.

You only need to download an applet once. Once you download them, they are cached to your disk, but when the applet codes change, you need to download the new version again. This action is imitated automatically through the browser.

Your client maintains security by connecting back to the same machine that has the Web site. If you deal with any other activities involving HTML pages, running applets, or any other online process, this must all occur on the same machine. Thus, you need to know if the application server and the Web server exist on the same machine. If the Web server is on another machine, then the application server must be configured with Tuxedo's JRLY to make certain your transmissions are secure.

Configuring a Web Server

Web servers are composed of three items that include the Web site address, the TCP/IP listener, and the file directory map. Your Web server can map objects to real files that include applets. Whenever an applet is downloaded to a browser, you have to determine how that applet is triggered through the HTML page.

Remember that you only need to download applets once after they are cached to the disk. If applets change, however, you will have to download the new version. Your web browser can determine if there are any updated files and can automatically download the update when needed.

Refining the Application Server

When you are using a three-tier connection, you are using hardware components that enhance the range of tuning and, as a result, many problems can emerge due to your higher complexity. You must worry about more than just the client and database server that must be refined to increase your performance; you also have to consider monitoring your system much more and maintain your application server client request's processing duties as well.

When you start your application server as part of your domain, memory is cached to the disk. When you boot your application server, a specific number of PSAPPSRV servers are also started. This means that each PSAPPSRV starts receiving database objects and caches them to the memory and disk too. This will require that you have an increased amount of memory available.

Every PSAPPSRV has its own memory and disk cache, so when you have quite a few PSAPPSRV around, you do not need to worry about sharing resources from one memory of disk cache.

Whenever an application server is terminated, the PSAPPSRV in the application server purges its memory as well as any cached objects. Whenever the application server is booted up again, every PSAPPSRV memory cache starts again. However, the application server PSQCKSRV does not support a cache, which means it always queries the database for objects.

The memory and disk cache is manifested for each client workstation too. This means that each of your client requests will look at its own cache of the memory on disk before routing any request to the application server.

Tuxedo Strings

Your Tuxedo connect strings were created for advanced configurations necessary to support dynamic load balancing. You can determine a connect string that permits a client to connect to another application server whenever it is not responding because it may be filled to capacity. You can use this type of functionality by selecting the client Configuration Manager.

You will find the Application Servers tab important, but you can input this information into the sign-on screen from the administration settings. It's useful to determine the Tuxedo connect string though the Configuration Manager. Figure 2.4 shows Tuxedo Strings, while the Configuration Manager is shown in Figure 2.5.

You can choose an option that will determine several application servers to which the client can connect. However, each application server will probably receive the same number of connections. You can use a special command to affect load balancing on your windows client so that you can control both the IP address and the port number.

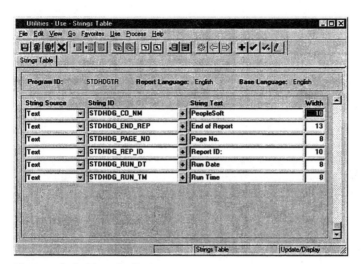

Figure 2.4 *Tuxedo Strings.*

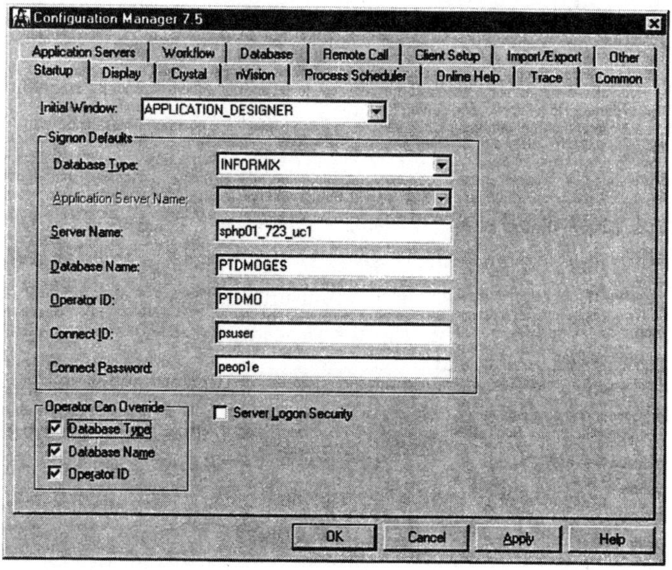

Figure 2.5 *Configuration Manager.*

These same load-balancing operations are important whenever the application server you have chosen is not available. This means your attempt to connect will not succeed. Therefore, the system will not attempt to connect you until the other application servers are designated. You must not embed space in any section of your connection string. It is important to note that the PeopleSoft system will automatically remove any embedded space prior to storing this value within the registry. Also, a certain number of application servers can be defined within the parenthesis group, but you have to watch carefully to make sure you input the right settings in the right command parameters.

When you deal with load balancing on Windows clients, you can select options that allow you to define a fail-over connection string. You can determine this type of command when you need to select the application server from the parenthesis group whenever ip1 and ip2 is not available. Your system can automatically try to connect to the designated application server, but if that application server fails, you system will try to make a connection through the next group specified and will continue to do so until a connection is made. However, if more than one application server is designated within any group, your system will move between them. If your application server fails, the system will try to make a connection to the next group and so on.

You may also find it useful to use load balancing on Web clients, but this requires that you install several Web servers. This is not like the Windows client that permits you to determine a Tuxedo connection string using the configuration manger. You have the choice to configure Web clients for multiple Web servers and have Web client connections to different URLs too. You can also configure several Web servers and have Web clients connect to a common URL. This means you can implement load balancing between Web servers through a network resolution setting.

Tracing

Traces are associated with both PeopleCode and SQL for a given client that runs on the application server. The settings can be controlled through the Configuration Manager. These types of trace files are compiled to the application server as opposed to the client.

You can trace network services so that the network can write all of its send and receive messages between the client and the application server. These files are sent to a directory file on the client machine. Some of the commands you may find include

- Clock time

- Send length

- Receive length

- Application services invoked

- Any special parameters

Tracing is also associated with logging so that you can send Tuxedo system messages to Windows NT's event log by setting the logging page in your system. One of the options you can choose is the logging option for the Windows NT Event log as well as the standard ULOG (Disk File). Should you use standard ULOG messages, you can choose the directory you put ULOG messages into. You may wish to activate some trace settings that are created only to check your three-tier performance of your system.

You can use a certain level of SQL for tracing any activities created by your clients within a given domain. You can set the value to be the same as the sum you want for given options.

TraceSQLMask is a useful parameter that sets a maximum level for SQL tracing for any activities created by a given client on your domain. These trace files are compiled on the application server, not the client. The idea is to enable the system administrator to see SQL created on the application server domain for a specific client, as opposed to all clients.

Users can turn on SQL tracing by setting a specified trace level through the configuration manger. They can set values that are transmitted to the application server, but only SQL created by the client can be captured. You can stop clients from activating the application server trace and eating up your precious resources when the application server uses TraceSQLMask as an administration control measure.

Should a client transmit a request to trace SQL, the application server can examine the value sent to the TraceSQLMask. Should the client value be less than or equal to the TraceSQL Mast, then the application server can permit the trace. However, if the client value is greater, then the application server will permit the trace up to the TraceSQL Mask value.

Trace files are recorded on the application server, yet no trace is shown on the client. You can set a specified level for PeopleCode tracing for any activities created by all clients on a given domain. You can set certain values to be defined in the configuration file. TracePC is the parameters value that displays within the configuration manager.

You can use network service traces on a client. Network traces can be defined on the client Configuration Manager trace settings. You only need to select the network trace and determine the name of the trace file. This type of trace will provide you with specific information on each client request within the application server. This type of trace gives you the elapsed time you need to complete the following values:

- Request string

- SQL statement

- Length of the request

- Length of the response

Remember that this type of trace is created on the client, as opposed to the application server itself.

Configuration Manager

The Configuration Manager is a PeopleTool that can ease your workstation administration by modifying the registry settings in one central location in your PeopleSoft system. The Configuration Manager allows you to set up one workstation to display your system and site environment. You can then export the configuration file that can be shared with all the workstations on your site.

The Configuration Manager is composed of several controls that allow you to establish your workstations for the Process Scheduler. You can then connect to an application server using online help and other modules. You are then able to use this tool by accessing the Configuration Manager's interface and the environmental settings that you can determine.

When we discuss the Configuration Manager, it is important to make some comments about its GUI interface. The Configuration Manager is simple and allows you to access PeopleSoft registry settings from one location. This saves you time from searching aimlessly through the registry on your own. This interface is similar to what you would see in a typical Windows environment.

Just clicking the standard Configuration Manager shortcut in your program group starts the Configuration Manager. You can then start the program online to access utilities, the Process Scheduler, the EDI Manager, report books, the application engine, and mass change. Figure 2.6 shows the mass change process.

PeopleSoft Configuration Setup

When you startup your system, you are confronted with options that enable you to customize the default values that

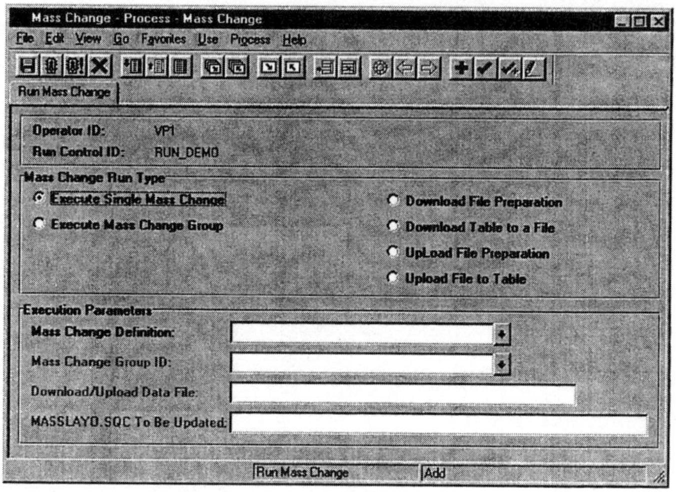

Figure 2.6 *Mass Change Process.*

alter the look of your sign-on process. These entries are
displayed on the sign-on screen, but you do not need to alter
any of these values unless you do not want the defaults. The
benefit is that you can select any PeopleTools or other
applications you wish to open after sign-on is complete.

You can determine what your initial PeopleTool or
application window will display when you log onto the
system. This can be easily accomplished by inputting the
specified menu name in the Initial Window edit box. This
list will give you the chance to select from among the menu
names you want. However, if you do not have sufficient
authorization to access a given menu, then you will not be
able to select a menu unless you know its name, because it
won't appear on the list. The PeopleSoft system will open
the first window you are authorized to access under these
security conditions. This prevents unauthorized users from
accessing information they are not allowed to see.

Your sign-on default settings enable you to customize
your default during the sign-on procedure. These types of
settings are apparent on the sign-on screen, but you only
need to change values if you don't like the default settings.

The system will need to authorize you to execute any changes to the sign-on defaults. You can best illustrate the relationship between startup and the sign-on dialog by examining the values that are displayed during the standard PeopleSoft sign-on dialog box.

Menu Options

When confronted with the configuration settings, you will need to define several elements that include the database type, application server name, server name, database name, operator ID, and the connect ID/connect password.

The database type is a menu list that allows you to choose the name of your RDBMS:

- DB2

- Oracle

- Informix

- Etc.

These items appear by default in the PeopleSoft sign-on window. You can then select APPSRV to log on to an application server instead of the database. You can examine all of your choices and then permit an operator to change your database-type selection as the sign-on dialog using the database type option in the Operator Can Override group. However, you choose the APPSRV from the following list:

- Database type

- Server name

- Connect ID

- Connect password control

All of these options are disabled and the system will acquire these values from the application server instead.

The application server name must be dealt with when you select the APPSRV from the database type list. You will need to determine the application server's name in this field. If you have defined your application server configuration and register it on the application servers tab, then you must do that before you proceed any further.

The server name is an option you must select when you input the name of the default database server in the server name field. This parameter is only permitted for the following DBMS's:

- Informix

- Sybase

- Microsoft SQL Server

- IBM's DB2

This system refers to any input where the user connects, but this is somewhat different from the other PeopleSoft releases where the server name field is called the Host name in the Unix server. Remember that the server name must be input in lower case in the Informix database. When dealing with the Microsoft SQL Server, the server name must be used automatically to create your ODBC data source name.

You can input the default database name when you select a valid database name. Similar to the database type, you can allow an operator to override the default selection at sign-on, but you must choose the correct option in the Operator Can Override group.

The Operator ID parameter is useful, as it allows you to determine the default Operator ID that is used to log into the PeopleSoft system. This parameter is optional, like all of your other startup parameters. You can, however, use the Operator ID parameter together with a PSUSER module that has a user-designated logon process. PSUSER code can help you both examine and modify the Operator ID value prior to logging onto the selected database.

Connect ID is a parameter ID that is shared for all DB2 and Informix systems. They are substitutes for your Operator ID in the logon process. If you enable this function, you must establish an individual operating system account and connect ID for all operator IDs in your PeopleSoft definition tables in your system. The connect password field is used to designate the default connect ID password for your systems.

Operator Can Override Parameter

One of the most talked about parameters in this section involves the Operator Can Override command. Many PeopleSoft systems can use multiple database types and names. You can use different selections in the Operator Can Override group to either enable or disable your operators from inputting

- RDBMS

- Database mames

- Operator IDs

The system only permits what you have defined at logon. Most of the time, you will not use any of these controls to stop users from trying to sign on to any other database other that your default system. The specific settings involved in this option include the database type, database name, and operator ID.

Should you choose the database type, the system will perceive that you want to grant access to override the database name and operator ID. This means you will have to go through options that will sometimes be automatically chosen for you. You must deselect either the database name or operator ID without first deselecting the database type. If you are responsible for configuring workstations that connect to both two- and three-tier configurations, you need to choose these parameters. You will also need to determine whether users connect to a two- or three-tier configuration during sign-on to your system.

When you choose the database name, the system will perceive that you wish to override the Operator ID. This means that the Operator ID button will automatically be chosen as your default. You can choose to deselect these parameters, but you must also disable the database name and database type radio buttons too.

If you only need to provide a user with the power to override the Operator ID chosen at logon, you can simply choose Operator ID. You don't need to worry about any other options, but you cannot disable the Operator ID if you have chosen the database type.

Server Security

Server logon security is an important function that permits your database administrators to modify a user's password on the server through a third-party SQL tool. All password changes are reflected in the PSOPRDEFN. If you choose server logon security, then you will notice that the set password button won't be represented in the sign-on dialog box.

If the database administrator alters the user's password to the server, the system will prompt the user to input their old password before signing on. If they do this correctly, then they are permitted to sign on and they will not be asked for the old password any more.

Should you deselect the server logon security option, notice that the set password button will be shown on the sign-on dialog box. If you modify a user's password beyond PeopleTools, that user will not be able to sign on.

Database Specific Logon Security

Every database handles server logon security differently. Microsoft SQL Server allows you to determine the server logon security settings the same way as Oracle. Informix, DB2 for MVS, AS/400, AIX, and ODBC, however, do not allow you to manually determine the server logon security settings. Instead, the server logon security is automatically disabled if you use the Connect ID. Under any other circumstance, it is automatically enabled.

Sybase doesn't allow you to manually determine the server logon security setting either. Server Logon Security is always disabled; therefore, you will not be able to modify a password outside of the PeopleTools or Sybase platform.

Working with Panels

One of the benefits of the PeopleSoft system is that you can choose the "customize" method, which controls how panels appear on your screen. You can modify the entire display size by adjusting the panel height and width. You can change the panel size, show a panel in the navigator, highlight a specific field, and even show the database name.

In order to determine the display size of your screen, you will need to modify the default size of the window as it is displayed with associated width and height fields. You can choose to have window display size of 640 x 480, 800 x 600, 1024 x 769, or even choose a customer size.

Integrating a specific, customized panel size into your system gives you a means of specifying the way in which panels are displayed, as though they were created for different-sized windows other than the one that is open.

You can choose to scale your panels to fit the window as needed. This means that if your display size is set to a certain resolution, you can open a panel designated to display the windows in another resolution. These panel controls are automatically scaled down so that all panel information appears on your screen.

You can use the clip setting to make certain your panel controls are always shown in their normal size. This setting is necessary if the panel is too large to fit onscreen. The scrollbar can also help in viewing the other screen real estate that is missing.

When dealing with screens, you can also modify your menu fields. You can select the highlight popup menu field so that fields with popup menus are highlighted to tell users that they are there. Note that this option is normally disabled, but you may want it on to show which fields contain such menus.

Another important screen feature is to show the database name. This function is helpful if you are performing several PeopleTools actions. It allows you to have an open panel and to have the database name you are connected to appear in the status bar on the bottom of the pane. You will also see the current panel name and its activity. When the database name is shown, you can also have which database you are connected to shown in the Window task bar when PeopleTools is running.

Display

As we move the discussion away from panels, we now delve into the navigator display. In this option, you can choose three different types of display options. "ON" is when the navigator will be displayed with each menu group you open. "OFF" is when the navigator is not displayed and the user will need to launch the navigator manually. "FIRST" is when the navigator is shown on the very first PeopleSoft instance and is not displayed after that.

Application Server Settings

Cache files are important in your PeopleTools implementation. Cache files record database object information locally and are automatically downloaded the first time you open a database object or perform a change to the master copy of the object on your database server.

On every database you use, you will only have one cache file directory that stores the cache files for that database. You can assign your cache directory using a single directory entry or even delete directories as needed. When a cache file directory is deleted or missing, the system automatically rebuilds it the next time cache files are downloaded to your system. When you work with your application server, you are effectively dealing with the configured application server that has a client that can connect. Note that before you input anything onto your application server, you need to have configured it first.

In order to effectively configure your system, you need to have knowledge of several different settings that will be involved for PeopleSoft's integration into your system. The application server name is used when you input a name for an application server that you have configured. This is the name that appears in the sign-on screen list. You need to select a name that is easy to remember for your site, but don't go over 24 characters.

You can input the IP address on the resolvable server name of your application server. This is designated in the application server field. You can define the IP address in the workstation listen configuration section of your PSAPPSRV.CFG when you install your application server.

You can also input the port number for the application server you defined in your application server name field. You can determine the port number in the listener element configuration section of your PSAPPSRV.CFG file when you installed and configured your application server. Note that the port number is an arbitrary number between 0 and 9,999 defined by site applications in your system.

The Tuxedo connection string is defined for your advanced configuration to support dynamic load balancing. You can define a connect string that permits a client to connect to another application server in the event that either one is not working or is filled to capacity.

Round Robin

You can optionally choose the round robin load balance. This option defines several application servers when the client arbitrarily connects. However, it is not likely that each application server will receive an equal number of connections. You can determine the IP address using either a dotted notation or using the server's DNS name. It doesn't matter which convention you use to input the address, but the slashes that go before the IP address are necessary.

Should the application server that you choose not be available, your connection attempt will fail. The system then cannot connect to the other application server designated with the parentheses of your command. You must not embed any spaces within the connection string because PeopleSoft automatically removes them before recording the value in its registry.

Round Robin with fail-over is very much the same as the Round Robin Load Balance. This option permits you to designate a failure connection string. Should the application server be chosen from the first group but not be available, the system will automatically try to connect to an application server defined in your second group. If that application server doesn't connect, the system will try to connect to the next group to the right until it connects. However, if several application services are defined within any group, the system will round robin between them. If your chosen application server fails, the system will try to connect to the next application server if you have one defined.

Working in the Workflow

The workflow setting is where you can define options and locations related to the workflow implementation in your system. Electronic workflow keeps track of assigned tasks within your business processes automatically.

In your workflow, you will most certainly deal with the Message Agent. You can determine several parameters for this function, including the server name that defines the name of your Lotus Notes Server that has mail-in databases. You can use the mail-in database to determine the name of the Lotus Notes mail-in database you want PSNOTES.EXE to inspect. Figure 2.7 illustrates how Lotus Notes can integrate effectively into your PeopleSoft system. This is the actual database where users can send forms to be processed by your applications. You can finally use the polling frequency to determine how often the Message Agent Monitor program inspects the mail-in database for new forms to process. These parameters measure units in seconds and defaults at 30.

Forms are important for determining the locations of the server name and mail-in database. The server name determines the name of the Lotus Notes server where forms are defined. The mail-in database determines the database on the previous server where the forms reside.

You can also specify a detach directory where PSNOTES.EXE file attachments on the incoming forms are

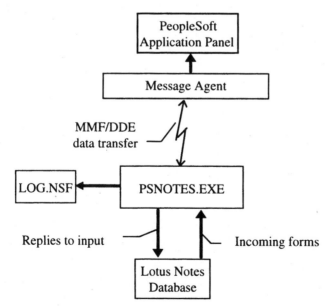

Figure 2.7 *Lotus Notes Integration.*

received. You can use PSNOTES.EXE to send fields that it cannot deliver to the Message Agent.

The Maximum Worklist Instance function establishes limits on the amount of worklist instances or entries that are displayed when viewing worklists. The default for this value is 250, but you can leave the edit box blank if you do not want any rows returned.

The mail protocol is useful when you want to integrate e-mail into your workflow. You will probably use the mail protocol group whenever you wish to determine what mail protocol your site uses.

PeopleSoft employs both the MAPI and VIM protocols. MAPI or Mail API is the programming interface that permits you to send and receive mail all over the Microsoft Mail messaging system. If this is the mail protocol that your site uses, then choose this option to configure your client to execute the PeopleSoft workflow e-mail generation. VIM is an acronym for the Vendor Independent Messaging Interface. This is the programming interface that enables you to both send and receive e-mail over a VIM-compliant messaging system (such as cc:Mail). If this is the mail protocol that your company uses, then choose this option to configure your client to run the PeopleSoft Workflow e-mail generation. Once you have determined your mail protocol, you can define the mail path that your site will use. Most organizations just place it in the Windows directory for easy access.

Conclusion

This chapter has provided a good introduction into very specific PeopleSoft tools. Armed with this general level of information, you can now proceed into the next chapter and see how the Message Agent plays a vital role within your corporate structure.

03

Message Agent

The Message Agent processes messages transmitted to PeopleSoft by external systems including interactive voice response (IVR) systems, e-mail, Internet, intranet, extranet, and kiosks. This also offers an application program interface (API) that enables third-party systems to integrate with PeopleSoft in a real-time manner.

Introduction to the PeopleSoft Message Agent

PeopleSoft's Message Agent is the best method to access PeopleSoft panel groups as well as the business logic that is tied with them outside of the PeopleSoft online panels. The Message Agent extends the capabilities of PeopleSoft data and business processed outside of PeopleSoft applications.

The Message Agent permits users in your company to use other third-party applications to process information in PeopleSoft panels. Figures 3.1 and 3.2 illustrate how the Message Agent functions within a third-party application environment. Instead of inputting or changing data within the PeopleSoft panels, users can input data through software applications they know and use everyday. They can use Message Agent processing to allow users to employ other processes that include Web applications and C++ tools.

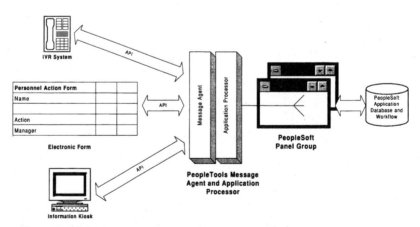

Adding Third-Party Applications to the Workflow with the Message Agent

Figure 3.1 *Message Agent and Third-Party Applications.*

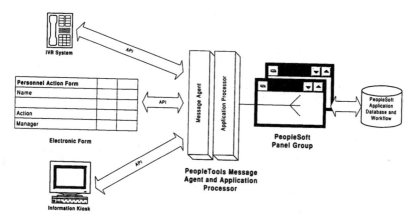

Adding Third-Party Applications to the Workflow with the Message Agent

Figure 3.2 *Adding Third-Party Applications to the Workflow with the Message Agent.*

You can add PeopleSoft processes using the Message Agent through:

- Database Agent

- OS/nVision

- Notes Forms

These items are used in several PeopleSoft applications for internal processes. However, you can also use them to acquire data from your PeopleSoft database or other networked databases. Message Agent sections give you information on Message Agent usages, processes, and programming and will act as a reference for Message Agent API calls.

Application Programming Interfaces (APIs) together with a message definition facilitate access to PeopleSoft panels. Message Agent API's give you the ability to write programs that reuse business logic.

Using the Message Agent in PeopleTools integration tools requires that you have a message definition, Message Agent client groups, and a Message Agent server.

Message Definitions

In order to allow programs to access a PeopleSoft panel, you need to create a message definition through the Application Designer. Message definitions create mapping from sets of fields in one message definition to those fields on a given PeopleSoft panel. You will also find other information that handles the control mechanisms when accessing PeopleSoft panels.

Message Agent Client Programs

Message Agent client programs are compiled using Message Agent APIs. Note that APIs are actually a collection of programming interfaces that permit the user to compile a specific program that is used to access a PeopleSoft panel through either the message definition or the Message Agent client. Programmers can depend on familiar OLE/COM and C programming interfaces.

Message Agent APIs enable programmers to write programs that can do the same types of activities that can be accomplished when accessing a PeopleSoft panel. Programs can be created for the purpose of providing the keys to a panel that are the same as a search dialog would find. In addition, you can also acquire the data from a panel field or even input the data into a panel field and save the panel.

It is important to note that PeopleSoft executes the same exact edits and security checks that any user must execute. These checks can also include executing business logic connected with a given panel. Therefore, if a panel has Workflow business as part of its contents, then the Message Agent can trigger the associated business event.

You will also find that the Message Agent server is part of the PeopleSoft application server. It operates as an

independent application server process and is administered
similar to that of other PeopleSoft application servers.

Building the Message Agent

In PeopleSoft Release 7.5, you will note that the release of
the Message Agent has been made to run as part of the
three-tier software architecture. Therefore, the Message
Agent now operates on its application server as another
server called PSAPISRV.

You can expect to find three common components
within the PeopleSoft platform that include:

1. Clients: Message Agent client programs

2. Application server: This can be either a Unix, Windows
   NT, or Windows 2000 server that perform PeopleSoft's
   server processes

3. Database server: This can run any of the supported
   RDBMS/platform combinations present in this type of
   ERP environment

Three-Tier Architecture

The Message Agent has a basic three-tier architecture that
is illustrated in Figure 3.3.

The Message Agent functions within the PeopleSoft three-
tier environment. This functionality benefits its users by
offering better Message Agent processing. Connections are
not limited to a specific Message Agent server process. This
means that when a Message Agent client program first tries
to connect to a Message Agent server, it does not necessarily
connect to a specific server, but it does connect to a specific
machine and port that has a Message Agent server operating
on it. As a result, the Message Agent client program need not
consume all of the Message Agent Server's resources.

Performance is increased because there are fewer calls to
the Message Agent server. The Message Agent is built such

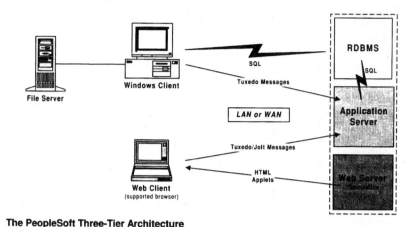

The PeopleSoft Three-Tier Architecture

Figure 3.3 *Three-Tier Architecture.*

that only a few of the client API calls are executed on the Message Agent server. Most of the client API calls that execute at runtime are local to the client. As a result, only a few calls are sent from the client to the server.

These servers can support several request processes, but only an external Message Agent request is processed at any given time. This means that you can achieve greater flexibility and performance, because if a problem occurs at any one Message Agent application server, then operational results do not affect any other Message Agent client programs. Since problems are localized, your entire operation won't shut down from any one problem. This model is very efficient and protects your entire enterprise from system-wide shut-downs.

Message Agent Benefits

You will find that the Message Agent is automatically connected to the Application Server as well as all of the administrative functions presented by the Application Server. You need not try to individually call up each

Message Agent application or execute several Message Agent connections. You will find that the Application Server's administrative process starts automatically when it is needed. In addition, you will find that since PeopleSoft Application Server administrative processes can operate on several Message Agent machines simultaneously, there is greater stability in your operating platform and less chance of system failures at any given point within your enterprise.

Message Agent Functions

Several things need to occur prior to the Message Agent completing any given translation task. The panel group must be made to meet a business user's requirements. The message definition for a given Message Agent application must be created or defined and the Message Agent API programs must be compiled. Finally, you need to be connected to an application server that has access to the Message Agent.

Message Agent APIs allow users to write an external programs that can function similarly to online PeopleSoft panels. In order for this process to occur, you must complete an outline that follows the same exact steps that external programs follow. This allows you to imitate the save functionality of online panels.

The following steps represent the best outline you can follow to imitate PeopleSoft panels:

1. You need to connect to the Message Agent. External programs need to connect to the Message Agent server and designate the PeopleSoft operator ID and password.

2. Designate the message definition that an external program must have. This means transmitting a message definition that is used by designating the activity name and message definition name that are both established by the Application Designer.

3. You must institute search dialog processing. External programs can perform search dialog processing by defining search record key fields, processing search records, and acquiring rows that are returned from a given search record. In addition, API sets acquire information regarding all fields and associated attributes on a given search record.

4. Check if you can find message definition field information. You will find that the Message Agent gives APIs for an external program that are used to designate both fields and their associated attributes in a given message definition.

5. You must then set message definition values. The Message Agent offers APIs that are used to set both the key as well as other input fields for a message definition should the program be inputting data into a PeopleSoft panel.

6. Then you can process message definitions. The Message Agent offers an API call for external programs that are required to process message definitions that return rows of data. These definitions input data into the panel and then save it.

7 . The Message Agent then offers APIs so that external programs acquire data for all fields within the message definitions that are designated as output.

8. The next step involves edit and prompt table processing. Note that few record fields have an edit table connected with them, as edit table lists have valid values for a given field. Edit tables and prompt tables are the same because in an online system, users can simply press the F4 key to show table and value contents. External programs can also execute Message Agent functions. Also, Message Agent APIs

are used to determine both fields and attributes regarding fields on both edit and prompt tables.

9. You must be careful to look for any error information, because if any Message Agent APIs return an error, the external program can receive an error too. Should an error occur, you can get the message name of the record or field so you can determine the best way to fix the problem.

10. Finally, the Message Agent gives you calls so that you can change the operator and set options and then disconnect when you need to.

Message Definitions

Message Definitions permit Message Agent client programs to access PeopleSoft panel groups. It is possible to create message definitions in the Application Designer (including activity on an object). You can map between Message Agent fields and PeopleSoft panel fields.

Message Agent designates which message definitions are used by a given message definition name. You must be careful to watch the panel where you input data, the action mode, and the search record definition, because whenever the Message Agent acquires data, it moves to the appropriate PeopleSoft panel in much the same way as you would move to a panel. It then selects the panel from the menu and the action mode from the drop-down menu, and it inputs key data into the search dialog box.

Several application panels have at least one scroll bar that allows you to display data from more than one row at any given time. PeopleSoft's Message Agent depends on several scroll-level management techniques that specify message definitions.

You must determine which data fields map to specific panel fields. The Message Agent acquires values from specific fields. It then inputs them into associated fields on the PeopleSoft panel. Several types of message definition activities are used with applications that include PS/nVision, Database Agent, IVR, Visual Basic, and Notes Forms.

Whenever a Message Agent receives data, it moves to the associated panel. At this point, the information the Message Agent needs to move to a given panel is entered when you establish the message definition. A message definition attributes dialog box shows you where information is mapped according to the following information:

- Panel name

- Action mode

- Search record definition

Working with Rows

The Message Agent can only update one row of data at any given time. You can add or update rows, but you must still process one row at a time.

In order to update rows within a scroll, it is important to follow an exact procedure that allows you to use a "SmartMessage" so that you can specify which message definition you need to use. You can then get the metadata that defines the fields within the message definition. This could refer to either the GetFieldList or the GetFieldInfo method within your OLE interface.

The next step is to set the values for the first row you need to add or update through the SetField parameter. At this point, you need to set the values for the key fields of your main record definition inside the scroll and any higher level keys.

When you deal with level 1 scrolls, you must remember to set values for the next row that you need to add or update using SetField. However, you need not designate level 0 keys for a second time; you need only provide new level 1 values. You can then repeat these steps for each row that you need to either add or update.

Using "ProcessMessage," you can process the row and use the GetField parameter to verify your results. You can then obtain values from the output fields that are determined in the message definition. Should there be an error, you can recall the text of the error message so you can correct it.

For each update you wish to make, you need to go back and set the values you want to add or update through SetField, process the row, and check the results again with GetField, as described above, for each record you need to add or update. Then you can disconnect from the Message Agent or begin another message. Should the message definition have the "Delete remaining rows option," then the Message Agent will eliminate any rows in the scroll that you have not added or updated since beginning the message in the first place.

When working with multiple rows, you can receive data from either an individual row or from within a scroll. You can do this by following the same type of procedure as when you acquire data from a panel that does not have a scroll bar. You can give the Message Agent values for all of the key fields that are important in identifying the row. Then use the GetField parameters to acquire the values from the non-key data fields that are designated as output fields within the message definition. If you are using a message definition that has the option of "Output all occurrences," then you can acquire data from all of the level 1 scrolls as long as the message definition includes both their input fields and output fields.

When you need to acquire data from all rows within a level 1 scroll, you must designate which message definitions you need to use via SmartMessages. You may also need to get the metadata that defines the fields within the message definition using the GetFieldList or GetFieldInfo within the

OLE interface. You must then set the values for the level 0 key fields, but this would not apply to any level 1 key fields though the SetField parameter. Note that a level 1 key field must be defined as output fields in the message definition. Only then can you use the ProcessMessage parameter to process the message.

You can then obtain the results for the first returned row using the GetValue parameter and can acquire the values from the output fields designated in the message definition. You can get the next returned row by using the FindNextOutputrow parameter and keep using that parameter again until you have processed all the returned rows. Afterwards, you can disconnect from the Message Agent or start another message.

Building a Message Definition

You can build a message definition through the Application Designer. It is defined and managed through business processes, and it can create a new message definition or alter your current message definitions.

A message definition can be created by either opening or creating a business process in the Application Designer. You can then build an activity inside the Business Process and the designer permits you to create message definitions on the activity map. When you create a message definition, you can designate each field within the mapping as an input field (a field with a value that the Message Agent maps from an external application to the PeopleSoft panel) or an output field (a field with a value that the Message Agent sends from the PeopleSoft panel to the output lists, making the value available to the external application).

Resolving Problems with the Message Agent

If you are trying to process a Message Agent transaction but instead receive a failed message error, note that there are easy ways of correcting these problems. During the installation process of PeopleTools version 7.5, the client only needs to have a subset of the PeopleSoft files in order to acquire access to the Message Agent and initiate Message Agent API functionality. Only minor differences exist between the installation of Windows and Unix. The client installation files are on the PeopleSoft CD and can be transferred to your file server so that you can install only what you need. This is a simple problem that just requires that you pay special attention to getting the right files for the right operating system.

It is possible to have several actions running at the same time from the Message Agent server for your application server. You can choose to cycle over the Message Agent server once a specific number of requests has been executed. This may be a prudent option if the Message Agent server crashes.

PeopleTools' 7.5 Message Agent structure can benefit from PeopleSoft's Tuxedo server functionality. Tuxedo can handle the queue management of client requests, server management, and monitoring functions.

You may experience problems by calling out program functions. Visual Basic programmers are advised to use OLE Automation Server APIs because you can build an OLE Automation Server object easily when you are familiar with the task.

OLE Automation Server

You can program an OLE Automation server by creating a reference to the type library "psmas.tlb" and then stating a variable "CmagAutoServer" within your program. You can then access its member functions (Connect, StartMessage, ProcessMessage, and Disconnect).

You can also program the OLE Automation server by stating a variable as a generic object and then setting the

variable to whatever is returned by the CreateObject
parameter. These procedures both achieve the same thing,
but you obtain better performance when you create a
reference to the type library above. It is possible for you to
call the C APIs from Visual Basic, but you need to state an
alias for these functions.

When programming in C++, you need only include
psmsgapi.h in your programs. This will give you access to
all of the functions and global definitions that are stated.
However, you must not include the header file that is
compliant for C++ compilers. You can optionally choose to
load psmsg.dll and acquire function pointers to the APIs
with which you need to work. Java programmers have an
easier time, as they need only create a wrapper code around
the C APIs.

You must be careful about PSMsgErrorText. If you see
messages from PSMsgErrorText that indicate a row exists
in the ADD or DATAENTRY module or that you have
more than one row existing for a search key, you have not
given sufficient key values necessary to access a specific
panel group or mode. You must then look at the type of
search record you have designated to access the specific
panel group. Some problems often result from not
supplying sufficient key values to the search record so it
can execute its tasks. You must make certain the Message
Agent does not have default values inserted into the search
record, as it is input with online processing. You may also
need to set values through the Message Agent yourself
without relying on any automation.

Working with the Configuration Manager

In order to find solutions to any problems you might
experience with your PeopleSoft implementation, you can
refine your possibilities and look for patterns. You can also

simplify your problems as much as possible by removing PeopleCode functions that modify your data. Remember the first things to trace include information such as SQL statements and Message Agent data. You need to look for a specific sequence of events that may have caused your error message. Under normal circumstances, you will notice SQL transactions to message catalog tables whenever an error occurs. The majority of the time, you can examine the end of the trace files in order to give you a good idea of where the error might have occurred.

Ask yourself if you are trying to validate a value by finding it on a table. Determine if you have any difficulty updating or inserting a row of data and compare any traces that occur between online transactions and the Message Agent transactions. You can then find the problem just by determining what is different that may be causing the error in your systems.

Error Messages

In order to understand the types of errors you may expect to see in your integrated PeopleSoft systems, this section will explain some of the more common messages you may see.

Unknown Form Field

This means that the field mapping that you used is not correct. You may be able to solve this problem by making certain that the field mappings use the correct case-sensitive routines.

Record Not Found in Current Panel Context

This means that the Message Agent was not able to locate the record inside the panel group. You can solve this problem by verifying that the record exists through examining the panel's layout.

Unable to Update Value

When the transaction was proceeding, the value you inserted for a specific field was not correctly saved. This means that the format of your data is probably not valid. In most cases, PeopleCode did not correctly execute for a specific field.

Record Field Not Found

This occurs when the Message Agent tries to locate the record.field reference on one your panel groups, but the system was not able to locate it. You can solve this problem by verifying that your message definition field mapping points to the proper record.field and that the panel group contains the appropriate record you need.

Bad Map Level Option

Whenever you have records at levels 1, 2, or 3, the Message Agent tries to acquire the level mapping information when it accesses data at any of these levels. This type of information was created specifically for your level mapping options within your message definition. You may also see this message if your panel layout is not constructed correctly.

Skipping Parent Key

This problem is not too difficult to solve. It means that the Message Agent was working through child records and searching for keys to define a specific row of data. Therefore, it will inherit key values from parent records.

Unable to Find Entry for this Map Level

This means that the Message Agent has attempted to find the record at a given scroll level but could not do so. You must make certain that you are mapping to the appropriate record's data-specific level. This means that the indentation in their field mapping provides you with a good overview of which types of records exist at a given scroll level.

Unable to Find Recfield

This means that the Message Agent found it difficult to find a record or field in our field mapping.

Could Not Find Record Field

In this type of error, the Message Agent has attempted to acquire the record and field that it must have to map data, but it could not get the data it needed. You can easily solve this problem by verifying that both the record and field exist within the database and the PeopleSoft panel.

Invalid Data Format

This type of error occurs when you try to insert the date field. You need to verify that they are all written in the correct format for the client on which they exist.

It is important to note that the Message Agent in PeopleTools 7.5 operates on the application server. This means that all the PeopleCode runs on the application server too. Thus, you may choose to operate the Validation Wizard with the Web option enabled, which enables you to verify that all of your PeopleCode can be performed on the application server correctly. You can then examine any values in use by PeopleCode functions, compare the online traces to the Message Agent traces, and determine what is different. By comparing these results, you can correct your errors quickly and efficiently.

Helpful Hints

You can also insert duplicate keys. Note that the Message Agent does not support records that contain duplicate keys,

so they shouldn't exist in your RDBMS. You can solve
problems with duplicate keys by adding another key to the
record so you have a unique set of key values that allows
you to identify each row. You can then remove any
duplicate key field attributes from your records.

You may choose to insert several level 1 rows. You
can insert several of these rows of data by using one
ProcessMessage call via the Message Agent. Although you
may not use this same type of process to insert several level
0, 2, or 3 rows of data in any given transaction, you can set
all of the level 0 key and non-key fields and then loop
through all level 1 key and non-key types of fields. When
you have gone through these steps, you can send a
ProcessMessage parameter to save all of your data.

You can use the #MessageAgent in PeopleCode to
separate any PeopleCode functions that are executed by
encapsulating specific lines of code through "if-then"
statements using the %MessageAgent parameter. Note that
the PeopleCode variable %MessageAgent will possess an
actual value when the Message Agent is used within a
transaction.

You can acquire multiple output rows when dealing
with only level 1 scrolls. You must make certain that the
level 1 records have the flag enabled for "Output All
Occurrences" in the same way you use Message Agent
types of procedures so that you can move effectively
through your output lists.

As you review these helpful hints to improve your
Message Agent integration tool, you must finally consider
performance issues. When inserting large amounts of data,
you can benefit from inserting several level 1 rows at the
same time. Although the panel group that you access needs
to have a specific panel construction, you can batch your
data up and reduce the amount of network access you

require. This will free up your network resources and enable you to increase your performance with less network traffic.

You can verify the search keys that are used when you are indexing. Make certain these keys are used to line up with indexes created for a specific table. If you have a record with indexes of a given set of fields, they are displayed in a certain order and you have a search record with specific values for those fields. Under normal circumstances, it will take you quite a bit of time to look for a record with the specific elements you need, because your database will have to execute a full index table scan that will consume a great deal of time. If you have a search record with values for the fields that you need, however, it will execute that lookup command much more quickly.

Conclusion

Now that you have a good idea how the Message Agent can play a vital role in your enterprise resource planning environment, you can now use the knowledge you have learned about PeopleTools integration tools and apply that to understanding the Electronic Data Interchange (EDI) Manager tool in the next chapter. These tools all function effectively together to provide you with a cohesive computing environment.

04

EDI Manager Tool

The Electronic Data Interchange (EDI)
Manager tool is used to define the data
mappings for EDI. In addition, it can
also be used as a general data migration
tool between PeopleSoft and files or
batches of data.

95

EDI Manager

The PeopleSoft EDI Manager, as shown in Figure 4.1, gives you the tools you need to manage electronic commerce transactions with your trading partners. The EDI Manager lets you establish and maintain data about your colleagues. You can also designate data mapping between transaction files and tables within your PeopleSoft database.

When setting up the EDI Manager, you must learn how you can integrate it with your electronic commerce implementation that helps you prepare your system and accept EDI transactions. It gives you benefits that enable you to designate conversion rules for your transaction data, designate your transaction types for your application processes, and establish partner relationships between external companies as well as internal business entities.

Electronic Data Interchange

The EDI standard offers a method of exchanging data between companies so they can perform electronic

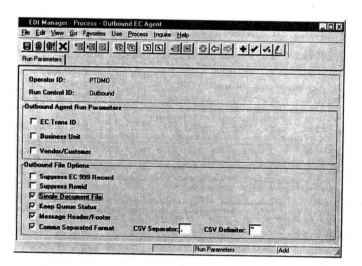

Figure 4.1 *EDI Manager.*

business. EDI provides you with a standardized format for transaction data. It allows porters to communicate in a common programming language. Should one organization require a transaction connection, it can extract the transaction data from its database and then translate it into the standard EDI format. It then transmits that information over a network to another trading organization or partner. The other partner company receives this EDI transmission and transfers that data into a transaction-processing application. The process involves several procedures, but the EDI transactions are enabled by your PeopleSoft application, as illustrated in the following illustration.

Outgoing Transactions

You will find that the procedure for outgoing transactions is similar to that of incoming transactions. You can run an SQE that extracts the proper data from the application tables, at which time it copies that data set to the staging label. An EDI Agent then creates PeopleSoft business documents from this data, at which time the EDI translation software converts the document into an X.12 or EDIFACT format before they are sent to your partners.

The procedure involves your data from PeopleSoft business documents and both incoming and outgoing staging tables. The entire step is executed by EDI Agents and is executed with respect to data mapping defined within the EDI Manager. You can then transfer data from the staging tables and the application tables just by executing the proper sets of data validation. Note that this step is executed by SQRs to process specific types of transactions.

PeopleSoft's EDI Manager enables you to designate mappings that the EDI Agents use to convert PeopleSoft business documents into data for the staging tables. In addition, you can use the EDI Manager to retain information regarding both vendors and trading partners linked with your organization.

When dealing with EDI transaction data, note that staging tables are only used as temporary storage areas. Whenever the EDI Agent works on a PeopleSoft business document, it copies the data into your database by adding the information into the staging tables. Then the application load process transfers the data from the staging tables into the application tables. Note that this process is transaction-specific.

EDI PeopleSoft Codes

When you work with EDI transactions from your trading partners, it is important to note that the majority of the data will be sent to you in code or in identification numbers. Anyone who sends you a transaction will have a trading partner and will have a transaction ID to identify the type of transaction.

PeopleSoft's database stores most of its information and data in codes of ID numbers too. The types of codes it can incorporate include the following:

- Business Unit ID

- Customer ID

- Employee ID

- Operator ID

Most of these types of codes are similiar to the information in the body of the EDI transaction. During process transactions, the EDI Agent duplicates the transaction data in the PeopleSoft database. At this point, the database converts the external EDI codes into PeopleSoft codes. In addition, outgoing EDI transactions are written out in the file so it can convert the PeopleSoft codes into codes that trading partners can use. You can also designate how an EDI Agent converts codes by using EDI Manager.

The EDI Manager can execute two types of conversions:

1. It can translate between EDI event codes and PeopleSoft action codes. These codes determine which type of action a transaction needs.

2. It can convert data values from any field within a given transaction.

Event Codes

Event codes are important within EDI transactions because they have the power to designate which type of action is needed by a transaction call. This means that event codes can determine if a transaction is either an entirely new, resubmitted, or an updated form of a transaction within your system.

Primary event codes (purpose codes) determine the transaction status. This means it can either be a new transaction, cancellation, duplication, or status request. In short, each and every transaction can have a primary code associated with it.

Secondary event codes (transaction codes) determine the transaction types. This means that a secondary event code can make some transaction types include these types of codes, while others do not. PeopleSoft can designate a specific action for a given transaction, however, through a single action code. This means that an EDI Agent can process an EDI transaction but requires an event code conversion into a PeopleSoft action code.

The EDI Manager enables you to find specific event codes that are translated into specific codes. You may choose to process transactions in different ways, depending on the specific trading partner that created them in the first place. In addition, the EDI Manager enables you to designate various event codes to action translators.

The EDI Agent uses specific methods to translate event codes into action codes. It can designate a set of recognizable primary event codes, secondary event codes, and action codes. You can choose to determine exactly which event codes are associated with specific action codes for a given trading partner profile. You must also define which trading partner profile you need to use for each of your associates.

Working with Values

You will find that data values in a given EDI transaction field may not always correspond to the values within the PeopleSoft database. This means that the EDI transaction can designate transaction codes through a given set of numbers, but the PeopleSoft database can only use letters to depict the same exact codes. In this type of situation, the EDI Agent must translate external values into associated internal values.

It is important to define your conversion data profile because it uses the PeopleSoft database table values and determines how that value will be recorded within PeopleSoft business documents. You can then create several conversion data profiles for the same table, yet you may have to establish various conversions for each of your trading partners to achieve this objective.

In order to convert data values for each partner, you must first designate a table within the PeopleSoft database that contains values that are different from those in PeopleSoft business documents. You may have to designate a trading partner conversion ID to each table to make this possible. You can then establish a conversion data profile that determines how internal and corresponding external values are used for each table value. When you use another trading partner, you are in effect using different values and must create one conversion data profile for each unique set of external values. Finally, you can define the proper conversion data profile for each trading partner to keep your information correct.

Working with EDI Transactions

When trading partners send you EDI transactions, note that its first record includes a transaction ID that will determine the transaction type. The EDI Agent will employ this ID together with the trading partner's ID so you know which inbound map is necessary to process your transaction data. Conversely, when you send an outgoing transaction, the EDI Agent will append the correct transaction ID in the first transaction record. This enables the person receiving it to know which type of transaction you have sent.

It is important that you determine exactly what transactions your system can process in the EDI Manager. Furthermore, you must determine exactly what transactions each person has the ability to execute for each of your trading partners. In order to achieve this objective, you must first create a transaction ID for each type of transaction that you want your applications to support. Then you must establish at least one pattern profile that lists several transactions each partner can execute. Finally, define a partner profile for each trading partner to accomplish your objective.

Working with Trading Partners

When dealing with trading partners, it is important to know exactly what the trading partner does and to whom it refers in your business dealings. A trading partner is a business that resides within an external company.

You can organize your company into several business units with PeopleSoft's financial applications. However, each unit tracks your data in a different way since each business unit works with different trading partners.

A trading partner should send an EDI transaction to a
particular business unit so that the EDI Agent knows where
the business unit should be forwarded to and whom to send
the transaction to once processing is complete. External
organizations often have distinct divisions, departments,
and units to which EDI transactions should be addressed.

Whenever you establish trading partners in your EDI
Manager, you must designate an internal and external
hierarchy in each organization. This means you must
designate entry codes for specific business types that act as
partners. You must then designate trading partner IDs to
every internal business unit for the external training
partners so that they can submit transactions.

PeopleSoft financial applications record their own
individual set of business units and trading partner IDs.
This gives them the capability to refer to multiple business
unit IDs for several physical units. You can then designate
trading partner IDs for your external organizations. In
addition, should you need to send in EDI transactions to
specific business units within an associate company, then
you need to define unique business entity IDs.

One final note about dealing with EDI transactions is that
PeopleSoft applications record their transaction information
inside PeopleSoft database tables. In order for an application
to execute an EDI transaction, it becomes necessary for it to
have the transaction data in its tables. Therefore, in order to
process an EDI transaction, it must first transfer the data
from an incoming EDI transaction set file into the
application tables. In addition to create the EDI transaction
that must be given to the trading partner, you must acquire
the transaction data from the application tables and get that
information into an EDI transaction set file.

You must define how your EDI Agent will transfer data
from the EDI transaction set file and the application tables.
You can do this by defining an electronic commerce map.
There are two types of electronic commerce maps:

1. Inbound maps that transfer incoming transaction data into a database

2. Outbound maps that create outgoing EDI documents from transaction data in the database

Business Documents

PeopleSoft business documents are in an ASCII file format and possess data for at least one EDI transaction. These documents have both transaction and control information that informs the system of the specific transaction type, where it was created, and how its specific document elements pertain to each other. Business documents are segmented into records, which are separated from each other through a line feed and carriage return.

Every record is reduced into fields of a specific length. One of the record fields is the Record ID (usually #1), which determines the record type, header, detail line, summary line, and any other information or record field you need.

The control record is the first business document record. This record determines the transaction type for the trading partners you deal with. It is based on the control record where the EDI Agent can receive the mapping definition for the designated transaction as well as the data conversion options. The EDI Agent can read the document records individually, but after each record that follows the control record, the EDI Agent reads the record ID field value and determines the exact record definition to use for parsing the remainder of the record.

PeopleSoft record definitions determine

- Location

- Size

- Data Type

This information is used for all the other record fields and the EDI Agent can then copy the data from the document into staging database tables. The EDI Agent follows a given set of rules whereby it deals with a new control record that is defined by the ID of 999. It can then receive the mapping definition for the new transaction type and report the process. However, the majority of transactions incorporate several record types that include the following:

- Header

- Detail lines

- Schedules

- Summary lines

- Other relevant information

Record layout inside a business document follows a specific pattern where all detail lines are connected to a specific parent of header lines and all must be the same as the parent record. It is important to note that the EDI Agent can process transactions made at a specific unit of work that the EDI Agent should use for entities such as purchases and invoices.

Keeping Electronic Commerce Flowing

Whenever you need to monitor your EDI processing, the EDI Manager should be used to perform continuous examinations of your electronic commerce applications. You will need to be able to utilize outbound maps, schedule EDI Agents, review EDI processing errors, and finally be able to examine your processing history at a moment's notice.

EDI Agents have the capability to copy EDI transactions between business documents and the database. EDI Agents come in two different types. The first is the inbound EDI

Agent that can process incoming transactions just by copying data from your business documents into your database. The second is the outbound EDI Agent that can create business documents from transaction data in the EDI staging tables. Note that EDI maps do not start the EDI Agent. You have to use a Process Scheduler request that informs your system exactly when, where, and how often you need to run each instance of the EDI Agent.

It is important to know how you can start at least one EDI Agent to process both your incoming and outgoing EDI transactions. In addition, you must produce outbound maps that the EDI Agent can use to run controls, start EDI Agents, and finally create your outbound maps.

Whenever you examine any task, it is important to consider that scheduling tasks depends on using the Process Scheduler. In order to schedule a process, you must inform your system exactly when and where the process should be executed. Run controls are important because they are involved in database records that establish setting values. You need not input the same value every time you schedule a process; you must instead save a run control with specific settings. Each time you schedule a process, you must choose the run control so that your system will establish the missing settings. Whenever you choose a process, the EDI Manager waits for you to input a run control ID. This allows you to use a current run control record, choose the update/display mode, create a new record, or add a mode.

Defining What the EDI Agent Needs

You can define what the EDI Agent needs whenever you create an outbound map definition. The EDI Agent must be able to extract data from the staging tables, but the EDI Agent must execute SQL statements that rely on your specific map definitions. When your system can process an EDI transaction, two EDI Agents must be functioning constantly (an inbound and outbound agent). You may wish to start another EDI Agent instance for tasks such as processing business documents that failed the first run through. Should an error occur at any point during the EDI processing, the EDI Agent can transmit a wordlist item to the EDI Coordinator.

What the EDI Transaction Does

The EDI transaction can enable you to receive any transmissions from other trading partners over the network. This can be anything like the number of transactions set for any amount of internal trading partners. You can mange all of the transaction data, but your file organizers must be set in several specific ways.

The package level of the top level of your company represents the complete transaction set file. It is made out to your organization the same way a mail package would be done. This type of package can be composed of at least one type of transaction group. Each type of transaction group can be a set of transactions that deal with the same type as well as with the same partners or associates of your organization.

It is important to note that every single transaction group will incorporate at least one individual unit of work (possibly more). Each unit of work is representative of a single transaction that you need to either commit or roll back, depending on your needs.

EDI Transaction Software

Third-party suppliers can give you software that deals with EDI translations and can create PeopleSoft business documents. These documents are divided into transaction set files and occur at each transaction group level.

Business documents normally include several units of work and often incorporate numerous transaction groups, according to how you have configured your translation software. However, it is important to note that PeopleSoft business documents do not include information regarding its transaction group packages or where they come from. It is important to note that EDI translation software can give you this type of information through external audit files. In addition, the EDI Agent has the capability to copy information into audit tables within your database. Accessing auditing information, however, requires the EDI translation software to record both the package and the transaction group information within an audit file. Only then can the EDI Agent process this file.

Conclusion

Now that we have seen how EDI can use agents to process files and facilitate operations within your PeopleSoft computing environment, we can enhance this discussion in the next chapter by examining workflow processors. It too can host several agents that have the power to run and control the workflow in your business process.

05

Workflow Processor

The Workflow Processor is a suite of online agents that run and control the workflow in your business processes. When these business processes are defined, agents are created to perform the business process tasks.

Business Processes

Business processes are important because if you need to perform a task within a PeopleSoft application, you must be able to access and utilize at least one panel. Most often, a task is composed of one single step. In many other cases, however, a given task may need several steps in which the user needs to execute an entire procedure in a specific order. Many of these steps can include

- Online transactions

- Using panels

- Manual processes

- Automated background processes

- Workflow routings

When dealing with application functionality, most business processes offer a process-oriented type of organization with features that support function-oriented menus. These processes simplify the procedures necessary to complete a given task. In addition, these processes provide a clear illustration of your workflow that will allow you and your users to view the exactly results of an automated task started from a specific panel within your PeopleSoft implementation.

Business processes provide several benefits that are better than menus. These benefits extend to the point where business processes offer a clear illustration of several steps within the task flow and everything it depends on. This means you can see exactly which user actions are necessary in order to create a unified procedure.

These types of business processes also function to demonstrate what they have been used for, as opposed to what functions they can execute. Users have the ability to navigate through panels simply by determining which transactions they can execute at a given time. These processes also provide a clear illustration of your workflow routings and how they are integrated into your automation.

These business processes are accessible by users through the PeopleSoft navigator. This is important because you can create business processes in the Application Designer by establishing an illustrative navigator map that can depict that ordered representation of business processes within an application.

Business process maps are useful for connecting you with users' business processes. These processes require security access from the user to reach the PeopleSoft applications. You will find business process maps a good visual method of navigating through icons connecting business processes or other business process maps to your console.

Graphically depicted business processes illustrate functions that make up your business processes. The PeopleSoft windows graphically depict the relationships between specific activities as well as any interdependencies that may exist in your activity sequence for a given process. Such activities explain the exact steps that are associated with application panels or external programs that make up an activity inside of a business process. Activities often include specific methodologies or procedures that deal with application panels as well as the following:

- Workflow routings

- Decision points

- Approval steps

You can see the best illustration of a workflow routing in an activity document. Users can simply select the workflow routing icon to show the task description. Figure 5.1 shows the activity routing icon within the PeopleSoft system, whereas Figure 5.2 shows the workflow routing icon.

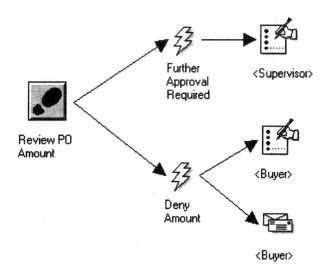

Figure 5.1 *Activity Routing Icon.*

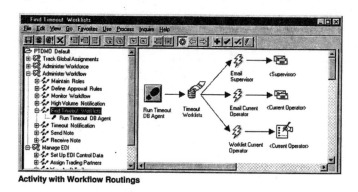

Activity with Workflow Routings

Figure 5.2 *Workflow Routing Icon.*

The Application Designer allows you to designate
business processes within an application. You can do this
by composing navigator maps, which define specific
component relationships and attributes that help define
your business process.

Two navigator map types exist that include

1. Business process maps

2. Navigator maps

The Application Designer maps exist as independent objects within the Application Designer, allowing you to employ normal procedures to execute the following types of operations:

- Open

- Save

- Delete

- Rename

- Project adding

Analyzing Business Processes

When you begin to compose business processes and business process maps within the Application Designer, it is important that your first step involve the analysis of automated business processes. Thus, you must perform the following steps:

- Define all component tasks

- Define how a task can be segmented into:

  1. Activities

  2. Steps

Analyzing a business process means you have to divide the work so you can develop a business process that is composed of an activity that has several steps or a step that has many activities. In order to accomplish your goal, you may need to establish individual activities when you need to separate work from one user to another user in another group. This means that all activities must incorporate steps for one individual user. This removes a great deal of the complexity involved when integrating business processes into your working environment.

You can create individual activities when there is a time delay between specific tasks for a single user. This means that users must have the ability to finish all of the steps involved in a given activity during a specific instance. You must also outline several individual steps in an activity. This allows you to make specific designations at each major panel or group that a user must finish. The concept and methodology behind creating steps within an activity for the user allows him/her to navigator more easily between specific PeopleSoft panels by using the "Next Step" and "Previous Step" commands within the PeopleSoft graphical Navigator.

Also try to create steps for panels that you consider to be of high importance. This means that if you see a panel you think a user will only use occasionally for specialized processing tasks, then it is not worth including it in a given activity. You may instead allow the user to acquire the panel through the menu or panel navigator buttons instead.

Using PeopleSoft's Navigator

Navigator maps come in three distinct flavors: activities, business processes (shown in Figure 5.3), and business process maps. Figure 5.4 shows business process maps within your ERP environment. Both the business processes and business process maps exist individually so that you can work in the Application Designer and incorporate several projects. Note that activities are an important component for your business processes so that you can both access and define these activities through the "Activity" icon present in the open business process.

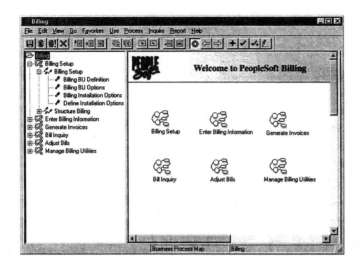

Figure 5.3 *Business Processes.*

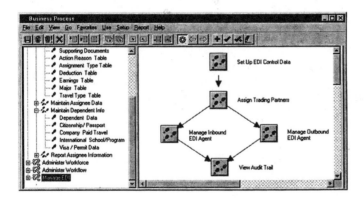

Figure 5.4 *Business Process Maps.*

Activity definitions are recorded individually so that the same activity can be used by several business processes. Although you cannot add a business process to a business process map until after the specific business process has been made, you can define the business process before anything else. PeopleSoft's Navigator has several benefits when you define

- Business process maps

- Business processes

- Activities

Using any of these features, you can define a universal set of Application Designer features that enable you to put icons on the map, move them, and even establish a set of properties for them. You can then display or hide your modeling systems or even control the map size's zoom display. In addition, you can maintain a level of control over the grid so you can align icons the way you want to and then navigate between business processes and associated activities.

Creating Maps

One advantage of PeopleSoft's Navigator is that you can create your own business process map. You can do this in the form of a graphical depiction of at least one (possibly more than one) business process. This type of graph or map functions as a path between the PeopleSoft Navigator and specific user maps. These business process maps can integrate several business processes as well as their associated activities that lead to other maps as well.

Map Security

At any point when you are responsible for adding either an operator or an operator class within PeopleSoft's Security Administrator, you must define what your default business process map will be for a given operator or operator class. The default map is usually the graphical representation that shows when a given user begins to use the PeopleSoft Navigator. In addition, this map will also explain what level of security the user has to have in order to access a given map. This can mean that a user has access to all of the maps or perhaps he only has access to some of the maps that are directly or indirectly connected to the default business process map.

When users move from one map to another, they begin at the default business process map to which they have access level security. This means that the user can have access to all of the business processes that show up on the default map. However, if the default map has connections to other business process maps, then they have access to all of the other business processes within their access domain as well.

This means that a given user can theoretically access all of the associated activities that correspond to a specific business process. Please note that this doesn't automatically give access to all of the activities present within a given PeopleSoft panel. This does, however, provide a starting point where the user has surpassed one very important access layer barrier and could possibly delve further into your system.

When the user does choose a given step, the system will examine his privileges to determine if that user has a sufficient level of security access to the panel that the user wants to access. The system begins by looking at the user's access rights to the panel in question in much the same way as if the user had chosen to enter through the GUI menus. It does this by examining a list of authorized menu items present within the Security Administrator. However, if the user does not have a sufficient level of access to reach the panel, the system will output a message error and will deny access.

Development and Workflow

If you need to develop or refine your applications, you need to follow a special procedure that will make certain you have some valid relationships between the objects you define, including

- Fields

- Records

- Panels

- Panel groups

- Menus

As you specialize your PeopleSoft application, you must determine exactly which objects will change as a result of any adjustments you make. When you can determine the impact of your changes, you can develop your application using the following procedure:

1. First design your application as your primary development step.

2. Establish your field definitions and create your project using PeopleSoft's Application Designer for the duration of this procedure.

3. Establish your record definition.

4. Create your SQL objects.

5. Establish your exact panel definitions.

6. Develop your panel group definitions.

7. Define your menu definitions.

8. Define your business processes.

9. Use the Security Administrator to enable your PeopleSoft security protocols throughout your system environment.

10. You can test the applications for your online system to make certain they work correctly.

Working with Workflow

PeopleSoft applications offer several advantages, but most importantly they can help you add a refined layer of automation to your business tasks. PeopleSoft provides you with workflow tools that can be integrated into several automated business processes. These tools can help you integrate several user activities into one centralized business process.

Workflow can also help you both refine and revamp your mission-critical business processes. This will help you achieve the following business objectives:

- Efficiency

- Reduction in costs

- Support of customer and personnel needs

Workflow is integrated into PeopleSoft's applications so that you can benefit from

- Workflow tools

- Electronic forms

- E-mail

- Intelligent agents

All of these elements function seamlessly to provide you with automated business process that include

- Procurements

- New hires

- Transaction approvals

- Automating common business processes

PeopleSoft enables Workflow to integrate with all of its other applications similarly to an open system. In addition, PeopleTools and Workflow tools function together to offer a simple development environment that you can use to customize your applications to meet your individual business requirements.

Workflow Defined

The majority of your daily tasks are probably part of much bigger tasks that use several steps and several workgroups functioning together as one unit. Whenever you go into one application, you must have a reason for using its function. The module will output a certain result that a third person must review and then the cycle is complete. This type of process is a workflow process and refers to a larger process that leads a cycle from one initiatory event to a completion event.

Nearly all business processes are, in one form or another, defined using the Application Designer and the workflow process. Workflow is generally used to call up processes that deal with several users as well as the data routing between one user group and another. Workflow tools also assist you in creating routings within your enterprise system environment. Due to the fact that the system itself realizes what your overall objectives are, it can automatically proceed to the next step in your workflow process.

Customer Example

The best way to illustrate the workflow process is to look at a customer example to see exactly how workflow processes can integrate within your enterprise. Let's say that a new company has formed and they have to hire some experienced people. This company advertises in the newspaper and are flooded with numerous resumes from people who all look qualified for selected positions. It is difficult, if not impossible, to choose the best candidate for the job.

The company decides to implement a special process for hiring employees in the organization. This process involves several manual steps. First, the resumes for a given job are tallied and reviewed in a special job request panel. Then the job candidates are reviewed by the company's HR manager who either approves or rejects each individual candidate. Should the manager approve the candidate, he or she goes to the training department to learn and become part of the organization. Should the HR manager reject the candidate, then the employee is informed by telephone or a rejection postcard. If there is only one clear candidate who meets all of the job criteria, he or she is automatically approved. Finally, the training department instructs the employee on company matters and confirms his or her new status as a member of the organization.

This example demonstrates how workflow is the overall process required to become part of an organization. In all of the above tasks, the business rules link every process of hiring the individual together into one unit. Each task that is completed during this process is called an activity, while every single condition that causes each activity is called an "event." The process leads from submitting the resume to being approved by the HR management to finally becoming part of this organization.

Automating Workflow

This entire process can also be automated. PeopleSoft provides you with a workflow that can be integrated into an HR department to automate the majority of this business process.

When a job candidate finishes his application, the system automatically sends his resume to the HR manager to be judged for a job position. When the HR manager approves the candidate, the system sends the resume and the HR manager's evaluation along to the training department. If the HR manager rejects the candidate, the system generates a rejection postcard that is immediately mailed to the candidate, informing him/her no positions are available. Finally, when the candidate does get hired, the system generates a worker profile for the person and makes him or her part of the organization by creating an e-mail account and entering the employee into the payroll computer.

This method allows the PeopleSoft system to offer its capabilities to non-PeopleSoft users who wish to benefit from the system's automated processes. This example company can benefit from the HR process by permitting users to write out a hire form in another application instead of going through the PeopleSoft panel. The system can automatically process the form, map its data into an application, and then start the hiring process. This can help enhance your business processes through the use of automated means. Figure 5.5 demonstrates how a form-based e-mail allows non-PeopleSoft users to send data to your PeopleSoft system.

What Workflow Has to Offer

You can see exactly how PeopleSoft applications provide you with a common database that allows you to provide information with PeopleSoft users in your organization. However, accessing the same data does not necessarily mean everyone is working together as a group. In the

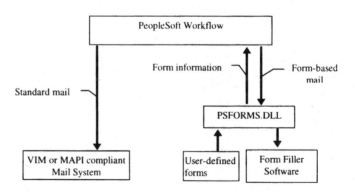

Figure 5.5 *Form-based E-mail.*

absence of automated workflow, you can perform a great deal of work beyond the system perimeter in an effort to group all of your activates with those of other users. This allows you to maintain the workflow throughout your organization.

Whenever a candidate enters a request to be hired from another position, the HR manager and training department do not know about it until they run a query or receive a personal message from that person. However, workflow makes it possible for your applications to do much more. Should you require an HR manager's approval for a specific hiring request, the system can automatically send that request to the proper person. It is not necessary to establish a supporting task that would send e-mail or route a printed copy of the resume to the correct person.

Workflow functions by killing any extraneous job tasks that are affiliated with controlling paper flow throughout your company. This process can effectively unburden employees of performing clerical functions to focus on more difficult tasks.

Workflow can also allow you to monitor your organization's work and improve how it is managed. It helps you by speeding continuous process enhancements. This means you can determine at any point in time how your business is changing and how to change your business processes to meet those changes. When changes do take place, you can use this methodology to implement new business processes and refine your organization into a more effective setup.

Workflow Tools

Workflow tools can significantly help you improve your tasks and automate several business processes within your organization. Instead of dealing with specific database queries for expired passwords or overdue products, you can set the system to automatically search for work that must be completed. Once it finds that work, it can create working items to cope with the demand. This procedure is good for tasks that do not require user involvement to proceed.

You can use the PeopleSoft Message Agent to incorporate other application vendors within your business processes. Users have the chance to send and receive information to and from other PeopleSoft databases using e-mail and forms that they know and can input data into easily. This procedure is good for tasks that involve non-PeopleSoft users with whom you need to exchange data to do business.

Workflow software has the capability to connect activities that maintain and facilitate the flow of your business processes. This type of work is helpful for tasks that involve several users or several workgroups functioning together to further a business objective or goal. When you combine all of these workflow capabilities together in your product, it is important to maintain your concentration on integrating Workflow into all procurement stages and approval cycles through the virtual approval application that PeopleTools has created.

The majority of applications from PeopleSoft offer several business processes that can help your company satisfy your organizational needs that include PeopleSoft Payables and PeopleSoft Human Resources. PeopleSoft Payables refines your voucher approval, verifying that your payments are made on time and that they are signed off correctly. PeopleSoft Human Resources incorporates several model business processes that you need for both hiring and firing employees, job changes, and informing managers of when employee reviews are due.

Conclusion

As we have seen, the Workflow Processor can provide you with the capability to perform several functions. You can deal with several tasks and know exactly which types of processes you can utilize in your system. However, knowing your workflow is only part of the solution. In order to realize its potential, you need to know how to use PeopleSoft navigation tools to move about your system and perform certain functions. You will find the next chapter an enormous help in knowing how to benefit from the PeopleSoft Navigational Array and use it to your advantage.

06

PeopleSoft Navigator Tools

PeopleSoft Navigator tools offer a graphical browser that provides your application users with a map of the business processes they participate in, enabling them to navigate or select application panels by clicking on activities they need to perform.

Data Tools

The PeopleSoft system offers several data integrity tools that ensure your information is correctly recorded in your system. These tools include

- SQL Alter

- SYSAUDIT

- DDDAUDIT

You will want to use these tools whenever you are performing activities that include

- Upgrades

- System customizations

- Integrity verification

- Comparisons to SQL objects

PeopleSoft doesn't care much for people making changes in the system at the database level. They do ask that you work via a PeopleSoft application or use their PeopleTools, which lessens your chances of encountering problems. The tools they provide will help you support a consistent level of information recorded in PeopleTools as well as the information recorded in your database.

Data Mover

The data mover is a PeopleTool that offers you an easy method of transferring data from one PeopleSoft database to another. You can move databases from one operation system to a database platform on another machine or another network. You can perform SQL statements on any database and it doesn't matter if the operating system or database platform is different. You can also control your database security and access privileges.

The data mover is very helpful in allowing you to

- Create scripts

- Edit scripts

- Run scripts

These types of scripts can integrate any type of SQL command and data mover command used for either importing or exporting database information. Note that the default file extension for scripts is .DMS (data mover scripts).

When dealing with the input and output panes, note that the input pane window is the location where the script you will open is displayed. The input pane is where you can both view and edit database mover scripts. The output pane window shows the script run results. Should you come across any errors, the output pane will show you where the script has failed.

Status Bar

When you have the status bar in front of you, something called the SQL trace is shown. You should really use data mover with the tracing turned off, so you can displace the SQL trace before starting the data mover in several areas including the PeopleTools utilities and the Configuration Manager.

There is an operating mode display on the status bar. It tells you if you are in regular mode or in bootstrap mode. When you are linked to the database in regular mode, the status will display a blank operating mode. The operating mode will display bootstrap if you are connected to a given mode. You must make certain that you know what mode you are connected to so that the database command can proceed correctly.

Data Mover Modes

As stated above, the data mover has two modes in which it can operate. This first is regular mode, which you will use the majority of the time when you log into the data mover. You can access this mode by entering your operator ID and password during sign on. Note that in regular mode all your commands are valid and can be used.

The second mode is called bootstrap mode. You can use this mode whenever you need to start the data mover with a password. In this circumstance, you are effectively launching in bootstrap mode itself, which is normally used for database loading. You can also use this function when no PeopleSoft security tables are defined. In addition, this mode is used for achieving several security tasks that grant user permissions or encrypt the user's password.

When discussing data mover modes, it is important to detail how scripts can contain several types of commands. Two commands in particular include the data mover commands and SQL commands. Database mover commands are used to both import and export database information or modify the database itself. These commands can control script performance or call up other data mover files and input comments. SQL commands incorporate both standard and atypical SQL commands used to modify the database for several different options.

There are very specific data mover commands. These commands are independent of any platform and are individualized to your data mover. These commands are used for

- Importing

- Exporting

- Controlling the run environment

- Renaming fields and records

- Database security administration

- Denoting comments

Data mover commands are straightforward. The ENCRYPT_PASSWORD allows you to encrypt any user passwords for access. EXPORT tells the data mover to choose record information and data from a record that inserts the result set within a file. You can make use of the export file created as input to migrate to another platform. This type of file can move easily between ASCII and EBCDIC characters and work with double-byte characters too.

GRANT_USER allows an operator to obtain permission to sign on to the system. IMPORT places data into a table that uses the export file information. If a table space or table does not exist, this command can create table space, tables, or indexes for a record just by employing the export file information.

RWMARK is used to make comments and REWNAME enables you to rename a record, a field in a record, or a field in all records.

REPLACE_ALL is like the IMPORT command because if a table does exist, you can use this command to drop the table and its indexes from the database. You can then develop the table and indexes though the export file information and then insert data into the table through the export file information. REPLACE_DATA is also like the IMPORT command because it can delete data from an existing table and then insert the data into the export file. REPLACE_VIEW enables you to redevelop a certain view within the database.

RUN allows you to perform a .DMS file form inside the data move script, but this file cannot have any nested RUN commands. When something is succeeded by a SET parameter, a forms statement can set certain conditions whereby the data mover can perform SQL commands.

Working with the Import Manager

It is often difficult to implement an application that transports data within your system. Since your current data may not have had any edits, you may have to define them within the Application Designer using PeopleCode. This means you may need to input data that satisfies certain rules in order to acquire a level of consistency and validity in your data.

The Import Manager will permit you to input one row of a data at a time. This means that it is not the same as when you work on panels that have access to multiple rows simultaneously. This is primarily why you can validate field values for field edits and PeopleCode that is designated within your application.

The concept in this section is to demonstrate how you can prepare your data conversion and use the Import Manager to develop an import definition to upload source information from one database to another in your application data tables. You can then learn to execute a sample import and review the result through summarized output. Finally, you can examine and anticipate several data interdependencies and special importing procedures.

Conversions

Whenever you develop an efficient conversion procedure, you need to establish specific operational objectives. Before you actually create your conversion procedure, however, you need to know exactly how to implement an effective management statement that can define your operational objectives. You must consider several factors that will be crucial to your conversion goal. You want to ask yourself exactly how much historical data you need to convert, does this data have any value, and if you need to rationalize code values or reorganize your data. In short, every point during your implementation and data conversion must be considered.

When creating a data conversion plan, you must do it in several stages:

1. Designate your implementation goals.

2. Create conversion stages that satisfy your priorities.

3. Incorporate time estimates for full conversion process.

4. Allocate time for tasks.

If you follow these procedures, you can proceed to create your data load routines. First, you must create scrub routines, which are programs that ensure you have achieved a certain level of data validity and integrity once you load your data into your tables.

In order to test your systems to achieve the best load time, you will need to execute several comparison tests to see exactly how much time is required for load job runs. This means you will have to determine whether longer or shorter load times will be most effective for front-end programming and data inspecting. You also must examine back-end data modifications because of load edits that were not completed.

You also must select a load method for each data set that will provide the least load time and the most ideal data integrity. However, you still must test your data after conversion. This means you will have to check your data integrity by examining rows online. PeopleCode can show you online errors that will flag any data problems, but you still must identify any inconsistencies and resolve your problems yourself.

One of the ways in which you can dig out potential problems within your organization is through data mapping. Several organizations don't really believe in data ownership or the types of relationships that exist between certain data elements prior to creating a conversion plan. So before you continue with your conversion plan, you must examine your business priorities and determine the best methods for mapping processes. Thus, you will have to define specific function areas that will incorporate the first stage of data conversion.

You can begin your data conversion by starting with one area and working toward other pertinent data

elements field by field. Next, you can examine your data
for any interdependencies to see if any data groups must
be integrated in the first converted data set. Once you have
mapped all of your data elements, you must determine
which data elements exist on each table and which of
those elements need data from other tables for either
searches or validation. You can then make certain that all
of your fields and functional data elements are consistent
between the source and target system. If any data is not
available in the source system, it must be included in some
way through other input methods before it is transferred
to the target system.

Once you have gotten into the conversion process, you
can use the Import Manager as both an editing and a data
validation tool. You can also use it as a data load method
as well. The Import Manager helps you make certain that
your data satisfies both online editing and formatting
requirements. It can assist you in identifying data rows that
do not satisfy your table insert rules. If you are working
with high volumes of rows, you may need a high-volume
load procedure that includes the use of load programs.

In order to determine the best method for your tasks,
you must examine the conversion procedure very closely.
This evaluation must include load times for each
conversion method and determine the load time as
opposed to the volume of data and validity requirements.
You must then examine if the conversion tool you need is
the best one for your initial data load, or if you can use it
for a runtime data load from another system. You can then
determine how the combination of these procedures will
help you examine all of our conversion levels and satisfy
your implantation objectives. Finally, you can test your
conversion methods to see which one can most effectively
manage the volume of data you have through the best
means possible.

Source Data

You can examine the source of your data whenever you need to. Data forms are often defined through the source program, so you can ascertain which format your data is in and integrate a format conversion into your system as part of the process of loading it onto the target system.

It is important to find out where the source data exists on your master files. This means that the source of your data is often not the same as that used for tables you are loading data into, and a data merger prior to a load is sometimes needed. You can inspect data field formats in both the source and target systems, but you may need conversion routines compiled to the form, which will be the same as what you have defined in the Application Designer.

You must also find out if your required data is available from automated sources. Sometimes a small data element set is needed by the target system but is not available from your source system. If this is true, you may have to input a data subset.

Defining Tables

In order to designate how tables are to be loaded during each phase of your implementation, you must select the implementation for your application stage to determine how data tables will build your data set. Only then can you decide which tables will need to be loaded and in what order. Since some data tables are used for both the editing and validation of data rows, they must be first filled with correct data. The edits against such tables can only be effective when data is imported. You can then inspect and verify your source data.

Note that the conversion of bad data will produce even more bad data. You must incorporate both data clean-up and automated validity checks prior to sending converted data into target tables.

Results

In order to determine if you are finally ready to convert your data using the Import Manager, you must make certain you have created a conversion plan, discovered which method is best, executed field comparisons and data element mappings, and designated test modules for testing conversion program code. You can then create a conversion contingency plan, if needed, then you can define your successful objectives, and create a countdown to going live. Finally, you can acquire the approvals you need for sign-offs on all of your programs and plans.

The Import Manager gives you a means for converting data from your recurrent files to your PeopleTools application data tables. Your record definitions will function as the basis for your important definitions. The Import tools have the power to automate the import file layer for both field maps and data loading for your application data tables. Import definitions incorporate both the start position and length; they work with both edits and data that are integrated into your system from external files.

The Import Manager has been created explicitly to upload file data from a specific fixed-length ASCII source file. The exact editing takes place throughout your import processes in the same way as data is input via the panel interface.

Importing data into your tables can have several edits or PeopleCode programs. It often takes a large amount of time to process those smaller tables that have not been edited very much. This means you have to make certain that:

• Data is loaded in the correct procedure.

• Effective dates are correct.

• Required fields are populated correctly.

The Import Manager executes SQL inserts, indicating that new rows of data have unique types of keys and can be input into an SQL table. Whenever you perform updates to an existing row of data, they cannot be executed through the Import Manager. However, if the utility deals with key values on the source file that exists on the target machine, you will acquire an error and rows will not be recorded to the database. Should you need to modify rows of data once the imports have completed, you can use SQL scripts using batch updates.

It is important for you to realize which PeopleCode programs will run when using the Import Manager. You must ensure that you examine all of your lists and determine exactly what PeopleCode can do during your import process. After performing your reporting script, you still have to know how to work with the target tables that convert name formats and fields and enhance your performance.

Working with the Target Table

A situation may arise in which you have to modify fields attributed on your target table that include

- Adding columns

- Requirements status changes

- Field changes

- Key structure changes

The system will look at these parameters and prompt you to execute specific changes to any important definitions that are available for that table the next time you attempt to execute the tasks. This means that the Import Manager will execute a comparison test between the target table record definition and that of the import definition prior to executing the given import.

When you have to perform work that involves importing data into a field that has a name format, you will need to convert the data to your mixed case format before recording it to your database. Should the data be in upper-case letters, you can execute a conversion, leaving the first character of each word capitalized so you can convert the remainder of the word to lower case.

If the data you have to map is in a mixed case format field, then the Import Manager will convert the data prior to recording the field, but only if the following conditions are true: The data is in upper case and must be converted to upper and lower case. This means you will have to make the first letter of each word upper case. In addition, there must not be any data conversion to all lower or all upper case. You can present this type of conversion by turning on the mixed case format in the Application Designer.

Increasing Performance

Once you import a large amount of rows, your database index statistics must be updated. Otherwise, system performance will be much slower. You can then update statistics for any problematic areas.

You can increase your performance even more by unloading the database to another hard disk. You can then use a disk defragment utility to reorganize the hard disk of the database server. Only then can you reload the database to your original hard disk.

Making Modifications

As users alter data within your PeopleSoft applications, you must note that these people are actually performing SQL statements. This means that PeopleSoft offers several statements that are important for updating data. You may not need to create more statements, yet sometimes you will need to create several more. This is why the Mass Change parameter was established.

Mass Change actually involves a SQL generator that allows you to create and execute customer applications. Mass Change can establish several statements that the users in your organizations can perform on certain business functions. Mass Change types are shown in Figure 6.1. These command statements include

- Insert

- Update

- Delete

Mass Change is very much the same as PeopleSoft Query, but the query can acquire data from the database, whereas Mass Change can update your database. You will also find that Mass Change is very much like the Application Engineer when it comes to producing results like database updates. Mass Change is different from the Application Engineer because it actually can create SQL and doesn't work on processing logic. Mass Change works very well in

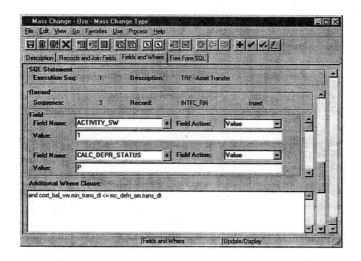

Figure 6.1 *Mass Change Types.*

helping you execute high-volume and set-oriented transactions. You can use it to copy data from one table to the next, archive table data, and execute transactions that are not supported through normal panels.

Whenever you implement Mass Change, you must focus on types, templates, and definitions. Types are the lowest type of components. Mass Change types define the SQL statements that must be created, recorded, or contain executing statements. Mass Change types are defined by application developers that know both SQL and database design.

Templates are created on the Mass Change types. These types of templates are used to determine which field will compose the WHERE clause of the SQL statements. It also helps you determine which fields can be hard coded with specific values. Note that application developers within your organization often define templates.

Mass Changes definitions are integrated into the Mass Change template. They are usually developed and performed by end users. Mass Change definitions are used to determine:

- Values and operators for each field in the WHERE clause

- Default fields

- SQL statements

- Assets (as shown in Figure 6.2)

When you define the Mass Change types or templates, you need to know SQL and database design very well, as these two functions will be closely linked. Your users will not need to add any types of Mass Changes types or templates, but when you create Mass Change definitions, all the proper information will use one type or template, with the exception of the field and operator values that are input into your system.

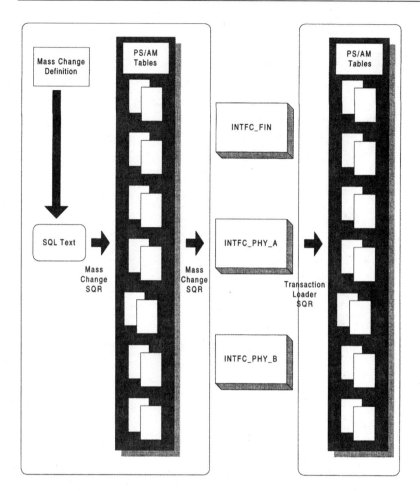

Figure 6.2 *Mass Change Assets.*

Mass Change types can specify the basic architecture of the SQL statements that the Mass Change definition will create. This works to explain

- How many SQL statements will be created

- Which records will be operated on

- How these records will be operated on

The order of these operations is determined by the way in which you set up your PeopleSoft system.

Mass Change types and templates utilize a PeopleSoft owner to achieve its goals. You can designate the owner for the system who will initiate the Mass Change types, but PeopleSoft will define the list of owners.

Creating SQL

In as much as PeopleSoft uses SQL and database design hand in hand, it is important for you to determine how to benefit from generating SQL. In order to accomplish this task, you need to know how to execute Mass Change-generated SQL statements that are based on the following factors:

- The information you input

- Type

- Template

- Definition panels

In order to know what type of information to offer, you must know how Mass Change itself uses information in your PeopleSoft system. It uses SQL action values in the records and join fields panel. You must inform Mass Change as to what kind of SQL statement it needs to produce. Record values determine which records and fields are used within this statement.

Note that the Insert and Select SQL actions function together. Should a SQL statement be composed of a insert type of action, the Mass Change will develop an Insert statement and use all its select-action records for the purpose of creating the SELECTG clause.

You need not worry about the sequence in which both Select and Insert happen. If there is more than one Insert action for a given SQL statements row, extra INSEWR clauses will be created to use the same type of SELECT clause. This means that Mass Change can establish several SQL statements using the information from just one SQL statement row in the system. Mass Change has the power to create several statements from one SQL statements row, but this relies on your records and SQL action choices. Whenever selections are displayed that have two Insert statements when Mass Change creates the SQL, you need to be careful. You must be wary of how you program multiple insert actions in one SQL statement row.

Normally, you should restrict panel selections to create only one SQL statement per SQL statement row. If you place an Update action record in one SQL statement row, you also need to put a delete action record in another. This must match for every command you put into your PeopleSoft system.

In some cases where inserts have the same SELECT clause, you can use them all in one SQL statement so that you need not establish Select records several times. Then if you have several inserts that all need a different type of SELECT clause, you must put each insert command into its own SQL statement row. SQL statement rows that have SELECT actions without an Insert command do not produce any SQL. You must choose your SELECT actions so that they are associated with one other Insert action.

Taking the SQL Definition Further

Mass Change templates take the SQL definition further, giving you control over which fields will be available for the user to designate when defining a Mass Change definition and when those specific fields will be used as a selection criteria or default. Specific fields are often used in the WHERE clause for the statment, but default fields are also used in the SELECT clauses within the INSERT statements and in the SET areas of UPDATE statements.

Mass Change Security

When you work with Mass Change, it is important to detail the level of security you need. You need to determine what specific Mass Change templates an operator can use for a given definition that must be created. You also need to know if an operator can execute Mass Changes to definitions online and how many Mass Change definitions an operator can use. The types of commands and definitions must be based on a template that has the same owner and operator. These commands include

- Open

- View

- Execute

As you use Mass Change, make note that this command has a great deal of power to change large amounts of data within your database. Therefore, you should not use Mass Change to write directly to your database. Instead, you should only write to intermediary tables that you review. You can then make appropriate changes and you can approve them, delete your changes, or modify them before making them permanent. You can then use another type of SQL to load the data into the database efficiently.

Whenever you process mass changes into your system, they usually are composed of a definition phase as well as a processing phase. You must first define the types of selection criteria and the changes you need to make to selected data. Only then can you execute a form of SQL that can execute your defined changes.

When you run Mass Change, you must select the Mass Change template you want and then use it to develop a Mass Change function. You should make a detailed outline of the criteria you want or need for choosing rows so you can identify the columns and values you need to change.

Then run the Mass Change SQL for:

- Select

- Change

- Transfer data

All of these can be done to the load tables. You can then preview the data to see that it meets your needs. Finally, you can run the transaction loader SQL to load data from the load tables and put it into your PeopleSoft tables.

When running the Mass Change, you are taking your Mass Change definition and moving it into SQL text. This text is then forwarded into the Mass Change SQR. After going through several commands and parameters, the information is sent to the transaction loader SQR where PeopleSoft tables handle the information from here on out.

Transferring Data

When you use Mass Change, you can download data from one table to a sequential file. You can also upload a data block back to the table from the sequential file. Both these methods are composed of preparing the file or table structure for the file that will be sent or received and creating the file for the table itself.

When you are using the download procedure to rewrite a specific field to show the new layout of a table you are downloading, this procedure actually rewrites parts of the Mass Change SQR so you can proceed with your transaction. You should execute this procedure on a local version of your Mass Change SQC, as opposed to your permanent network copy.

The file you are updating will have a specific field where you can determine the actual copy of the file you need to rewrite. You may only need to alter your SQR environment variables to make certain you can run a local copy of the Mass Change.

When dealing with uploads, you will find that the general procedure is pretty much the same as the first one when it comes to downloading. The Mass Change SQR must rewrite itself so it can load the data. You need to mark the file to be uploaded in the Download/Upload data file. You must note that this file will contain a copy of the file you are making changes to and is actually the one you will download with your actual table information.

Once you have finished your download process, you can then download the data to the sequential file on your system. Note that this file is composed of the specific SQC file you created and the table data. Your job is to determine the filename where you can store this data in the Download/Upload data file. You must know where this file is in case you need to upload the data again. Similarly, when you complete uploads, you are ready to upload the file data to the table from which it was originally downloaded. You can designate this file in the Download/Upload data field.

Whenever you set your SQR environment, be sure you are working on a local copy of it with Mass Change. Many people have problems when they update the local SQC file, but they use the network file SQC file's copy instead and wonder why the changes are never made. You must make certain your SQR environment variable settings are correct for the file you want to use.

Resolving Problems

If you have performance problems on many different database platforms, you will have to do a great deal of extra processing because you will have to work with more SQL table row inserts in log mode. This is often more difficult than row updates in update mode. Furthermore, you will have to cope with update mode requests that exclude all of your flagged rows, which occur from errors in future transaction set-edit requests.

Anytime you deal with online error correction problems, note that they are used in combination with PeopleCode "SetReEdit" functions. In this problem, update mode rows are flagged to be in error and can be acquired in online error corrections with the re-edit function of all your panel input fields. This effectively provides some field-level methods that will help you define edit errors without having to worry about increased processing problems involved in creating log mode details in your system.

One final issue that you will undoubtedly see involves detail reporting. When you work with TSE log entries that provide a high level of batch-detail reporting functions without additional edit table joining, you need to look at how log table columns are defined by the user (see Figure 6.3). If you have an edit tables field that can be integrated in the field-level TSE log table definition, then you must deal with them. If you have any edit errors that are designated by certain field names and values that have full table key fields, then you must include them as well.

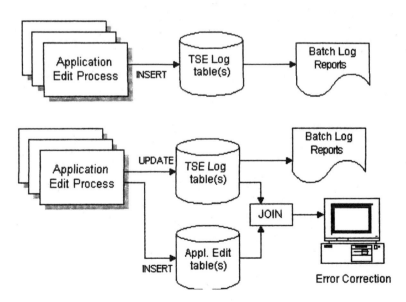

Figure 6.3 *TSE log.*

Whenever your users create a reporting procedure that deals with the management and production results from log tables, you will gain some important benefits for offline analysis as well as batch correction for any edit errors dealing with high-volume transactions.

Application Server

PeopleSoft integrates its client/server architecture in both a two- and three-tier configuration. The concept behind this section is illustrated by the differences and benefits for each of these platforms. This information will allow you to determine which configuration is best for your site.

The PeopleSoft application server is the cornerstone of the PeopleSoft 7.x three-tier architecture. It was created specifically to reduce your LAN traffic and greatly enhance your system scalabilities. One of its most common uses is the application server and three-tier configuration that the application server creates for all of your SQL that is different from the SQL generated by the client.

Two- and three-tier connections differ with respect to the server that you connect to at sign on. In a two-tier configuration, the client connects directly to your database server. In a three-tier configuration, however, the client connects to the application server, which is what will sustain connections to your database server.

PeopleSoft applications are run in a two-tier environment where all the online applications function on the client using data that is acquired directly though SQL calls from individual database servers. PeopleSoft supports three-tier transaction processing, but sections of the application logic move from the client to the application server where it then talks to with database server. You can segment the application logic between the client workstation and the application server. This is called application partitioning.

The application server is the cornerstone of the three-tier architecture. It uses Tuxedo, BEA System's transaction monitor, and can manage and monitor client transactions as they proceed. The three-tier configuration involves a client workstation that transmits requests to the application server where the Tuxedo system is. It can then schedule a service that might include a save or a panel group build.

BEA Tuxedo software (shown in Figure 6.4) can be used for both Windows OS and Web clients (standard with PeopleTools). The Windows client can only connect to the two-tier or three-tier mode using a logon screen option, but the Web client only connects in three-tier mode. When you are in a three-tier mode, several components make up your system:

- Client

- Application server

- Database server

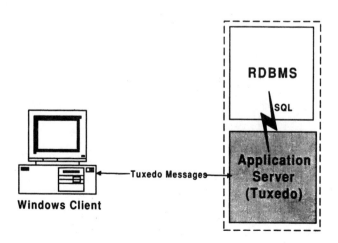

Figure 6.4 *BEA Tuxedo.*

Windows and Web clients support the Unix Message
Agent client and can be used only with the Message Agent.
The PeopleSoft application server can work on either a
Unix or Windows NT computer that has BEA's Tuxedo
middle projects as well as BEA's Jolt. BEA Jolt Install is
shown in Figure 6.5, while BEA Jolt is shown in Figure 6.6.
The application server may or may not be on the same
machine as the database server. The database server can
function on any RDBMS-supported machine.

Finally, the Web server can only work if you support
PeopleSoft's Web clients. There is also a Web server
directory and a Web site you have to consider that
functions solely in HTML and Java. These items must also
be maintained for each PeopleSoft database.

Working in a Three-Tier Environment

In many three-tier environments, you will find the
Windows client working with two-tier connections and
sending SQL directly to the database server. There are also

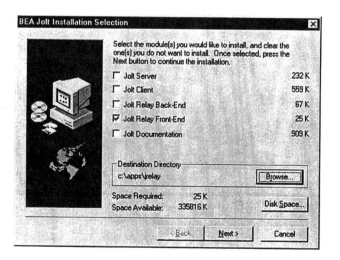

Figure 6.5 *BEA Jolt Install.*

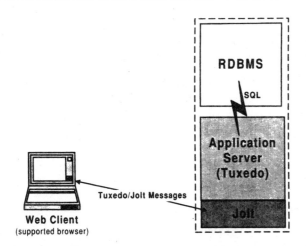

Figure 6.6 *BEA Jolt.*

times where the Windows and Web client will work together in a three-tier connection and will send Tuxedo messages to the application server that runs the SQL against the database server. However, there is a very important difference between the Windows and Web clients for the source of your client's binary information. Windows clients connect in a two-tier or three-tier environment, depending on the file server that provides binary files including DLLs and EXEs.

The Web client will have client binaries such as Java class files and will exist in the PeopleSoft applet that is downloaded from the Web server. The database, application, and Web servers will work together in the same machines. You will see a logical three-tier configuration where each of the application and database servers work on physically different machines.

You can also create an environment in which your application server exists on another machine, instead of your database server. This type of separation is called a physical three-tier configuration. You can choose either a physical or logical three-tier configuration to best suit your needs. If you have an application server on the same machine as the database server, then you are following PeopleSoft's recommended procedure. If your application and database servers are on different machines, make sure your application server is connected to the database server by a network that will provide you with a great deal of throughput.

Why Two- or Three-Tier?

In your computing environment, you can implement a two-tier, three-tier, or combination-type environment. You can configure which users will log on to the two-tier and which will access the three-tier environment. This choice, however, will rely on the type of transactions that the users need to do.

Certain advantages and disadvantages come with each configuration. Its advantages include less network traffic, increased wide area network (WAN) performance, and fewer maintenance duties of client workstation configurations because database connectivity is not necessary with the client. You can allow Web client connections and maintain the capability to scale the system to satisfy your increasing user demands. You can do this by:

- Reconfiguring your application servers

- Installing application servers on more powerful computer systems

- Using several application servers

Having a two-tier system enables you to offer a much simpler computing environment. It only needs the client workstation and database server components to be installed. Your system administrators are not required to invest time in learning new application server administration tools. Finally, you need not worry about buying extra machines or upgrading your current machines for use as application servers.

Special differences exist between a physical environment and a logical three-tier one. You may choose to configure the physical or logical environment, but PeopleSoft recommends having your systems rely on the database and operating system you currently use, instead of upgrading to another one. If you change, you leave yourself at risk for losing precious system functionality, so it is better to stay where you are.

In a physical three-tier environment, you have physically different machines within your system configuration that include the client/workstation, application server, and finally the database server. In a logical three-tier environment, you have two different machines within your configuration, including the client/workstation and the server where both the application and database server exist.

Workstations

PeopleSoft supports Windows and will work with Windows/C++ tools as well as Java-based web clients. The Windows client offers a high level of desktop integration with your other Windows applications that include:

- MS Word

- MS Excel

- E-mail

You have the flexibility of configuring your Windows clients to connect to the two-tier configuration, database, or three-tier application server. Windows clients use three-tier connections and work on any TCP/IP connection with a client using any Windows product (NT 4.x, 95, 98, and 2000).

The standard Web client can operate on a subset of transactions that can also be run on your Windows client. Web clients can support the use of universal applications, which enhance Web workflow and are created to integrate well into your current corporate intranet. Web client connections need a supported browser on the workstation and it must also have access to a Web server that has PeopleSoft applets and HTML.

Application servers must use BEA's Jolt to support Web client connections. Jolt performs the communication between the Java environment and the Tuxedo application. When you install Tuxedo through PeopleTools, Jolt automatically installs as part of the standard installation. It doesn't matter whether you select to configure or enable Jolt; it depends mainly on if you deploy the Web client. If you don't, you need not worry about the Jolt installation.

Web clients permit you to access both PeopleSoft applications and universal applications. You gain access through the Web server; all you need is a Web client that can offer a supported Web browser and a TCP/IP connection and can access the Web server that has HTML and applets. You can access the PeopleSoft client bin directory, but this is not necessary for the Web client. Binaries are needed to run applications in a browser. They can be acquired by downloading Java applets from a given Web site, while applets are class files that are the Java equivalent of .EXE and .DLL files. Therefore, if you want to use the Web client, you only need to have a Web server working with your Java applets .HTML and .JAR (sets of compressed Java Class files) file types.

Components

Since several different types of components comprise your physical computing environment that houses the application server, including the database server and client, several types of components function together on the application server. These components work together to answer a client transaction as fast as possible. However, you need to know how the application server functions before you configure it. This means you should understand Tuxedo and Jolt.

Tuxedo is a BEA System transaction monitor. It supports the three-tier processing you need and is used by the application server. You can configure the application server to support both Windows and Web clients by using the PSADMIN utility (shown in Figure 6.7).

If you can enable Web client connections, you will need to configure Jolt and its counterpart, the Jolt Internet Relay (JRLY), shown in Figure 6.8. Once you are familiar with these tools, you can bring an effective application server online to deal with your computing tasks in an efficient manner.

Tuxedo is the main tool that processes requests from both the Windows and Web clients within your system. Windows clients send a request to the Tuxedo listening

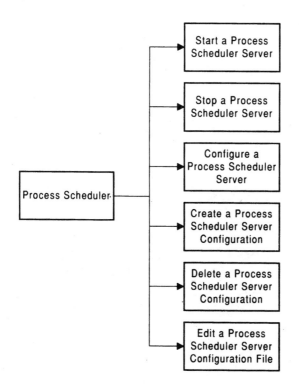

Figure 6.7 *PSADMIN.*

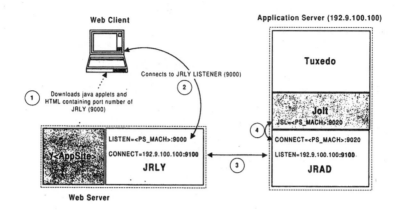

Figure 6.8 *Jolt Internet Relay.*

device, while the Web client sends a request to the Jolt
listener. The listener then passes the request to Tuxedo, but
it doesn't execute the processing. Instead, it schedules the
server processes that execute their own transactions. Server
processes execute application logic and send SQL to the
RDBMS. This server is a C++ program where each
application server process establishes and supports its own
database connections.

JOLT

Jolt is actually a product that works with Tuxedo on the
same machine. It receives Java requests from Web clients,
but is not an individual product because it cannot function
without Tuxedo. Web clients connect to the Jolt port, not
the application server. Jolt is the communication go-
between for Java and C++ computing environments. When
Jolt sends a Web client request to the Tuxedo application
server, it is the same as when a Windows client requests it.

The JRLY or the Jolt Relay Adapted (JRAD) offer secure
methods of processing Web client transactions over the
Internet or an intranet. These connections take place at the

Web server or application server; both are different machines. Figure 6.9 demonstrates both JRLY and JRAD in the PeopleSoft system.

When the Web and application servers are on the same machine, the JRLY and JRAD are not needed. When a Web and application server are on different machines, you will need to use the JRLY and JRAD. The latter is installed automatically as part of your standard Tuxedo and Jolt installation. The former must be installed separately.

The JRLY is composed of a program and a configuration file that must be installed on the same machine as the Web server responsible for providing self-service applications. JRLY is used when the Web server and application server are separated. Both JRAD and JRLY are required to offer a secure application server connection. JRLY is an executable file that exists where the Web server is located. A connection between JRAD and JRLY is established at one central contact point that you can secure, but this is not the same as a Web client connecting directly to the application server. Most often, the Web server is used with JRLY and

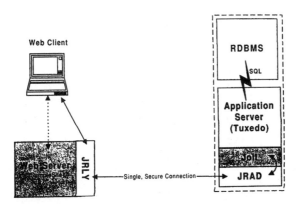

Figure 6.9 *JRAD and JRLY.*

they will both be external to the firewall, while JRAD is on the application server inside the firewall.

JRAD is actually a listener process that exists on the same machine as the application server and was created to receive JRLY messages. You can configure JRAD on the application server through the PSADMIN utility that is composed of the JRAD listener and the JRAD connection; both match the JOLT port number for your system.

Dealing with the Application Server

When you configure your application server through the PSADMIN utility, the application server domain must be configured for each database you have in your three-tier environment. You can have as many relationships as you need between the application server domains and the database, or you may have a one-to-one relationship.

The easier method involves the configuration of one application server domain to one PeopleSoft database. You can become more complicated and configure several application server domains where each domain can connect to the same database, but you cannot have a single application server domain connected to more than one database. If you have three databases, you will need to configure three separate application server domains, with one for each database. However, several application domains per database may be required for increased performance.

When you have an application server domain start a set of server processes, remember that each server process actually establishes a persistent connection to the database. This type of connection is like a plain SQL pipeline, which is used by server processes to send and receive SQL requests for clients connecting to the application server. The RDBMS, however, will see each server process as representing one connected user, or it may reuse the same connection for several client requests.

Processes

Whenever you look into the application server, you must always deal with listeners, handlers, and processes. It is important to deal with various services that make up the unified application server processes, as it will help demonstrate each server's function. You need to know how to configure and refine your application server. You must know how to configure multiple workstation handlers as well as when to execute this task to best meet your site's requirements.

In a standard environment, your RDBMS will use SQL as the carrier to process within your application server. Both Windows clients and Web servers send information back and forth into this cycle to support the system routines in a given organization. To more fully illustrate these concepts, you need to examine the following server processes about your PeopleSoft system.

The workstation listener (WSL) is a process that can monitor the Tuxedo ports for your initial connection request from the Windows clients within your system. When the WSL accepts a connection from a workstation, it sends that request to a workstation handler (WSH). Then the workstation interacts with the WSH to which it is assigned. The WSH can process requests it receives from the QSL, but the port number for the WSH is chosen at random.

The Jolt station listener (JSL) works only with the Web client connection and can process and monitor the Jolt port for connection requests sent from the Web client. When the JSL accepts a connection from the Web client, it directs the request to the Jolt station handler (JSH). Then the Web client works with the JSH itself. The JSH only applies to Web client connections that can process requests from the JSL. However, the port number for the JSH is chosen within Tuxedo in a sequential order.

The Jolt Repository Server (JREPSVR) can translate Jolt requests to Tuxedo server calls, but this only applies to Web client connections. The Bulletin Board Liaison (BBL) is the main Tuxedo engineer.

The PeopleSoft Tuxedo Authentication (PSAUTHO) verifies clients at the login time by choosing the client values from the PSOPRDEFN table. The PeopleSoft Application Server Manager (PSAPPSRV) can create and record panels, execute PeopleCodes, process messages, and support all non-conversational client requests.

The PeopleSoft Quick Server Manager (PSQCKSRV) is much like the PSAPPSRV, but it can process all the shorter, non-sensational client requests. The PeopleSoft Message Agent Server Manager (PSAPISRV) can handle server processes as well as all Message Agent requests. The PeopleSoft SQL Access (PSSAMSRC) is much like the PSAPPSRV, but it can process all conversational client requests.

Note that you can configure several WSHs capable of supporting 60 client connections. In the same way, you can also configure several server processes that include PSAPPSRV or PSQCKSRV to handle predictable client workloads.

Tuxedo can produce incremental server processes that are used to support increasing client requests. It has the capability to configure several server processes, including incremental ones that combine with the application server's scalability. Even though the names and port numbers of specific components affiliated with the Web client and Window client connections are slightly different, the mechanism itself is the same.

Windows Clients

You can expect to see a certain level of events that will take place in the Windows client connection to the application server. It will detail several components that must deal with each event and provide an explanation as to why they occur.

The client is the primary event that deals with Windows NT 4.x or Windows 95/98 machines, which will send a process request that takes the form of a Tuxedo message.

The WSL designates each application server with a port number and acts as the central point of contact for workstation clients. It listens for client requests, receives them, and then sends out connections to the appropriate workstation handlers. The WSH can assign a client and route all the messages to a given port. When the number of WSHs increases, it only needs to reconfigure the domain to handle extra users.

All client request messages take the form of a service name and its associated parameters. The Tuxedo Bulletin Board Liaison (BBL) and its server processes execute a given service on the part of the client. Should the server process be busy working on a client request, the next client request waits in the queue or is routed to another server process that is available.

All PeopleSoft services are created to work with several different service types. PeopleSoft services take client requests from SQL and run them again the RDBMS. The RDBMS has the power to process SQL requests and return results to the PeopleSoft service that sent the request in the first place. Only then can the proper PeopleSoft service send the results to the workstation through the route from which the request came.

Web Client Connections

Just as I listed the sequence of events that occurs with Windows client connections, you will find the Web client connection to the application server as well as the component that is responsible for each event. Web client connections are similar to those of the Windows client, except for the fact that the client can connect to the JSL, instead of the WSL. Web clients automatically try to connect to the 9000 port because that number is hard-coded into your HTML.

The client/browser is your primary component. The browser runs on a supported workstation with a specific URL for a Web page with HTML applet tags. The Tuxedo Web Listener then receives the incoming request and permits the client to view a specific Web page. That Web page has the PeopleSoft applet tag that determines parameters, including the following:

- JOLT port server

- Self-service application to be executed

When the client starts the given applet, the Web server only needs to send information within the applet tag to the browser. The browser then downloads the information from the applet target that determines the JOLT port as well as the self-service application that needs to be executed. When this information is downloaded, the browser doesn't need to work with the Web server to maintain this connection.

The JSL is similar to the WSL in the Windows connection. Every application server that is Jolt-enabled has a port number designated as the Java station listener. Note that the JSL is a central contact point for Web clients. It can listen for client requests, receive them, and then send connections to the JSHs. The JSL designates the Web client request to a JSH and Web clients can then route messages to the JSH until the client logs off or has a timeout. The JSH can receive the transaction request from the JSL and transmit the message to the JREPSVR, which acquires the Jolt service definitions and then sends the service definitions to the JSH. JREPSVR is a BEA process that can reformat the Java message for Tuxedo.

Tuxedo's Bulletin Board Liaison (BBL) can receive a client request and place it in a queue for a specific server process. PeopleSoft processes the request in the queue from the BBL and then runs SQL against the RDBMS. Finally, the SQL request is processed and returned with a result from the PeopleSoft service that sent the request. This final step takes place in the RDBMS.

Conclusion

Navigator tools are an important factor in your system. Without the ability to know how every facet of your system works, you will not have the power to effectively integrate elements into your system. But what is the most important item that *must* be integrated into your networked environment? The database is the most important part of your ERP solution. The next chapter examines the database agent and explains in great detail how it functions and how you can benefit from its integration into your corporate computing environment.

Database Agent

The Database Agent monitors the
PeopleSoft database to identify items
that need to enter the workflow for
processing.

165

Developing Database Agents

Database Agents are essentially workflow programs that
execute functions that involve running a query against your
databases. It can then send those results to the Message
Agent. This is a straightforward function that is combined
with other workflow tools, but it can greatly enhance the
types of automation tasks that can be used in your system.

Database Agents can be used in combination with the
Process Scheduler. They allow you to monitor your
database table for specific conditions that can trigger
business events. If you need to develop a database agent
that queries for a given task, you can schedule it to run
once a month or for whatever duration you need. Figure
7.1 illustrates the Process Scheduler database agent that
works in your PeopleSoft environment.

When the database agent locates the parameter you
need, it sends that data to the Message Agent. The Message
Agent then inputs the data into a panel that creates
worklist entries for the proper personnel. The benefit is
that this entire process can proceed without any user

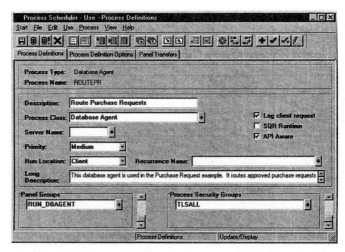

Figure 7.1 *The Process Scheduler DB (Database) Agent.*

intervention. This is demonstrative of the fact that the database agent executes any query that you define using the PeopleSoft Query tool.

Database agents perform direct tasks, but they are very important within your workflow. When you perform predefined queries regularly, they can inspect your database every so often for data that is pertinent to a given business process. It can then send that data to the Message Agent, which can respond automatically to your needs.

The majority of business process routings are triggered when a user inputs data onto a PeopleSoft panel. In many cases, the system will create an approval request whenever the user inputs a new task. The system will instantly respond through its workflow procedure. Sometimes you may find it more useful to trigger a given routing based on a specific event that does not involve user intervention. This can often be useful for any other worklist entries. The database agent can enact certain routings to deal with any processes that the Process Scheduler needs to handle.

Events that are not started by a user can also trigger certain routings. The PeopleSoft Query tool can enable you to compose a query that inspects for data that must be processed. You can also use the Process Scheduler to schedule a database agent to perform a query on a regular basis and imitate a workflow even when a certain condition occurs. However, when you start the database agent, user intervention is no longer needed.

Databases and Triggering Events

Business events are not triggered directly by database agents. PeopleSoft Workflow enables you to trigger business events only when you either input or save data on a panel that has Workflow PeopleCode. Database agents do not have the power to input data on panels, but agents can server the Message Agent as well as users.

Indirectly, database agents can trigger business events. They do this by sending the query results of the Message Agent through an associated message definition to map query results to a PeopleSoft panel. When the panel has Workflow PeopleCode, the business process is triggered when the Message Agent saves its panel. However, the database agent query returns several rows of data and it can locate several items that must be dealt with immediately.

The Message Agent sends the rows to at least one other Message Agent one row at a time. This means that if you have several Message Agents running, the database agent can divide the workload such that the Message Agent can call up the panel group that has triggered the business event for each row.

Batch Processes

A few activities can be executed as online processes, whereas some processes require querying the system before you can perform them in the background. These background or batch processes can be scheduled to run now, later, or recur as often as you need. They can also process several items all at one time; but they are not the same as other online processes that usually work one item at a time. You can offload these items to a server such that time-intensive tasks do not consume all of your computer's resources.

Batch processes are problematic in some ways because they connect to your database directly, as opposed to working though your panels. This means that if you need the panel processor to verify your inbound data or have it perform a custom PeopleCode, you may not want to use batch processes to update your database in the background. However, you trigger business events by saving data on a given panel, and batch processes cannot imitate a workflow.

The above types of restrictions do not bind database agents because they are more like online processes. Database agents can input data through PeopleSoft panels through the Message Agent as its go-between. They are like batch processes because they can handle a batch of items, but you can have an agent execute a batch of line processes. This means that if you have a batch process that transfers information between two organizational departments, you can make the system send you an e-mail whenever the manager of all associated departments confirms a data transfer will take place. Batch processes cannot trigger the e-mail routing. This means that creating the e-mails manually would be far too time-intensive. However, after the batch process is competed, you can execute a database agent that can query the system for data transfers and then send an e-mail automatically to each manager.

You could alternatively replace the batch processes with a database agent to make your data transfer occur much more easily. However, since the database agent inputs data though the normal asset transfer panel, it can trigger an e-mail routing as it executes the transfer itself.

How to Add a Database Agent

The database agent program itself can benefit you by adapting itself to your workflow. You can make your database agent trigger a specific business event, but it must first send data to the Message Agent. However, if the Message Agent has to transfer that data into a panel that has Workflow PeopleCode affiliated with it, then, besides the database agent, you will have make certain you have a message definition that can map the query results to a panel. That panel must then be able to trigger the proper business event.

In order to add a database agent, you must first determine the data you want the database agent to acquire. Before creating the database agent, it is important to determine what you need. If you create an agent that is meant to monitor the database, you are looking for data that reveals what you need to do. You can then create a panel that will gather all of the information you need to begin your business process. In order to trigger a business event, you need to know which panel you can use to give the system the data it needs to route work items to the next workflow step. This means that your panel must use a record definition that has Workflow PeopleCode so it can trigger the event you need.

Your next step is to form a query that can acquire the information you need from the database. Since you know which data will trigger a business event, you can use the PeopleSoft Query tool to form a query that examines your system for the proper conditions to acquire the data you need. Queries usually only acquire the essential information you need from the database. However, the Message Agent will send this essential overview information to the panel, which then acquires the rest of the data for this item.

At this point, you can actually create the business process that will work with the agent's data. In order to determine exactly what steps you need to take when the database agent finds its data, the Application Designer can designate business process and the events that make up its components.

Remember to integrate an activity with the database agent. This is important because, as you complete the setup process, your area essentially defines a message definition that informs the Message Agent about the manner in which it can transfer data from the query result set to your PeopleSoft panel.

Now that you have all of the primary information set for your goal, you must test the database agent. In order to do so, you must execute the database agent program. This enables you to determine if you can actually get the results you need. The database agent can acquire the proper data it must have to perform the right processes when it is triggered to do so.

Once the test is complete, you can add the database agent to the Process Scheduler. When you have determined that you have acquired the results you want, add the database agent to your Process Scheduler. Then you can determine which panels your users can run from the database agent and how frequently the system can run them. Finally, you can run the database agent and reap the results from your hard work. This allows you to determine how well your effort translates into your practical implementation.

When it becomes necessary to add database agents to the Process Scheduler, you must follow a certain procedure for scheduling a database agent. This procedure is the same as that for any Process Scheduler process.

You must first designate your process-type definitions. These definitions determine the general parameters that all database agents share. You must also create a process definition. Whenever you add a database agent to the Process Scheduler, it is important that you include specific information about the agent you are using. This means you have to detail exactly:

1. What the activity name will be

2. What the message definitions will say about the database agent

3. How frequently the Process Scheduler will run it

Executing Database Agents

Now that you know some details for adding the database agent to your Process Scheduler, you know how to make it available for you needs. However, the one thing you don't know is how to schedule the agent to run. In order to initiate the database agent, you need to start it just like other scheduled processes using the Process Scheduler

Request box. Remember that database agents function only in three-tier modes. This means that if you try to imitate a database agent process in a two-tier mode through the Process Scheduler it will not function.

In order to designate database agents to a given panel group, you must add the database agent as well as any other scheduled processes to the Process Scheduler. You can then define the panel group with which users can imitate the process. This means that when users choose the run command from that specific panel group, the Process Scheduler Request box will display all of the database agents as one process through the request.

When you want to schedule a process, you can use the Process Scheduler's run control. This allows you to use the panel group to define the database agent so it can both define and run control records. However, the query that your database agent executes does not have any runtime bind variables; you can define the database agent so that it uses a panel group that does create run controls. This means that your system will acquire all of the run control information it requires form the Process Scheduler Request command structure.

Should a query include runtime bind variables, you must try to establish a run control record definition that includes the following:

- Required fields

- Panels for the user to input fields

- A database agent on the panel

Enhanced Functionality

One of the nicest features that the PeopleSoft database agent can provide is the Remote Report Delivery feature. It has a function that allows users to acquire reports through an e-mail message or an electronic form. They can also receive the report back through e-mail too. The system can use a database agent to look for completed reports that must be delivered to the person who requested it.

Remote Report Delivery works when a user sends a formatted message to a mailbox that the system is monitoring. The system uses the Message Agent to add the repot request to the Process Scheduler, which then prints the report and places it in a specific directory. The database agent then queries for the completed report. When it finds the proper document, it transmits an e-mail message to the person who requested it with an attached report.

In order to obtain specific functionality, you must look into message definitions to determine how you can make the Message Agent access a specific panel group in the Update or Display mode. Message definitions work in much the same way as when a user chooses the update or display mode. At this point, the system would display a search dialog box. The Message Agent can then map the Instance ID to the search key field and the system obtains a report request that lists all of the information from the panel group. Finally, the Message Agent can save the panel group so that the system can execute all of the PeopleCode affiliated with that function.

Route Controls

Route control query roles have runtime bind variables that point towards the control types they use as well as the values for specific types. This means that if you define a single route control type to use, you can map a value from the panel group that triggers the routings as well as map the user list role too.

When a business event is triggered, the application agent (as shown in Figure 7.2) can bind a query's bind variable by using data from the panel group that triggers the event, run the query as it checks each user's route control profile to see if it meets selection criteria, or route the work item to specific role users within your organization.

When you define your route control, remember that you must define route control types, as these elements identify specific details that will form your routing decision. You must then create route control profiles, which determine the value range that exists within a given route control type. You can then define route control profiles to role users so you can determine what areas they need to concentrate on.

Virtual Approver

The most common approval processes deal with several types of business rules. These rules often consist of situations where personnel approve a purchase for a certain amount of money through departmental approval or management approval. These types of rules are often integrated in the Workflow PeopleCode program. Several

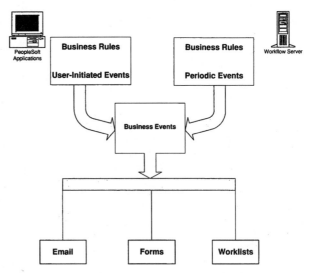

Application agents trigger business events and routings based on rules

Figure 7.2 *Application Agent.*

logical statements reside within PeopleCode to examine the data on a given panel. This often includes panels where employees input certain requests to determine if the conditions are appropriate for inputting a work item into the workflow.

You can also designate specific approval rules within PeopleCode that require some expert types of coding. You can implement rules so that your code undergoes several test conditions. You would need to determine the following types of information:

- Who is working on your system

- How much they can approve

- How work items need to be managed

- How you can modify rules

- How PeopleCode can help you modify rules

Virtual Approver enables you to specify certain approval rules based on several panels within the Workflow Administrator. However, don't be confused about the Virtual Approver not relying on PeopleCode. Instead of using PeopleCode to compile code, you can use the Virtual_Approval and Virtual_Router commands that are part of the Virtual Approver. This type of common approval function examines several approval rules to see what times you need to gather additional approval on. You may also need to check the following ideas:

- Which items need approval

- How to change a rule

- How to change information in the Workflow Administrator

- How the Virtual Approval plays an important role in your business processes

In essence, Virtual Approver is very much like route control. Both of these functions permit you to record application data on database tables, instead of having to code directly on the business process definition. This means you can customize routing with the need to redevelop your business processes.

Virtual Approver makes certain that all approval process use the same type of interface. This is important because you need to create them using the same type of tool. You can then automate your approval process with steps that either recur in parallel or one by one. You must make certain it has complete access to all of your workflow functions, such as routing through query rules. Since your approval rules are recorded on a table, you can use this concept so you can customize them as you need to. You can also specify all of your approval rules in one centralized panel group. Finally, you can designate various approval rules for different types of business processes or even use several types of rules for a given process.

As you are working with Virtual Approver, it is interesting to point out exactly what kinds of information the user sees. When you have designated approval process for a given transaction type, Virtual Approver functions in the background with the application agent. These two combined resources define exactly what transactions must require additional approval so they can route the transactions to next approval stage.

Users can input transactions following the same standard procedure. By doing so, they are inputting data into the PeopleSoft application panel. When the user saves the panel, Virtual Approver can look at the approval rules that you have designated to determine what type of approval is needed. Should the user have the authority to approve a transaction, Virtual Approver can change the transaction status to "Approved" and will not enter it back into the workflow. However, if the user does not have the correct authorization, he or she must follow the rules that are set. This may mean that someone would need to approve the transaction, so the user would see a warning message saying that the transaction needs the manager's approval. It then asks the user if the request should be entered into the workflow. If the user accepts this option, then Virtual Approver transfers the request to the worklist of the person who must approve it. The transaction is usually sent by way of an electronic form and retains a "pending" status until the proper person approves it.

Developing an Approval Process

The methods described in this section help you determine the best ways of creating an approval process. However, it is important to point out that these types of processes are virtually the same as many other business processes. You need to define the following items as usual:

- Roles

- Events

- Routings

The biggest difference, however, is that instead of specifying your business roles by compiling PeopleCode programs, you need to define them through the Approval Rule Definition panels present within the Workflow Administrator. You will use a different type of PeopleCode function to connect the approval rules to your panel. This means that you can use business processes that use the Virtual Approver to route control as well.

PeopleSoft applications come standard with many common types of approval processes. These processes are used with Virtual Approver so you can refine business processes. Often you will have to customize your existing processes, as opposed to creating new processes.

In order to customize the approval rules for your current business processes, you can open the approval rules and update them with rules that are needed for your individual business needs. This is why using a table-based approach is important in your approval processing.

When you use Virtual Approver to implement business processes, you can make important use of your list roles that are associated with certain organization levels. Virtual Approver can use various roles within your organization to determine the authorization levels for a given user. It is important to make certain that you establish the roles correctly in your organization, as it is illustrative of the various levels within your company and is made specifically for certain types of users.

When you deal with approval rule sets, you are defining several rules that allow your work to be approved within a given business process. It is also useful to give your business processes several approval rule sets.

When you define an approval rule set, you do so in the Workflow Administrator. You can then input the name of the business process you wish to add approval rules to, but if there is an existing business process, you can define it within the Application Designer. You can then enter a name for the approval rule set you need to define. Your system will use both the business process name as well as the approval rule set name as key elements. This enables you to designate several approval sets for the same business process.

You can designate various approval rule sets for various business units. This can be done even when the general business process is the same. When the application agent needs Virtual Approver, it determines the best approval set to use at that time.

Dealing with the Database

Whenever you implement your three-tier environment, note that your database connectivity must be available on the application server only. This means that you can acquire several important configuration advantages that only a three-tier connection can offer. One advantage is that the workstation administrator need not install and configure database connectivity for each client workstation that needs to send transaction requests to the database server.

For three-tier environment users, there isn't any need for any database connectivity software on the client. The PeopleSoft application server must maintain the SQL connection to your database in this three-tier environment. When you configure clients to have the option of determining a two- and three-tier connection at log on, you must require database connectivity for the client. Two-tier clients require database connectivity software.

Whenever you install or administrate your system, you must install database connectivity software to the client whenever you run the application reviewer. In addition, if you need to install a database or load stored statements using the data movement, you will also log on in two-tier mode. If you log on in three-tier mode, you can choose to run the Process Scheduler locally. However, if you log on in three-tier mode, you can run Crystal using Process Scheduler. Crystal uses application server functions to run SQL statements that don't need database connectivity.

Whenever you deal with database connectivity on your application server, remember that both Windows NT and the Unix application server must have database connectivity software to support SQL connections with the RDBMS. You can then install the connectivity software you need along with other utilities for your RDBMS.

Working with the Batch Server

Whenever you deal with the application server in your PeopleSoft environment, you must determine where your site's batch server environment will exist. The idea is to further illustrate the relationship between the application and batch server. When you install your batch server on any application server supported within your PeopleSoft environment, you can optionally select your batch environment to meet your individual corporate needs. Whenever you deal with your database platforms, you must have at least two different options for your batch environment location.

Whenever you install the Process Scheduler on a system that does offer support for the database, be careful because some systems do not offer support for the application server machine. You must have the ability to configure and administer the Process Scheduler, but you may not have the power to configure an application server domain, even when the application server menu options appear.

You will not be able to erase the PSADMIN's application server menu option because it may not be indicative of your ability to configure an application server on your machine. PSADMIN is shown in Figure 7.3.

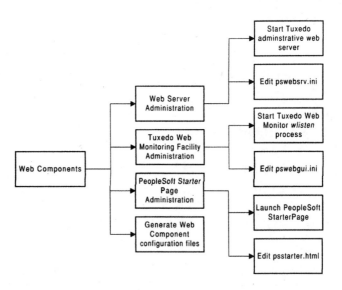

Figure 7.3 *PSADMIN.*

When you deal with the application server and Process Scheduler, note that PeopleSoft version 7.x uses PSADMIN. The PeopleSoft Server Administration menu interface helps you configure and administer both the application server and Process Scheduler. You can use the PSADMIN tool to configure the application server, but PeopleSoft integrates the Process Scheduler setup procedure into PSADMIN and offers a menu interface for configuring PeopleSoft parameters and administering the Process Server Agent.

The application server and batch server have PSADMIN as one central and common interface. PeopleSoft's application server uses Tuxedo to both send and receive requests from the Windows and Web clients. It sends SQL requests to the database server through persistent database connections that are maintained by application server processes.

The Process Scheduler is an independent entity that queries the database table for queued requests and starts COBOL, SQL, and other processes. Each SQR program will send SQL requests directly to the database server, but Crystal can run local SQL requests for the application server to be processed in three-tier mode.

Defining Your Three-Tier Environment

As you begin your work with your PeopleSoft three-tier environment, it is important to determine how each component is defined as well as how it will fit in with your organizational flow. An applet is defined as a small Java program that is part of the Web page you view. Whenever users access these pages, the applets are automatically downloaded to the browser where they then run. An application server domain is actually a collection of:

- Servers

- Services

- Resource managers

Every single application server domain is configured to connect to one database.

PSADMIN

This chapter has discussed several areas where the PSADMIN plays an important role. PSADMIN was created to be a unique configuration administration tool to ease the configuration and administration process for:

- Application servers

- Process Scheduler servers

- Web servers

PSADMIN was also created to be a user-friendly interface for Tuxedo's configuration administration command-line interface, yet as you look closer into PSADMIN, you will note that it functions more as a front end to the Tuxedo native configuration process. It gives you a nice way of creating an environment that users can work in. Users can also use it to configure several application servers through the central home directory. You gain further benefits in that it uses the same interface whether you are working on Unix or Window NT. It makes Tuxedo operations easier and is most helpful in commands that include:

- Boot

- Shutdown

- Status checking

PSADMIN enables you to both configure and administer your Process Scheduler servers, and you can also configure and administer the Tuxedo Web server for your PeopleSoft implementation.

Note that when you use the PSADMIN utility you are actually choosing several of the menu items that best illustrate the action you need to take. This may include inputting the correct number of command lines into the system, but you may also be able to benefit from the command-line options that PSADMIN can provider.

An important sidenote for PSADMIN involves looking at its hierarchical menu structure. Many of the menu items you choose in the PSADMIN utility provide several layers of extra menu items. Instead of just searching through the PeopleSoft architecture on your own, you can use a straight method to make yourself understand the menu structure within this utility.

Domains

As you integrate the application server into your PeopleSoft implementation, you need to have a domain created specifically so you can administrate it effectively. This means you can create a domain and determine its environment settings within your application server so it will work in your system appropriately.

Understanding Parameters

PeopleSoft's database name is also known as the DBName. It is important to note that this parameter is case-sensitive, so you must be careful when defining the names. DBType refers to the PeopleSoft database type. This can often include such databases as:

- DB2

- DB2/400

- DB2/ODBC

- DB2/Unix

- Informix

- Microsoft

- Oracle

- Sybase

Should you input the wrong database type, PSADMIN will prompt you with a list of valid choices. In this field, the values must be all in upper-case letters.

The OprID is the operator ID. This means that the operator must be defined in the PSOPRDEFN and must be authorized to start the application server by setting the columns and tables. This does not necessarily give the OprID any special capabilities, but it is able to start the application server. This value can be set using the security administrator or native SQL tool.

The OprPswd enables you to input the password used by the OprID that will allow you to gain access to the database. The passwords are recorded in the PSOPRDEFN and must all be made in upper-case letters. There is a certain logic to the Operator ID and password being written in upper case. They are written to ease the system administration burden. Customers often find it is difficult to connect to the system because they input their Operator ID or password correctly but forget if they made the first letter upper case.

The ConnectID is an important parameter for the DB2/Unix and Informix databases. This is essentially a Unix username and password that is recorded in upper or lower case. As a PeopleSoft user, the puserPw is used to perform the startup connection to the database. Your username has a specific authority to connect, but the connection is not necessary when the customer selects certain Unix usernames for your PeopleSoft OprID. The connect password or ConnectID password is the Unix name password that can be listed in any case.

The serverName is necessary for both Sybase and Informix but is not really used in another database. It is the name that the server will use in the PeopleSoft database once it is installed. It is also case sensitive, so you must be careful that all names function correctly in your system.

Certain parameters also function in the workstation listener configuration section of your system. The address parameter can automatically resolve the address for any machine name that PSADMIN can acquire through the system API call. You need not change this value unless circumstances change. You can determine the machine's IP address and a resolvable name or DNS name. You may wish to configure a file to run on the application server or another machine.

The port is useful when you want to designate a four-digit port number at which you can use the WSL. Port numbers are unique numbers between 1,000 and 16,000, but they cannot be used by any other service or the numbers won't function as valid ports.

Encryption of your data messages between the client workstation and the application server can also be used to protect your data from being intercepted. If you use 128-bit encryption, you need only copy the PeopleSoft file server files. There are specific settings appropriate to your encryption. The value of 0 means you have no encryption, the value of 40 means you have 40-bit encryption, and the value of 128 means you have 128-bit encryption.

Min and max handlers are the workstation handlers (WSH) that are started at boot domain for a given domain. Each WSH can support as many as 60 connections, but if the number of min handlers equals the number of max handlers, then the Tuxedo will not automatically start incremental WSH for you. The max clients per handler determines the most client workstation connections that each WSH can support.

The client cleanup and timeouts can determine the amount of time in minutes that client connections can stay idle without any work requests before the Tuxedo terminates a client's connection. The client can disconnect from the client without the user's knowledge, but the user can still just click to reconnect whenever he or she wants.

The Init timeout is the value that determines the amount of time in seconds that the Tuxedo permits a client connection request to bind to a WSH prior to terminating the connection. Tuxedo compression is important, as it determines the least amount of data a message can handle for the client and application server before data compression begins. This normally is indicative of the network buffer size threshold where compression is used between the client workstation and the application server.

Compression often increases performance for transactions over a wide area network (WAN), but it can hinder performance over a local area network (LAN) because most of the processing is devoted to compression and decompression. You could use a default threshold of 5,000, as this sets the balance between a WAN and a LAN. Your network request and response message of 5K will be compressed, but anything under 5K is not compressed. The client connection mode parameters enable you to choose from options such as:

- Retained

- Reconnect

- Any

These parameters are responsible for permitting connections from clients. The retained parameters indicate that the network connection is retained for the whole session. The reconnect parameters indicate that the client can establish a connection when the idle timeout is reached. When that happens, it can issue a reconnect parameters command so that the client can reestablish a connection when the idle timeout is reached. The any command indicates that the server will permit the client code to request a retained or reconnect session connection. A listener address indicates the specific machine that has the application server running on it.

Domain IDs are used when you want to input the name of your application's server domain. It does not need to match the name you indicated when you created the domain. This name is useful for the Tuxedo Web monitor, as it designates the application server domains on each machine. You should neither go over eight characters nor should you use upper case in any database names.

The Add to Path command should be used for database connectivity. If your database connectivity directory is not specified in the PATH, it can be set by determining these parameters. When dealing with Unix, you do not need to input this default to the current directory nor the current path.

The restartable command parameters enable you to indicate whether or not the Tuxedo can restart server processes, with the exception of BBL processes when the server is abnormally terminated. This is somewhat analogous to the kill on Unix boxes or the task manager in the Windows operating system.

The TracePC parameter establishes a specific level of PeopleCode tracing for any activity created by all of your clients in a given domain. Any value that might be useful is designated in the configuration file. TracePC values are shown in the Configuration Manager on the Trace Tab. The TracePCMask is a parameter that maintains which PeopleCode Trace options are requested by clients' machines and will be written to the trace file itself.

Database Option Parameters

The database option lets you determine specific environment variables that can increase your system performance for your DB2/MVS and Sybase implementations. The DB2InputMessageSize allows you to set options that will be enabled when you execute DB2/MVS through your Centura SQLNetwork. You can input specific values for your configuration and then the Input Message Size controls the absolute maximum size you can use for the input message bugger. This setting will directly manipulate your client's ability to send host messages.

The DB2OutputMessageSize is used to set options that will only be permitted it you are running DB2/MVS through the Centura SQLNetwork. You can input specific values for your configuration and can set the output message size with the maximum size permitted for the output message buffer. This setting also has the capability to affect the client and the way it receives host messages.

The SybasePackeSize option is useful, as it enables you to set the TCP packet size. The least amount you can use is 512, while the maximum number is 65,538. The default packet size is 512, but you can execute any packet-size changes. You need to make certain you can execute all of the associated Sybase server changes too.

The Min Instances parameter determines exactly how many servers will start at boot time, and the Max Instances parameter determines the maximum number of servers that can be started. You can use Min and Max at the same values and make them both a value that can deal with peak periods of usages. These values are normally 1, due to the PSAUTHO service being very fast.

The Recycle count determines how often a server will be run before it automatically terminates through the exist command. When it does terminate, Tuxedo automatically restarts the server, because servers are sporadically recycled to clear buffer areas. The time you need to recycle a server isn't very much.

The option that allows Consec Service Failures to be used for dynamic server process restarts for server failures. You can input a value greater than zero, whereas "0" disables it. The numerical value you input is the number of consecutive service failures that causes a recycle of the server processes. This is a good error-handling routine that permits a server process to terminate if it encounters several consecutive fatal error messages from service routines. These types of errors need not occur consecutively, but if they do, it means the server process must be recycled immediately. In fact, you will see retry messages every time the client machine encounters this type of error.

One important feature you will need to know is how to validate your sign-on with the database. This parameter is used for an added authorization level-checking method. You can enable these parameters with a value of 1 or disable it with a value of 0. Usually, this option is disabled, but when your users try to connect to an application server, the PSAUTH servers make certain that users' operator IDs and passwords are recorded in the PSOPRIDEFN. The request to connect will not succeed, however, if the password is not there, but when you do have a verified sign-on with the database option, the PSAUTHO will try to connect to the database through the Operator ID and password. These elements are part of the database connection string, and if it's OK, it disconnects and the regular Operator sign-on method is used. Therefore, if you want to connect to the database, you must have a valid account of your operating system of the RDBMS.

Note that when you are dealing with either DB2 or OS/390, which is MVS, the Operator ID and password must be defined on the MVS system as the user log-on ID.

Application Server Process Definitions

The PSAPPSRV executes some important functions that include loading panel groups and offering in-memory caching for PeopleTools objects on the application server. Each of these types of process servers has the capability to maintain their own individual cache.

PSAPPSRV also provides you with the Spawn option. When this value is set to 1, it is enabled, and when it is set to 0, it is disabled. Tuxedo is used to start more PSAPPSRV processes as well as PSQCKSRV as they become necessary. You can use this parameter by setting the previously defined Max Instances value to be greater than that of the

Min Instances value. If you have a Min instances value set to 2, while the Max Instances is set to 5, the PSAPPSRV would start two PSAPPSRVs at book time and then have three more PSAPPSERVs ready to work with the increase in your transaction requests.

The service timeout parameter is used to determine how many seconds a PSAPPSRV will wait until a server request is received before it times out. Service timeouts are recorded in the TUXLOG as well as in the APPSRV.LOG. When a timeout does occur, the PSSAPSRV stops and the Tuxedo automatically returns with the specified process.

The recycle count parameter is used to determine how often each server is executed before it is terminated by the system and immediately restarted. Servers are sporadically recycled to clear busy areas, but you must make certain that the values are managed by the server itself in order to work efficiently.

The Max Fetch Size usually defaults to 5000K, but this parameter sets the maximum memory used by the server to record fetched rows for transmission prior to sending the result set back to the client. When the memory limit is filled, the client receives the rows that are received from the system but issues a "memory buffer exceeded" type of warning. Therefore, you will find it better to maintain the default values. However, PSAPPSRV can support non-conversational transactions so that this type of parameter gives users a good means of dealing with high-volume throughput due to the necessity of larger volumes of data.

The Max Fetch Size can also default at 32K and can determine the most memory used by the server to recode memory fetched for a transaction before transmitting the results to the client and refilling the memory buffer. When the memory limit is filled, the server can send rows to the client and then place more data in the buffer and transmit those results to the client until the query is complete.

PSSAMSRV is an important parameter that supports conversation transactions. This parameter gives your users a simple method of refining performance by setting several network trips that are needed for a given transition. These values cause unlimited memory to be used, so only one round-trip is needed, regardless of how large the value is.

It is important to note that the PSQCKSRV parameter is a quick server that is used to copy the PSAPPRSR and execute quick requests. These types of requests include non-transactional read-only SQL requests too.

When dealing with the server, you may have to choose some special server process options in order to succeed. Once you input all of your previous parameter values for your application server, PSADMIN will ask you several process options that you can define to assist you. If the system prompts you to move quick PSAPPSRV services to a second PSQCKSRV, you can enter the domain, which will be accessed by only a few clients. You can input a yes answer to activate the PSQCKSRV in any situation when you need to obtain the best transaction throughput possible. If the system asks you if you want JOLT to be configured, remember that the JOLT listen is necessary to support your Web clients. If you are not using it to deploy Web clients, then you need not worry about configuration JOLT.

The system may also ask you if you want to configure JRAD. If JRAD is used to support Web clients within your advanced configurations, then you may wish to accept this default unless you are trying to configure JRAD and the JOLT Internet relay at the same time.

Whenever you are confronted with the edit configuration/log files menu, you can choose several options that allow you to view the application server as well as the Tuxedo log files. You can even edit the PSAPPSRV.cfg file yourself if you do not want to use the PSADMIN interface. One of the benefits of this PSADMIN's configuration is that you can run it from your text editor so you do not have to manually use or view application server configuration and log files. In addition, you don't need to have your text edited, specifically mentioned in the environment settings.

PSAPPSRV.CFG

Whenever you have to deal with the PSAPPSRV.CFG file
that has all of your configuration settings for an
application server domain, remember that the PSADMIN
interface gives you several prompts so you can edit and
alter this file within a specified structure format. The
majority of the time, you can edit the PSAPPSRV.CFG file
yourself in a manual text editor so you can gain greater
control. However, when you edit this configuration file
yourself, you will see that it is very much like editing a .INI
file in your Windows files. In fact, all of the parameters in
the file are grouped into two sections. You can then review
all of the terms and correct them as you need to.

Working with the Process Scheduler

PeopleSoft enables you to configure and administer your
Process Scheduler server agent using the PSADMIN. It
doesn't matter if you wish to run batch processes on the
application server because you can use the PSADMIN
utility to configure both your Process Schedulers and
process server agent.

In order to determine the best menus and options to use
for PSADMIN, you need to make certain you configure
your Process Scheduler server by starting the Process
Scheduler server from the administrator menu. You can
then create a Process Scheduler server configuration and
configure the Process Scheduler server itself. When you
have both added and configured a Process Scheduler server,
most of your administration tasks deal with either starting
or stopping a Process Scheduler server. The PeopleSoft
server administration menu is an exercise in Windows NT
and Unix. You can access the Process Scheduler
administration menu that is associated with the action you
need to execute.

When you need to start a Process Scheduler server, you can choose the appropriate option from the Process Scheduler administration menu. You can start the Process Scheduler server for a given database by entering the number of the database you want in the database list. You can alternatively stop the Process Scheduler server just by executing an application server option using the PSADMIN. You need only choose the appropriate option format from the PeopleSoft Process Scheduler administration menu. You can then stop the Process Scheduler server on a given database just by entering the number of the database list that is associated with the database you want to stop.

When you are working with Windows NT, it is important to note that you will often see a COBOL output window appear on your screen. Only a few seconds later, the Process Scheduler server will stop and its output window will disappear from your NT task bar. This is due to the fact that the server does not stop automatically. The PSADMIN was created specially to execute a stop, as opposed to immediately killing the server option. This gives the server a chance to refresh the request to stop and then terminate its process. It depends, of course, on your server's sleep time, which can vary from a few seconds to as long as half a minute. You can also verify your server's status with the process monitor to confirm your operations.

Configuration

You can also configure the Process Scheduler server similarly to application and Web servers. You can use the Process Scheduler administration menu to choose a text interface that will allow you to input parameter values for the Process Scheduler server.

You can enter configuration information for a given database within the PSPRCS.CFG configuration field as well as the PSADMIN. This allows you to obtain an interface to manage the PSPRCD.CFG file for your operating system parameters.

Integrating Web Components

Whenever you need to deal with the deployment of a Web client, you must have your web server deal with your HTML files. You can use the PSADMIN to configure your Tuxedo's Web server functions for your specific environment. The Tuxedo Web server may not be the best one to use for a full-scale production environment, but it does have several advantages.

Refining a Three-Tier Environment

As you work within your three-tier configuration, you must remember that your administration objectives can only be achieved or improved by making certain your configuration settings are optimally tuned to increase your performance. It is important to determine how both HOLT and JOLT Internet Relay work within your Web deployment.

Refining Your Workstation Environment

When you are working within the three-tier mode on a Windows family client workstation, you must remember that you can use both PeopleTools and the Configuration Manager to execute workstation changes. You can also determine your unique application server name, which is designed in the client's Configuration Manager in the application server dialog box. The application server name is actually a user-designated name that is affiliated with a given IP address on the application server machine as well as the port number that is used by a specific application and server domain. Remember that the application server name is *not* case-sensitive, so it need not match the application server name that is designated with the PSAPPSRV.CFG file settings.

Users in your organization can designate a resolvable DNS host name or IP notation in the Configuration Manager when establishing the client's application server name. Users can use one of these notations directly without having to use any specified characters when specifying this host name.

Connecting to Three-Tier Mode

If you need your client workstation to connect in either two- or three-tier mode, you can accomplish your objectives through the following methods. One important note that will help you acclimate to your three-tier environment is that connected clients will always see a hourglass, as opposed to the SQL lightning bolt whenever you wait for a transaction to complete.

As we discuss different options that run in three-tier mode, you must consider both Crystal and nVision. Both of these products can operate in three-tier mode. This means the client can transmit SQL calls to the application server, whereas the results are returned to the client in the form of a message. As opposed to a two-tier environment, Crystal and nVision would normally run on the client machine and execute SQL directly against the database server. These two products function differently in a three-tier environment where they run on the application server. Crystal is used in either a two- or three-tier environment, but Crystal will not function on the client unless you schedule it to run with the Process Scheduler (PSNT).

Due to the fact that Crystal can transmit SQL to the application server, you must note that it does not fully benefit from a three-tier configuration. However, ODBC (needed for the Crystal interface) does not have to live on the workstation. This can effectively eliminate several administration tasks. Most of the time, Crystal performance can be enhanced when used over a WAN because you can send messages on a WAN and make Tuxedo use packet compression to reduce the number of route trips needed. Crystal usually works the same in a three-tier environment as it does when connecting in a two-tier one.

Sharing Resources

PSADNUN provides you with three distinct sizing models where you can select options from the application server configuration utility. When you create the application server domain, you can choose from three sizes:

• Small

• Medium

• Large

All of the size models are based on the total user population as well as a special number of server processes that you need to support your users. The idea is that these models will provide your customers with a good point from which you can configure your application server.

In order to more fully illustrate what these size designations mean, small refers to a user population between one and 100, medium refers to a user population between 100 and 1,000, and large refers to a user population of 1,000-plus users.

In order to determine how many server processes you need to support your user population, you must consider overriding your original values using the PSADMIN utility. The numbers of server processes you can configure will depend ultimately on the number of elements that affect your user population and the types of users you have. You must consider if you have more causal or power users.

In order to determine your system kernel configuration setting, you must work with your application domains as well as the size of each domain configured for your machines. You need to begin with the concept that your existing system values are illustrative of the system requirements before configuration application domains. You must deal with all of your existing system values that include RDBMS requirements. You must increase your existing values with addition requirements that come from the application server domain size your need to configure. IPC resource parameters are illustrative of those that most customers need to review or modify depending on their environment.

When you are working with a large application server domain configuration, you will be supporting thousands of connected users. You may not choose to use a PeopleSoft small, medium, or large model designation. In this event, you will be using custom configuration parameters · through the PSADMIN utility. You can configure your application server before you boot the application server access special command-line menu options to determine your estimated shared resource requirements for your configuration.

As you deal with your system kernel configuration parameters, you can look at the number of processes per domain that you must set. You can then use the maximum number of process values for each small, medium, and large domain model you define. If you use a medium domain model of 200 processes, you may want to alter your PSAPPSRV.CFG to add extra maximum value for each server process you need to determine in order to satisfy your total number of business processes.

When working with large domains, you may need to examine your system kernel configuration parameters to determine how many current connected users you have. This means you may have as many as 1,000 users connected at any given time. However, with this large amount of users, you can expect that many of them are idle or not working on any active transaction execution.

What Is a Semaphore?

All processes that work in your Tuxedo application need a semaphore. Semaphores can be used as system resource locks that process uses to acquire control over shared system resources such as memory.

Whenever an application server is booted up, the number of semaphores configured in the operating system is checked. If the boot fails because the configured number of services is not set to a high-enough value, then the semaphore parameters may need to be changed, depending on:

- The number of application servers configured

- The number of databases

- The number of resources consuming semaphores (that is, database instances)

- How many other software programs are consuming system resources

Processes Communication

Business processes communicate with the system processes by using routing messages. Message live in the message queues and this queue supports several messages. Your system can have several message queues. This can include using Tuxedo messages when a client request is received by a WSH that has the power to route a request to another process (such as PSAPPSRV) that can use that message most effectively.

In order to define process communications more effectively, note what the following parameters mean and how they can effectively apply to your PeopleSoft environment.

MSGMNI determines the number of individual message queue identifiers. Every application server instance (PSAPPSVR) must have at least one message queue. This number is reduced if MSSQ sets are used where several server processes share one single queue.

MSGMAX indicates the maximum message size in bytes. This value must be large enough to support any Tuxedo application service.

MSGMNB is the largest message queue in bytes. This number must be large enough to deal with the total size of all messages that are on a queue and have been taken off by application servers. Any messages longer than three-quarters of the MSGMNB must be sent to a file instead of to the message queue. You should avoid this problem because it can decrease your performance.

MSGMAP is the number of entries in the control map used to manage your message segments. If this is the same as the number of message segments for MSGSEG, then it should be double the size of MSGMNI.

MSGSSZ is the size of the message segment in bytes. It can help you eliminate wasted space in your system.

MSGSEG is the number of message segments in your system.

MSGTQ is the total number of outstanding messages that can be recorded in the kernel. It is the maximum number of unread messages at any time.

These processes also take place in the shared memory. Whenever you deal with the Tuxedo environment, shared memory is important, as it can be used for the bulletin board as well as the control tables of the WSL.

The parameters associated with shared memory include the following:

SHMMAX is the maximum shared memory segment size in bytes. This number illustrates the largest shared memory segment that can be allocated. Note that these processes can attach to more than one segment size of SHMMAX, however.

SHMSEG is the maximum number of shared memory segments per process. When you deal with your system configuration, the maximum number of shared memory allocations for a process to attach to is determined by multiplying SHMMAX by SHMSEG. This results in a value between six and 15. A value of eight represents most current system settings.

SHMMNI is the maximum amount of shared memory identified in your system. Tuxedo needs at least one identifier per BBL and one more identified if the WSL is functional.

As you refine your kernel in Unix, you may also expect to see the following parameters that will be useful in your efforts:

ULIMIT refers to the maximum file size that these parameters can set. The values must be sufficiently large enough (4 MB or larger) to install Tuxedo and build application servers.

NOFILES refers to the maximum number of open files in a given process. The Tuxedo server needs a minimum of four file descriptors to function correctly.

MAXCUP is the maximum number of processes that can be run for every standard user. The Tuxedo system processes include both server and administrative processes that can function with the UID determined in the application's UBBCONFIG file. MAXUP must be big enough to permit all of these processes to run.

NPROC is the maximum amount of system-wide processes that can be run.

NREGION is the number of region table entries to allocate. Most of the system processes have three regions:

- Text

- Data

- Stack

Other regions are required for each shared memory segment as well as each shared text and data-attached library.

NUMTIM is the maximum number of STREAMS modules that can be pushed by the Transport Layer Interface (TLI).

NUMTRV is the number of TLI read/write structures that need to be allocated kernel data space.

Dealing with Large Application Domains

If you have a user population that involves more than a thousand users and many of them are power users, then you may need to perform advanced analysis and OPV planning. In order to accomplish this goal, you need to know the number of database instances you wish to plan for adding PeopleSoft. Only then can you determine the incremental effect of each instance. You can examine your system by looking before and after you utilize your shared resources using the Unix and NT ipcs command when starting database instances.

You must try to examine how many application server domains you need to configure. You can have a 1:1 ratio or a more complex relationship between the application server and the database. If you are either in production or in testing, you can designate several application servers for fail-safe conditions. However, you may not want to use individual machines to perform system operations. You should, however, determine how many server processes you need.

PeopleSoft 7 requires customers to configure their Unix kernel to employ a specific TCP/IP device. If you do not use it exactly as they specify, you may not be able to start the WSL at bootup. You will find that the digital Unix kernel configuration and build procedure allows you to create a kernel using the configure command and asks you to choose from system V devices, stream packet modules, its own transport interfaces, or even ISO 9660 compact disc file systems.

When you conncct to the client, you need to make certain the Tuxedo server permits your client workstation to connect to the application server. You need to start whenever the client request is received by the QSL.

One option you may need to set using the Init Timeout parameter is the PSADMIN configuration. If you set it to a value of 8, then the Tuxedo will allow workstation clients to multiply this value by the SCANUNIT to determine when to execute client connections to the application server. Note that the application server must be reconfigured to utilize the new values that you have issued to the system. This means that if the Init Timeout is 7 and the scan unit is 10, the Tuxedo server will allow 70 seconds for the client workstation to connect to your system.

You may have to consider processes that wait in the queue. This is when the client requests can stay in the queue waiting for the server processes to become available. You can use the BLOCKTIME * SCANUNIT parameter values to achieve your objective in the PeopleSoft application server UBX file. The application server must be reconfigured for a new value to take hold. This means you need to consider the client workstation requests that are queued for a certain length of time based on the blocktime and scan unit equations above.

You must also consider the maximum transaction time and in-database time. In the former, you must deal with server processes that are allowed to process a transaction prior to the terminated server process. You can set commands and parameters using the service timeout parameters. In the latter, you can set the value using whatever means are available in your database management system.

Configuration Parameters

PSADMIN allows you to configure the application server and prompt users for several different parameters. It can automatically calculate some parameters, but whether these items are determined by the user or automatically, these settings are recorded in the PSAPPSRV.UBB as parameters flags. It is important to discuss these parameters, how they are computed, and give you a better idea of why it may be useful to manually edit the PSAPPSRV.UBX files when you configure large domains.

Both MaxServers and MaxServices are parameters that are designated in the PSAPPSRV.UBB file. When dealing with PeopleSoft 7, you must examine both parameter values that are set automatically and determine the values needed by the PSADMIN. The idea in MaxServers is to set the sum to the maximum number of servers that are designated as:

- WSH

- JSH

- PSSAMSRV

- PSAPPSRV

- TMSYSEVT

Should you increase the MaxServers, you may also have to increase the MaxAccessers too. However, MaxServices are a sum of the number of designated services. PeopleSoft provides a default value that can possibly be too small for customers to configure large systems.

Adding Another WSL

One WSL can support several hundred client connections because it can support such large columns. The WSL has the capability to receive a client workstation's initial request; it can then deal with the management of that client for all future WSH connections. Once the initial request is complete, the client connects to the WSH, as opposed to the WSL. You can use the port number that is internally defined by the Tuxedo server.

Times will occur when the number of client requests is very large and a great deal of client connection wait

timeouts are displayed. You may wish to imitate multiple
WSLs to deal with the increase in client requests.

Security

It is important to learn how to most effectively deal with
security issues in your three-tier environment. Several concepts
deal directly with three-tier environments that include:

- Data encryption

- Self-server

- Web clients

- Applications

As a PeopleSoft user, you have the ability to encrypt data
messages that are sent between the client and the
application server. As a North American customer, you can
permit both 40 and 128-bit encryption. International
customers can permit 40-bit encryption.

Forty-bit encryption is provided by the PeopleSoft
Tuxedo server through the CD that is sent to international
customers, whereas 128-bit encryption is provided through
the North American PeopleSoft CD-ROM.

The BEA/Tuxedo client workstation binary files are
found within the PeopleTools installation. These files exist
within your workstation for file servers. There are 40- and
128-bit encryptions of client files. PeopleSoft provides a 40-
bit international customer version to support two line
codes. North America uses 128-bit encryption, but in order
to do so, you have to copy the 129-bit files to your client
directory and overwrite the 30-bit .dll file.

It is also important to deal with application server
security. When you boot your application server, the
Operator ID is determined in the configuration file,
PSAPPSRV.CFG. It must be authorized to start the
application server. This type of authorization is given by
the setting in the STARTAPPSVR column within the

PSOPRDEFT. When it has a value of 1, this authorizes an operator to start an application server. In addition, you can provide authorization through the security administrator in the options group when you define an operator.

The security administrator helps you provide authorization to start an application server. However, this does not either directly or indirectly provide authorization or privileges outside the ability to start the application server. You must deal with clients connecting to the application server to send their operator ID and password. In addition, the application server uses these values to inspect the authorization in PSOPRDEFN when you deal with two-tier connections.

It is important to use upper-case letters in three-tier mode for both the operator ID and password. The upper-case lettering requirement is a means of easing the log-on process for users. In this method, users can enter their ID and password without having to deal with upper or lower case for the input data. This means that PeopleSoft automatically translates information into upper case. However, users who connect in both two- and three-tier modes need to have upper case for both the operator ID as well as the password.

You must also learn to deal with security in your Web server and Jolt. Once you connect to the Web site, you must deal with your Web client. When you do, you will be asked to provide a sign-on with both your operator ID and password, which is similar to what you have come to expect within your Windows family client log-on.

If you permit encryption on your application server for Jolt, then your application server's configuration would illustrate this fact. If you use Jolt 1.1v2, it creates a 128-bit RC4 session encryption key at log-on time if you have 128-bit software. International customers have a 40-bit key and the session key is sent over the network in a message protected by a 56-bit DES encryption.

You can imitate a temporary session key that is used to encrypt the sessions data. In fact, your complete security level allows you to utilize an equivalent 56-bit DES encryption. You will find that Jolt will support a more secure key exchange algorithm to sustain a 128-bit level of encryption for your systems.

You can use firewalls to place a wall between two networks. Most of the time, this wall stays between an internal network or trusted network and an untrusted external network, like the Internet. Firewalls look for both incoming and outgoing packets with regard to a set of rules that the administrator defines. These rules can either let users through or block them. You can also use a more complicated and secure type of firewall in the application gateway.

Many application-gateway firewall products use application proxies. These programs are developed for specific Internet services that include:

- HTTP

- FTP

- Telnet

These services work on a server that has two network connections. One connection works as the server to the application client, while the other works as a client to the application server. Both of these services examine network packets for valid application data.

Application proxies are more secure than packet filers. Many application gateway firewalls have a function called "network address translation" that stops internal IP addresses from being displayed to users beyond the perimeter of the trusted network.

Firewalls also allow users to see publicly accessible Web servers but protect access to Web server information that you don't want anyone to tamper with regarding internal contents.

Authentication is achieved through IP addresses that are defined for each client, server, and network device. This means that if you want to provide users with access to important internal files and data through the Internet, you need to be able to authenticate the user. Authentication allows your users to verify themselves as who they say they are by going through several methods of identification. Passwords are the most common method of authentication, yet users often do not protect their passwords well and they can sometimes be guessed.

As you discuss Web server security, browser security is also important, as it allows users to access the resources of any client that is running the application. Netscape is one Web browser that institutes Java applet limitations that prevent access to any client fields, don't listen to network sockets or requests, and can only open network connections to the same IP address where an applet was downloaded (that is, a Web server).

Applets can also be killed when the Web pages are purged from the cache. In addition, applets that have the same browser may not necessarily have the capability to communicate with each other. You may also benefit from using the Jolt Internet Relay (JRLY). It is a component that has the capability to route messages from one Jolt client to either a JSL or JSH. The benefit is that this makes it possible for you to have to have both the application server and Tuxedo on the same machine that has the Web server too.

Dealing with the Database

When you deal with some of the relational database systems that PeopleSoft system can support, you must also deal with extra registry settings that can be altered through the Configuration Manager. These settings allow you to improve or regulate the performance statistics of your system.

Some of the parameters you must deal with when working in your database include DB2 message size and the Sybase packet size. The DB2 message size is measured in bytes and this set of options is only used if you are running DB2 for OS/390 through the Centura SQLNetwork. You can input values of the input messages size that deals with the maximum amount allotted for the input message buffer. This setting deals with your client's ability to send messages to the host. The output message size is the maximum amount you can set for the output message buffer. This setting only deals with clients that have the ability to receive message from the host.

The Sybase packet size option allows you to define a TCP packet size. It has a minimum value of 512 and has a maximum value of 65,538. Although the default is 512, you can make changes to the packet size, but you also have to remember to make changes to the Sybase server too.

You may need to deal with the upcoming versions of PeopleTools as they move into future releases. If you do, you will need to convert images to a new format that may need greater amounts of storage space. If the images are bigger than the record size limit in your system, you can compress the images to meet your storage limit.

When you compress images, you must convert and compress them to your platform limit. This limit will allow you to convert and compress images to fit your database platform limit value in the image size limit field. You can choose to convert and compress images to the image size limit too. This option is useful in that you may need to upgrade to a different database platform. For this selection, you need only to define a value in the image size limit field. You can alternatively choose not to convert but can compress images to the image size limit. You will find this choice good for images that have been converted, but you need not convert them to satisfy your new platform size limits in your system.

Setting Up the Client

Whenever you are responsible for installing your PeopleSoft workstation, you must be aware of your configuration so that your system will run correctly. The client setup (as shown in Figure 7.4) is the point where you can choose several options that will directly impact workstations and call up client setup processes.

This configuration setup allows you to select which shortcuts will appear on your workstation's desktop. You must realize that there are other points where you can input important workstation values and defaults. You need to make certain that all of your setup windows have the proper values for your site when you are working with the Process Scheduler and your startup routines.

When dealing with client shortcuts, it is important to determine how they will affect your system. PeopleTools can add icons to launch programs in your PeopleSoft environment. You can use the application design to add icons for your PeopleTools development settings and then add the Configuration Manager to permit you to edit registry settings important to your system.

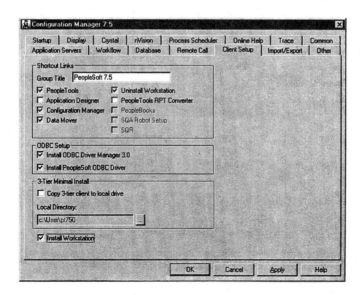

Figure 7.4 *Client Setup Tab.*

If, for some reason, you have to remove your workstations, you can use the uninstall workstation option to uninstall the most recent client setup in your system. This is important if several settings change and you need to reconfigure the machine from scratch.

The PeopleTools RPT converter calls up individual programs that can convert your RPT files from previous PeopleSoft formats to the most recent 7.x format, depending on your version. However, you only need to run this program when upgrading from older PeopleTools versions. Remember that when you back up your old RPT files, note that the converted program will greatly alter the system.

The SQA Robot Setup program allows you to use the SQA robot to test the applications you create. This allows you a good foundation, making certain your application will work correctly in your system.

Small Install

You can choose the three-tier small install option to install a minimized version onto your three-tier window workstations. The client setup will execute the three-tier install, but this will involve duplicating fields to a user directory on your three-tier client workstation. You will find this will be a good method of creating needed shortcuts on the workstation's desktop. When working in this field, you can use the local directory edit box to determine the directory where you need three-tier files installed. You must make certain you have adequate disk space on the client workstation before trying this type of installation. This means at least 80 MB of free space on every three-tier client workstation.

One of the other setup options you need to consider is the ODBC setup in your PeopleSoft Open Query. This option installs the ODBC driver manager with the associated Microsoft ODBC drivers you need to execute in combination with the ODBC Driver from PeopleSoft to allow Open Query to function on your system. If you have Microsoft ODBC drivers on your client, they may be older or newer than the ones from your PeopleSoft system. Note that if you do have the Microsoft ODBC drivers on your system, this procedure will overwrite your urgent drivers. The client setup installs the ODBC driver manager and any earlier versions are destroyed. However, if your Microsoft drivers are newer (from installing a new Windows client), then PeopleSoft will not overwrite newer drivers.

When you are installing Workstation, you must choose specific options in your client setup. You only need to select the client setup function once you have executed all of the proper sections determined in your Configuration Manager. If you do not select this option, the client will not run.

Configuration Manager Settings

The import/export settings (shown in Figure 7.5) allow you to complete several operations from your PeopleSoft system:

- Export files

- Save to a file

- Define environmental settings

- Import former settings that have been exported

All of these features are useful if you need to configure several workstations that have similar settings in your PeopleSoft system environment. Figure 7.6 shows the Configuration Manager.

When you export to a file, you will write all of your current configuration settings to a file. This is an important function whenever you want to establish several workstations that are all similar with respect to their environmental settings. Remember the filename you provide with the confirmation file, but make certain you apply all of your revised settings to your exported file. This allows you to make certain the exported configuration file will illustrate the current settings for executing changes.

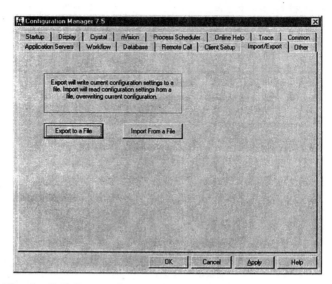

Figure 7.5 *Import/Export Settings.*

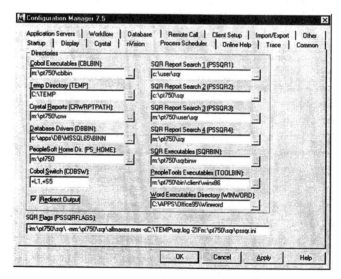

Figure 7.6 *Configuration Manager.*

When you import from a file, this will give you the same services for the export file, only in reverse. When you export to a field, this permits you to save your current configuration settings in a file. You can import from a file so that you can import former configurations saved on your workstation. You can import an older saved configuration file so that you can override all of your existing environmental settings.

Quality Application Runs

Specific settings affect your PeopleSoft quality application runs that are used on your Quality database in combination with the local database directory and the SQR output. The local data directory allows you to input the location on the client that explains where database files are used for current analysis. You can use the SQR output to input the path for the SQR that must populate the analysis data fields.

You can determine specific settings for your Quality server and other PeopleSoft products. You can use the Import/Export function to populate the Quality server environmental settings with associated values.

Issuing Commands

The Configuration Manager has provided you with several tabs in which you can choose and assign values to all of your system parameters. Also, certain command line options can be executed within the Configuration Manager that are very important. You can use these commands to implement certain functions within your system and execute certain sign-on tasks. These commands are often in the form of pscfg -<command function>.

The specific command line structure takes the following forms:

- Import a file: pscfg –import:<file>

- Export a file: pscfg –export:<file>

- Run Client Setup: pscfg –setup

- Running the quiet client setup: pscfg –quiet (This means that all output messages are recorded to a log file.)

- Disable ODBC Driver Manager Installation: pscfg –nodbc (This means the command is only valid when used in combination with the -setup command. It disables the installation of ODBC 3.0 drivers during the client setup process. You can use this command when you don't want to use ODBC 3.0 drivers installed on the client workstation using the setup option).

- Disable PeopleSoft ODBC Driver Installation: pscfg –nopsodbc (This means the command is only valid when it is used in combination with the –setup command. It disables the installation of the PeopleSoft ODBC drivers during the client setup installation. You can use this command when you don't want the PeopleSoft ODBC driver installed on the client workstation when you use the –setup option).

Uninstall Workstation Parameter

When you want to erase all of the PeopleSoft settings from your registry or just uninstall the entire workstation, you can use the command pscfg –clean. This command will effectively remove all of the workstation items, including the registry settings, cache files, shortcut links, and even the PeopleSoft program group. However, you must be certain that you do indeed wish to remove all of these items before using the –clean command on your system.

Utilities

Several system utilities can help you perform administrative functions that can be integrated easily into your system.

You can use these utilities to:

- Send system error messages

- Find help context numbers

- Set DDL model defaults

The PeopleTools utilities allow you to locate tools used to achieve some of these tasks. These utilities deal many different tasks, such as:

- Tracing PeopleCode to track and debug PeopleCode programs

- Recording cross-references (database object relationships)

- Options for system settings

The Utilities menu gives you the option to benefit from performance monitoring as well as the ability to trace PeopleCode (shown in Figure 7.7) and Trace SQL (shown in Figure 7.8). These tools not only help you monitor the PeopleSoft system, but they allow you to fine-tune it so you can increase performance levels and increase system

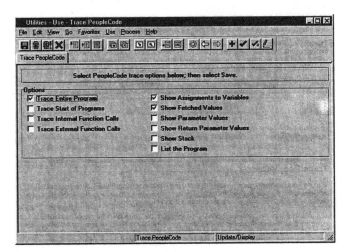

Figure 7.7 *Trace PeopleCode.*

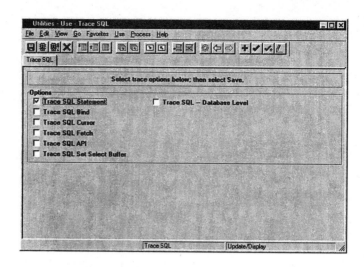

Figure 7.8 *Trace SQL.*

efficiency as it integrates with your daily business processes.

Text control involves two main features. The first is a message catalog that allows you to manage PeopleSoft system messages. The second is the strings table that allows you to translate SQR column titles.

Control tables help you both organize and control process-sharing throughout your entire system. It offers you utilities that include

- TableSet IDs

- Record groups

- TableSet controls

System settings are useful in that they allow you to use three primary utilities in the "USE" menu that include

1. PeopleTools options

2. DDL model defaults

3. Query security

All of these tools help you manage several PeopleTool system settings.

You will find that record cross-reference is a utility that maintains the capability to identify several database objects that include

- Panels

- Views

- PeopleCode

International settings deal with

- International preferences

- International field sizes

Both of the previous settings allow you to change your system so that you can function anywhere around the world.

You can define system data through a utility that was created for your PeopleSoft system administration. Users will have no reason to use this utility. Web client security must also be maintained, and you have two panels to help you establish Web client security profiles (that is, PSOPRALIAS and PSOPRALIASTYPE).

Utility processes are very helpful within the process menu. You can use the system audit to call up the SYSAUDIT.SQR. This file identifies any system inconsistencies. You can also change the base language that your system uses through the base language tool, depending on your global presence.

Increasing Performance

In order to maintain your application operating efficiency, you must monitor and refine your system every now and then. PeopleSoft provides you with several Trace utilities called

1. Trace PeopleCode

2. Trace SQL

Both these tools allow you to trace your online operations. They can be helpful whenever you are dealing with performance problems in your system. They can eliminate problems you might think are degrading your system's components, such as the following:

- Operating system

- Network

- RDBMS

All of these PeopleSoft utilities allow you to determine exactly which types of performance issues you need to deal with to increase your system operations. Most often you can use these utilities in conjunction with the Configuration Manager to provide several additional tracing options so you can gain better process control over your system. You can also activate or deactivate these utilities when you are online, a feature that the Configuration Manager does not support. This is why these special utilities are very helpful in your system operations.

Trace PeopleCode enables you to develop a file that can display the formation of your PeopleCode programs that are processed from the moment you start a given trace. This option can create your system performance, but it helps you monitor and record all of your PeopleCode actions. The benefit is that the report it gives you is very comprehensive.

You can select options on the panel that are associated with the Configuration Manager trace options. These choices from the panel do not always mesh with those made in the Configuration Manager.

Configuration Manager settings are recorded within the Windows registry and are used every time you sign on to the system. It provides you with special utilities panel settings that only deal with your current online session. When you do set these parameters, they will override whatever settings you have defined within the Configuration Manager.

Using the panel to control PeopleCode tracing is very advantageous in that it allows you to activate and deactivate it without the need to restart PeopleTools. You need not reset your Configuration Manager settings and your options are not activated until you have saved the panel within your system.

Trace SQL provides several benefits in monitoring your SQL system activity. You can execute Trace SQL by itself or together with Trace PeopleCode. The selections in your Trace SQL panel must be the same as the options you specify in the Configuration Manager Trace section. Note that these choices that are printed in this panel do not always show what changes have been made within the Configuration Manager.

Controlling Text

You can use two different panels to control text display types in your system.
These include:

- Messages

- SQR reports

Whenever you are confronted with PeopleSoft error messages, they are always recorded in the message catalog and are organized by your message set numbers. Every message set is composed of a category of messages that deal with everything including

- PeopleTools message bar items

- PeopleCode runtime messages

- PeopleSoft payroll

- PeopleSoft General Ledger application messages

PeopleTools employs some of these types of messages, but some applications use other types of messages that are called by the order of the following functions:

- Error

- Warning

- Message box

- MsgGet

- MsgGetText

- Integrated PeopleCode functions

The Message Catalog panel allows you to do the following:

- Input descriptions for each message

- Define security levels

- Input message text

- Input explanations

The message set description and sort description both refer to panels designed for simple and effective identification.

Every message is composed of at least one row of messages defined by the message number. All messages are defined severity parameters that determine exactly how the application processor will respond after receiving the error message box.

You can modify the system functionality to allow users to modify the processing capabilities based on the user's concept of the severity of the error. Some of the error types deal in varying degrees of severity. If the severity must be reserved for only the most serious message problems (such as a critical error), then the process must be stopped or the machine needs to be shut down. This would occur in any situation where all of the PeopleTools messages have a severity level of "Cancel." In most cases, you will use another severity level.

Whenever processing has stopped and data cannot be saved until the error is corrected, you are dealing with an "Error" condition. If you have an information message where processing still is functional, then this is only a "Warning."

The final parameter is the explanation text that appears whenever a user uses the explain button in the error box. This provides you with a detailed explanation of why the message was created and how you can resolve the problem. You can also add your own messages and message sets to deal with customized functionality within your system. You can also edit the message that PeopleSoft provides. Most of the time, PeopleSoft reserves all message set numbers up to the level of 20,000. However, if you have an added message set or edited a message set with a number that is less than 20,000, it may be overridden by more recent updates to your system.

Controlling System Settings

When you are working on the system control utility group, you can use it to control several factors, including:

- Performance

- Access

- PeopleTools

- Application processes

You can use the PeopleTools options to define:

- Language preference

- Change control settings

The DDL model defaults give you control over the operator of the data move as well as other functions associated with the data administration tasks in your system. Finally, you can control query access with the query security features PeopleSoft provides (see Figure 7.9).

The specific panel for PeopleTools deals with several system settings that are too specific to have their own panels. It offers you language settings and a base language control field box to determine what language PeopleTools displays and accepts, such as:

- Record definitions

- Panel definitions

- Messages

- Database objects

You can also use the "translations change last updated information" box to translate utilities, update the system, and translate objects to the data, time, and user ID of the person doing the translating. You can use its general

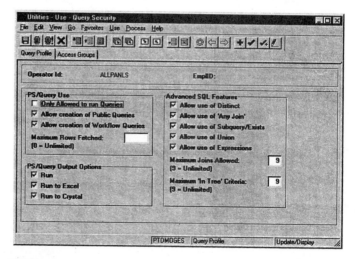

Figure 7.9 *Query Security.*

options boxes to control the background disconnect time. This value is actually used in the default value for security administrators. You can determine the number of jobs allowed for your HRMS system that support employees with concurrent jobs or have more than one enrollment set.

The Multi company organization allows more than one organization to make up your enterprise. These options will directly determine how the application process displays employee record numbers as well as all other company-related fields in the search dialogs and panel. If you choose the multi-currency dialog, fields are defined in several different currencies in your application so that you can work within your application windows.

You can add new operators through the security administrator. The system will just automatically provide new operators with select-level access to all of the three PeopleTools SQL tables at log-on time. Should you use a SQL security system and not want PeopleTools security administrators to execute any SQL grants, just disable grant access.

DDL Models

You can use the DDL model to support your DDL model statements and default parameters for the data mover. These options allow you to choose the panel and provide a build function in the application designer.

The DDL model default panel allows you to scroll through the different statement types and platforms designated in the PSDDLMODEL table. You can also change the DDL model attempts as well modify DDL values through commands that include:

- Add

- Delete

- Change

You can also institute sizing sets when you wish to deal with several DDL model versions of a given database platform. This means you can have one sizing set used throughout the development phase when you have tables that only test data. Alternatively, you could have a separate sizing set used during the production phase when tables have a great deal more data in them.

Query Security

You can designate query profiles that enable your users to access specific work items through a query. Specific users in your organization can execute existing queries, but they cannot create new queries. When you allow users to execute a query, you may not wish to restrict certain query types that they create. You can also define certain output options to create queries. In order to create new queries or run current queries, your users must have sufficient access rights to the record definition used in queries. When you create query trees, you can grant users access to them so you can both grant and restrict access to specific query trees or certain areas in the access group panels.

Dealing with Settings

International preferences allow you to establish panels to change operator language preferences determined in your operator ID profile in the Security Administrator. If you deal with currency values that need large numbers, you can specify fields that are longer than those in the standard application. You can then use the International Field Size panel to enhance amount fields within your applications.

Refining Performance

Your PeopleSoft configuration is different from other configurations. Many systems have several common components that include:

- Hardware

- Network

- Operating system

- Database software

When your PeopleSoft system experience changes, you can refine the performance of all these elements to optimize your application programs. In order to do so, you need to assign at least one person to refine application performance. You can create a team that can be composed of a special performance tuning team and must deal with all of your performance tuning components. Many organizations must deal with more that one task at a time. In order to best compose your team, you can specify specific jobs and responsibilities.

Your hardware and software decision-making team establishes system-wide performance and can include all departments that must deal with performance issues. The Database Administrator (DBA) must install, maintain, and refine your SQL RDBMS. The LAN/WAN system administrator installs, supports, and refines your network. There are three different types of administrators:

- System administrators, who install, support, and refine the operating system.

- Workstation administrators, who install, support, and refine workstations.

- File server administrators, who install, support, and refine the file server.

Application developers, programmers, and systems analysts all work together to develop, support, and alter the application systems. They work to refine performance at every step.

Finally, application users develop application system performance techniques for all applications and goals to deal with performance-tuning. The entire performance team must deal with system performance for the complete system. Their primary task is to increase performance; job titles and responsibilities come secondary to this goal. These people must be able to work with their fellow team members without any problems. You can achieve the best performance-tuning ideas through collaboration and common effort.

Several objectives can be achieved to help you increase performance. You need to carefully examine your performance goals early during the system installation before you even buy your computer and software.

Your objects are usually realized as a direct result of the negotiation between the application system users and the designers. All of your performance uses must involve administrator input to succeed.

You need to determine several factors before you can realize your performance issues:

1. Can the database server support batch and online performance increases?

2. Can your database and operating system be tuned to support to a larger processing load?

3. Can you schedule batch jobs effectively?

You can achieve your goals by developing performance-tuning directives. When dealing with PeopleSoft's HRMS batch process, you can work with batch payroll jobs to run at off-peak times. PeopleSoft HRMS online procedures can be implemented so that all of your HRMS online queries will run at a certain time on the network when the user count is low. Performance increases also result when you select your system hardware and software. It is important to choose a system that is both fast and can process larger amounts of data.

You can increase your system's performance by providing several tools that will help you refine your batch and online processing tasks. It is important to obtain tools that allow you to monitor:

- Your network

- Operating system

- RDBMS

Several different tools can be used to monitor your system performance. Specifically, you can monitor the following:

- Oscilloscope monitors

- System management utilities

- Operating system commands

Monitoring Your System

Several monitoring utilities can help you gauge your performance. Trace SQL is one tool that enables you to log several elements of information about the SQL activity called from PeopleTools and from batch COBOL on either the client or server. Trace PeopleCode traces information about PeopleCode programs run on the client or the server. DDDAUDIT and SYSAUDIT (shown in Figure 7.10) are SQR components that examine your PeopleTools records and makes certain they are synchronized with your RDBMS tables.

The Message Catalog utilities assist you in deciphering system messages. This functionality helps you monitor your system performance and increase it by providing you with essential information.

The Statistics Reports lets you see the timing statistics of your SQL statements from your PeopleSoft COBOL programs.

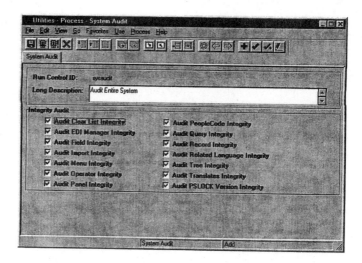

Figure 7.10 *SYSAUDIT.*

The Process Scheduler helps you define the level of detail within your message-logging levels. In addition, it offers a high level of logging aid in troubleshooting system performance. It also offers low-level logging that helps you save disk space and enhance your system performance.

The Application Reviewer is used for extensive debugging of anything you compile using PeopleCode.

The Application Engine Trace helps you trace and debug your applications. You can then execute background SQL processing against your data.

GUIs

You will find numerous SQL RDBMS monitors are available for your PeopleSoft system. The Windows GUI monitors are most effective because they offer you several benefits of standard terminals. They have full screens that can monitor several database statistics in many windows. They can also function with scalable graphics on your client applications. Since you are using these applications to monitor your performance, it gives you the ability to examine several detailed statistics and events, which can then be saved to a log file.

You can run your system to achieve several benchmarks that you don't usually have time to monitor over the long term. It can log files from important events and file them for review at a later point in time.

Powerful Performance Tools

You can use powerful performance tools on your workstation to execute important tasks that include:

- Database monitoring

- Monitoring the operating system

- Monitoring your network

- Monitoring your file server

These types of monitors can use agents for gathering data so you can install items on each LAN/WAN you need to monitor within the standard Windows GUI. You can check your network at any time you want, but the best method is to measure your network performance with a fully functional network sniffer so you can use a single operating system or SQL RDBMS to check network performance at any given time.

Quick inspections on Unix systems can be made by using the ping command. You can also develop a SQL RDBMS network test just by making a set of test tables that only you can access. You can then execute test queries against your tables at any time. Your system will record any connect and execute time against the number of users on your database, network, or server.

Spreadsheets are valuable tools, as they can monitor and plot your standard usage patterns. They can provide you with qualitative data that enable you to qualify which functions run during your test systems, including:

- Payroll

- Batch

- Online employee data entry

- Word processing

You can link these types of operations with your performance statistics to acquire a good level of processing workloads into your day-to-day system usage.

Regardless of the test you use, it is important to talk with your network administrators to examine network navigation paths that are plotted from your client to your server. This information will be invaluable in helping you find network problems, finding a good means of fixing them, and enhancing your network's performance. You can also use spy logging tools to help all of the different network application layers in your system to determine which functions are experiencing performance degradations.

It is important to verify that your performance monitors are calibrated correctly so that all of your tests are meaningful in helping you plot your performance accurately. Should your operating system monitor inform you that your database field is experiencing a communications bottleneck, you can check this information with the database monitor to see if it is true. Figure 7.11 shows the database monitor and how it is integrated into your system. If you have two performance monitoring tools that are not in agreement on your results, then you can determine how to use these tools so that you can analyze their data output to see if it is correct.

Primary Performance

One thing you must check involves the constant state of change that computer systems undergo. You need to examine the following:

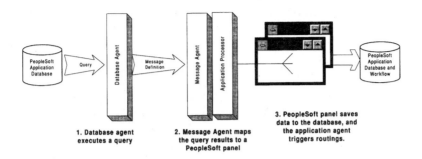

Figure 7.11 *Database Monitor.*

- Technology changes

- Data loads

- Network loads

In order to keep track of the constant state of change prevalent in the computer industry, you must constantly refine your system performance while remembering that your system may change as fast as you refine it to compensate for system performance lags.

Sooner or later your system performance will not be as fast as it should be. If the slowdown becomes unacceptable, your performance concepts will no longer be sufficient. This means you will have to determine a new level of acceptable performance for system users and define "baseline" performance, which is the minimum level of acceptable performance that you can effectively use.

In order to set baseline performance, you must test your business process operations when no other users are logged on to your network. You will first need to fetch the file server and database server operator. The next step involves comparing this level of performance with your system. You can then retest and compare your system results against a minimum, average, and full load during standard business hours. You can then test these results to keep your performance objectives clear with respect to actual versus perceived system performance on your systems.

Performance Objectives and Goals

You can establish certain performance goals for certain system components. You can then inspect your baseline performance to determine if your personnel are tuning the system correctly. You can then institute a plan to help implement performance-tuning methods to help you achieve your goals.

Your personnel can try ad hoc performances to increase single application performances as well as full system benchmark requests. Full system benchmarks will be more helpful than ad hoc requests, but more planning is required to use them effectively to increase your system performance.

Batch benchmarks and online benchmarks are two very different animals. Batch benchmarks define whether a setoff application can function with your processing windows. Online benchmarks help you determine if your application performance is good enough for your system requirements.

Most importantly, your performance tuning team and your entire workgroup are most effective in dealing with the performance issues within your system. They know your computing environment and they can most effectively deal with increasing your system performance in a timely manner.

Performing Ad Hoc Tuning

When you are ready to perform ad hoc tuning, you need to gather information so that your users can provide you with a report explaining what you need for determining which programs in your system are affected by performance degradations. You can then do some interesting background research on all of your system changes. You need to determine:

- How your configuration has changed in a way that might affect your system performance.

- Which components require more disk space.

- How many new users have been added to your system.

- What the users are doing.

You can also examine your system and database administration requests in recent months. Furthermore, check all of the monitors to review your system settings. Then you can create an operating system and network report to determine how resources are being used.

You can examine your SQL queries and see how they function against your:

- PeopleTools

- Application tables

- Database system tables

You can determine problems by running DDDAUDIT as well as your SQL scripts that report RDBMS fragmentation and growth. You can use space usage utilities and determine how effectively your system is working. You can then inspect your optimizer statistics and see if they are current as of your last data load and your current one.

Inspect your RDBMS initiation parameter settings and determine if they are current for your database usage. Inspect your RDBMS cache area and see if it is the correct size to satisfy your message configuration. You may also wish to leave your performance monitoring on until you determine and overcome system performance problems.

Remember to ask your users questions and determine if any intermittent or constant problems need to be considered in your performance issues. You should then try to reproduce the problem to determine which program is affecting performance. Users should keep a log of all the tests and carefully examine performance monitors to determine how system functionality changes with respect to new applications introduced to your system. Then reexamine your system to determine if you can isolate the problem. If you need help, you can always contact both PeopleSoft and your database vendor to determine if the problem is caused from a recent software upgrade. Most of the time, performance problems have refined workarounds to ensure you can examine your installation file and log your problems to see if any other user or customer is experiencing the same problem.

At this point, you need to examine your performance goals to determine if you have met your objectives. Are your goals achievable and have you done everything possible to accomplish them? Review your objectives to determine how well you've done and keep moving forward.

Benchmark Tuning

Now let's examine your application performance-tuning staff. Create a plan that will deal with associated staff members and make certain that they are all part of your plan.

You should begin by establishing your baseline performance statistics. In order to create the numbers you need for installing your applications before the system goes into production, define your spreadsheets and track your statistics. The baseline you define will help you choose your performance-tuning benchmark goals so you know what your current performance level is and what you want your future one to be.

Then create written performance statements that allow you to make certain that your personnel understands that your baseline performance is acceptable. You can use a server-posted document to provide your personnel with access to performance-tuning benchmarks. You can maintain a log of all discussions and problems associated with your business processes. This allows your workers to stay in constant communication in the event any questions come up.

At this point, you can develop a benchmark founded on a solid baseline performance set. You can maintain a useful performance monitor that can inform you of changing benchmark results on your system. You can examine the system that is being tested so you understand how the data flows throughout your system.

When you have gathered all your benchmarked statistics, you can apply them to your batch and online business processes. You can acquire all of the statistics for your different data-load levels. Only then can you plot the straight-path increase of your data-load statistic level to produce accurate benchmark results. You can then perform large data-load tests and refine your performance tests over a larger period of time to obtain the best results possible.

Finally, you can go over all of the benchmark results with your entire team. You can examine your performance situation and determine how close you are to achieving your objectives. If you are not as close as you would like, you can inspire management to work harder to achieve your performance objectives.

You may wish to look at more indicators besides those of total system throughput. You can include the following in your comparison:

- The operating system

- Database performance statistics

- How the OS and DBMS communicate

When you deal with online performance, consider the following important factors:

- Network

- Database

- Operating system tuning

System Prioritization

It is important to set certain priorities when executing performance tuning operations. This can be achieved by developing easy performance-tuning settings and working with each component that will provide the best performance return for your effort.

You can establish performance-tuning goals by selecting a certain business process and then ranking the components in order from most important to least important, according to urgency. You must list the component, detail the specific problem, and then outline a possible solution to help you achieve your objectives.

Sometimes you may need to settle for a compromise for your performance-tuning efforts. This may include establishing specialized programs or scripts for programs so you can optimize your system environment.

The following functions can be accelerated:

- Inserts

- Updates

- Deletes

However, query functions become slower when the above processes are running.

DBAs can execute scripts at periodic intervals that can analyze all database indexes. This makes it possible for you to acquire statistics that are always current with data that changes frequently.

As you work with PeopleSoft components, you can allow your applications to be fine-tuned for performance on several platforms. Note that these customer hardware and software configurations are different with each implementation. Therefore, you may have to further fine-tine your environment to cope with changing conditions.

PeopleSoft batch and online application performance goals are different with respect to their approach and reach into your system. Batch application tuning is executed at the database server, meaning it doesn't need tuning for:

- The network

- A client

- The file server

You can execute the majority of online tuning at the client workstation as you perform online applications.

It is your goal to try and eliminate as much conflict as possible between batch and online tuning for your systems. Note that performance tuning always includes finding the best match for system performance and functionality.

PeopleCode Trace Settings

You can deal with PeopleCode Trace settings to record a file that will display several elements of information regarding the PeopleCode processed when you initiate a trace. This option makes your system run slower because it must use more of its processing resources to monitor and record all of your PeopleCode actions. However, its monitors are produced through a detailed report.

PeopleCode Trace runs differently on different operating systems and in different modes. In a two-tier model running on Windows 95/98/NT clients and servers, you can activate or deactivate PeopleCode Trace through the Configuration Manager. Figure 7.12 shows the database tab within the Configuration Manager. In addition, you can activate a smaller version of PeopleCode Trace from the PeopleTools Utilities window in your system software application.

When you are working in a three-tier mode, you can permit the client to work in a manner similar to a two-tier mode. The trace file, however, is written only on the application server and not on any local machines. You can control the specific client-tracing options you enable and

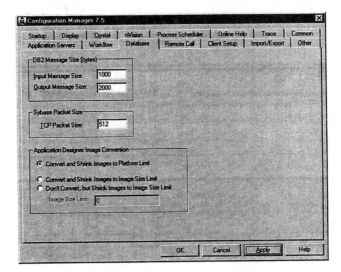

Figure 7.12 *Database Tab in the Configuration Manager.*

establish system-wide tracing levels within the application server's PSAPPSRV.CFG file too.

DDDAUDIT/SYSAUDIT

The DDDAUDIT and SYSAUDIT are actually SQRs that have SQL SELECT statements. They are used to ensure that your PeopleTools tables are synchronized with the SQL data tables in your database. You must be sure to execute these scripts prior to, during, and after performance-tuning benchmarks sessions so you can monitor your data state.

Message Catalog

You can be working with PeopleTools on your applications and suddenly see certain error messages. Specific status messages will appear on the title bar of your applications whenever background processes are running. The errors, title bar, and other message errors are all recorded in the Message Catalog. This utility program can help you determine what these messages mean so you can better monitor your system performance.

Working with Reports

One of the benefits of dealing with batch statistics reports is that you can set the COBOL statement time in the PTPSQLRT. It enables you to offer summary statistic reports that explain how much time has elapsed for the SQL statements performed in batch processing. This report provides you with an easy and effective means of monitoring your SQL performance within your PeopleSoft implementation. It explains exactly how much time each SQL statement will take to run. These time intervals are shown in seconds of elapsed time as well as a percentage of your total time. This allows you to examine queries that might pose a problem.

Dynamic SQL is used to report on a given time span. SQL Trace can report separate dynamic statements. You can work to enable this feature, but your application must determine specific SQL fields before executing the appropriate command.

You can save timing reports from every run in your system, but you can also compare statistics to locate any potential discrepancies that may exist. This is very useful once your application is experiencing performance problems due to a new software release or if system storage increases.

You should make a note to execute COBOL statistics timings with the option of always leaving them on. You can permit this report on Windows clients and servers through the Trace panel within the Configuration Manager. Note that the statistics report is appended to the same file as the COBOL SQL trace output.

Application Design

As you customize your PeopleSoft applications, you always need to remember how your performance tuning will be

affected. The application database you work with was
created via PeopleSoft's Evergreen Easy CASE Entity
Relationship diagramming tool. This means you may need
to use the "Easy CASE" product for developing your
database ER diagrams as well as tracing any changes you
make to your system. These diagrams have the capability to
record both primary and foreign key fields to provide you
with an overall picture of your system when you begin
tuning SQL statements and database indexes.

When you work with some SQL optimizers, you will
find that some of them follow every rule about reusing
cached SQL statements. When you have SQL syntax in
your system, it may need to be the same that is used in user
applications. Although your database may have the power
to support shared SQL pool areas in the memory used to
cache pre-parsed and analyzed SQL statements, you may
have problems if you do not create and adhere to SQL
coding and naming standards for enhancing performance in
your system.

Indexes are something you should use whenever you
design or gather SQL scripts into your system. These
indexes have the power to interrogate SQL database data
definitions and create detailed cross-reference index
reports. They can assist you in refining your application
and providing you with a means for executing application
modifications.

You will find that PeopleSoft provides a "demo"
database with pre-defined and sized indexes. Notice,
however, that the settings in the demo database are not
always good for your individual production system. You
have to consider the following factors when considering
index performance in your PeopleSoft system:

- Optimizers

- Placement

- Sizing

- Balance

Optimizers that are cost-based can choose data access paths with respect to their used and storage statistics. These statistics can define the current data load and distribute it in your database systems. Optimizers based on cost are different for every database since they are individual entities and have minds of their own.

Optimizers based on rules can execute decisions built on the presence of specific indexes and SQL syntax used to drive queries. Some of these databases utilize costs for rule-optimizing, depending on whether or not there are certain statistics for a given table and its indexes. Optimizers are important in working with distinctive databases. They are provided from one release to the next, but performance issues can increase or decrease with each respective release.

Indexes that are placed correctly in the system can be taken advantage of by most optimizers. This means that both cost- and rule-based optimizers can check for indexes on specific columns (that is, they can drive a query).

The majority of SQL optimizers function well with highly selective indexes. The primary key index is very selective because its columns are unique, but none of them are null. This means you should try to avoid large composite indexes that incorporate mostly null columns.

Indexes of a certain size and storage setting are created by many SQL databases. Just like tables, you will find you need to keep dynamics, extensions, fragmentation, and chaining to the lowest level possible to prevent disk communication bottlenecks that would decrease performance. Since index sizing is important, it plays a vital role as your database grows, rebuilds, and resizes. You can examine your index so that it will illustrate the current behavior of your transactions.

Index balance plays an important role when you have B*Tree storage facilities. Whenever data is altered in your database, the elements of the B*Tree can be unbalanced like a tree in a strong windstorm. This can leave you with cumulative degradation in your overall system performance.

Operating System Tuning

Whenever you have to tune your operating system, you must work with complex behavior patterns. In order to determine how to prevent your operating and network performance from degrading, make certain you have a sufficient amount of hardware resources available for your system so that business processes and tasks can run smoothly. You need to thoroughly examine your system format to determine if your hardware is capable of supporting your anticipated data load and growth patterns.

You can use load-balancing including RAID (Redundant Array of Inexpensive Disks) and striping to eliminate disk communication bottlenecks. The major cause of most SQL RDBMS performance problems occur when the input and output communications are blocked. Most of these performance problems can be eliminated, however, just by efficiently using your disk capacity in combination with good configuration planning.

Disk resources often fill up quickly and this parameter is often the most difficult to reconfigure when it is filled with data. You can tune each process or transfer in the disk setup to achieve the best control over performance.

When using OLTP, aggregate transfer performance is even more important to your system operation. Many problems can be solved by segmenting file systems by usage lines and processes. You can take batch processes and create files that have increased block sizes. Then each process can be tuned so that ILTP usage is optimized and you can produce files that have reduced blocks. This ultimately allows you to fine-tune your aggregate communication bandwidth so you can maximize your performance.

Memory is an important consideration. You need to carefully configure your operating system memory to ensure that your processes can run more quickly. When dealing with Unix, you may need to alter the number of memory parameters and then rebuild the kernel to take advantage of your OS changes.

Databases and Disk Resources

The majority of SQL databases experiences high gains in performance when the data is balanced throughout many different physical disks and controls across your entire system. Your databases should be created using a minimum of four different disk drives and controllers to properly diversify storage resources. However, I recommend using as many as possible to increase your performance.

DB2 and Oracle are two database examples that allow you to separate data into several different partitions or tablespaces. When you are dealing with large databases, you have the option of creating one table per partition or tablespace. When dealing with smaller databases (or don't want to partition your databases like me), you should separate the following:

- PeopleSoft distribution software

- SQL RDBMS distribution software

- Operating system software

- Database data

All of this information should be put into their own disks and controllers.

When you are using a database that involves archiving, make certain to use five different disks. Four disks is the minimum, but five would take the following form:

1. EXEs REDO system control

2. Data TEMP control

3. Index control

4. Rollback export

5. Archive

You may find you gain even better performance by placing your entire operating system, database, and application file onto one disk and then using that one disk per each database file type. In this type of configuration, you require seven different disks if you are archiving; if not, take one off and make it six.

Once you have distributed your file, you may still have disk bottlenecks. If this is so, you may need to use RAID level 5 or even consider operating system striping. Both of these disk structures offer performance gains that are superior to what balancing can offer.

Striping and RAID

Many operating systems can support a level of automatic assistance for striping data throughout multiple disk drives. This method allows an operating system to look at several database disks and consider them to be one or more logical drives. The method makes it easier to perform backups.

When you stripe your database disks, you can effectively reduce disk bottlenecks while maintaining an active level of data separated on their own driver with their own controllers. If you do not have a cross-platform standard, however, you may have problems with striping. If you lose one disk in a stripe set, you may also lose all of the data for a logical disk. Yet if you maintain these factors and keep everything running effectively, the result is that you will increase your performance substantially.

RAID offers you a standard disk structure that enhances fault tolerance and increases performance in your configuration. The benefit of RAID is that it can integrate data striping as well as shadowing without using too many overhead processes. RAID is becoming well supported and can successfully integrate at least two physical disk drives into one single, logical drive on your network.

Dealing with RAW Devices Under Unix

Unix system administrators often experience problems when using RAW devices whenever the SQL RDBMS can support these kinds of items. Even though RAW devices have several administrative drawbacks, they have the power to allow your system to bypass the Unix bugger cache and increase performance for your SQL RDBMS.

When dealing with your benchmarking studies, you can designate all of your PeopleSoft job processes to be assigned to the same process priority. Some databases work well when all the database background processes have the same level of priority.

In terms of utilizing CPU resources, you can use one of the CPU activity-reporting tools to determine how much usage your processor is experiencing. Unix systems often allow the user 60 percent of system activity; most system work should only account for about 20 percent activity.

If you have too much CPU system utilization, you will find the cause is an improperly configured system or program that doesn't use resources effectively. You can solve this problem by distributing processing tasks through several processors to ensure they are neither under- nor overused.

If your system has several concurrent processors, you can check your operating system to see if it has special performance modes that can either improve or (in the wrong mode) degrade your system performance. You can utilize functions that include a processor's affinity/binding, which stops a process and its data from migrating to another processor, consuming precious resources. You can also reconfigure your operating system kernel to be very light and not consume too many extra tasks that would decrease performance.

If you have a CPI that uses 100 percent of your resources, then you have a performance problem and the PCI will be of little or no use at all to you. If your CPI is just not doing any work, then the problem may not be the CPU. Most often, you will be experiencing problems such as

- Incorrectly configured/scheduled job processes

- Inefficient utilization of memory

- Inefficient utilization of disk input/output

This means that your CPU may not necessarily be slow, but the disk input/output devices may be severely degrading your performance causing all sorts of problems.

Memory Problems

You may also be experiencing problems with too much swapping or paging from internal memory saving processes. These types of tasks can severely degrade your system performance. In fact, if you do have this type of problem, you may not have sufficient memory or your system is not configured correctly.

Swapping usually takes place when a business process has exhausted all of its memory resources. When this occurs, the system tries to swap the memory contents to another program or to another disk. This means you may have to add more space when your swap report says you have a certain level of swapping activity for a specified time interval. You'll also need to check to see that you have sufficient swap space and that it is configured to have the least amount of disk input/output (I/O) conflicts.

Whenever you add users or programs to your system, remember that you must increase the available amount of swap space. Whenever swap space is set too low, you will see processes slow down significantly or even stop. Some new processes may not be started, but you'll need to make certain to stop any unused background processes within your system to free up as many system resources as you can. You can also look at your bugger cache to create a setting that is about one-third less than your total system memory with a swap file that is two to four times the amount of your available system memory.

Another feature that is similar to swapping is called paging, but this is not as severe a problem. When there is an insufficient amount of memory, only certain pages of your system are swapped out. Most of these programs include SQL RDBMS that use least recently used (LRU) algorithms that can page data to the disk with respect to the time the data has been idle within the memory. Try to keep paging activity to the lowest level you possibly can and monitor the system for a certain amount of time to make certain you have a baseline level of performance. Whatever conventions you use for swapping memory, try to implement them as effectively for paging as well.

Disk Requests

To effectively promote your PeopleSoft integration, your system uses disk request queues to process input and output requests that are waiting for a disk device to become available. When your disk can support an average queue that is greater than two, it must be looked at immediately. If you have a busy level that exceeds two-thirds of its capacity, your disk is extremely busy and must be looked at. No matter what the situation, you may need to add a disk drive and a controller to redistribute your I/O through more disks. Just remember that if your operating system and database can support asynchronous I/O, then use it so that your processes can continue after a write is executed because your input/output waits will decrease as well.

Increasing Network Performance

Networks are the heart and soul of your company. They have grown to serve complex configurations. Some of the nodes on a LAN/WAN may have faster hardware or software than others, providing one section with greater performance gains over another. Some nodes on your network may have shorter network access paths to the PeopleSoft application and database files, while others do not.

You will see different levels of performance between users of different geographical locations within a standard diversified organization because of the differences in speed from one network workgroup to another. Some networks increase but are not reworked to deal with an increase in client/server applications. This means you must be careful to look for any potential bottlenecks that can degrade performance for strategic gateways and router points within your network.

Making certain your network has a decent level of performance is the most difficult system component to deal with, because tuning requires that your techniques must change rapidly to meet your changing computing needs. In order to eliminate many network problems, you will have to isolate and replace certain elements in your system.

You should use the largest media bandwidth that technology has made available to date. The level of bandwidth is the result of your hardware and software combination. You need to examine communication bus speeds at the client and the server; make certain they are as fast as you can make them. Then choose the smallest network packet size (1,024 bytes) and implement fiber optics (FDDI) whenever you can in your network connections.

You must also monitor and balance your network loading as efficiently as possible. Networks are often segmented in many different subnets. This means you need to balance the number of users present on each segment to achieve the best possible level of performance. Think about redesigning your network to deal with other usage patterns. You may need to tie together specific clerical users and database data-entry workers on the same network note. However, depending on your system setup, you may not find this to be an effective approach. Alternatively, you can try to configure the client and server nodes with respect to function and proximity to respective data sources. This effectively helps you cut down on long network navigation paths and collisions.

Finally, you can put all of your hard work to use by running controlled tests on your system. You can establish a test that will transmit a specific packet data length from one node to another and then record the controlled data results. You can execute this test with your LAN/WAN either minimally or completely loaded. This means you can send one simple SQL statement for a client to another server and receive a fixed-length result. At this point, you can compare this data to the test executed with real work on your system. You can even consider executing practical SQL tests within your network's listening devices to determine how well data travels across your network.

Refining Your RDBMS

Make certain your PeopleSoft database administrator monitors your SQL RDBMS regularly so he/she can determine if you are experiencing any performance bottlenecks. Preventative maintenance is often the best method of making certain that more severe problems don't happen. In fact, some SQL databases are sent to you with either a full screen or a report-based performance monitor. These tools, however, are available from a variety of sources.

Be careful because most performance monitors have to deal with a certain level of processing overhead in order to run effectively. This is because they use shared resources on your system. This sharing can cause some GUI monitoring calculations to become more complex, which could be the source of some of your performance degradation when you plot your system bottlenecks.

When you tune your SQL databases, make certain you balance your database disk distribution. This is an important step because it enables you to acquire significant performance gains just by making sure you are effectively distributing your database disks throughout your multiple drive devices.

Inspect your system to determine if your database supports:

- Striping

- RAID

- Asynchronous I/O (suplexed, multiplexed, or concurrent I/O)

You should then try to (as effectively as possible) balance the CPU processing load in your PeopleSoft networked system. Your database cache buffers can also be tuned in order to increase performance as much as possible.

Finally, you can try to avoid deadlocks and excessive locking just by following these careful steps. If your SQL queries appear to be running slowly, you can use the SQL Trace utility to look at these indexes on all of your accessed tables and sort them by individual queries. You can inspect your system for any glaring indexing problems that might include:

- A lack of indexes on join columns

- Driving columns listed in the "WHERE" clause

Since each SQL RDBMS optimizer is an individual entity, you need to examine its behavior closely before you can understand and modify it. You can then query the cardinality of each table accessed within a query that is not performing as well as it should. In order to accomplish this task, you can execute several queries that can count the number of individual values in your index volume. You can then report this result as a percentage of the total number of table rows within your system. The next step is to make an informed decision on how well your database is performing in your PeopleSoft environment.

In short, you are completing a process in which you start to create index cross-references using SQL query scripts. You can try to determine if you have met your performance goals and if you are on track. Then you can query all tables for selectivity and cardinality.

The next level of this procedure is to use the "explain plan" to locate index inefficiency for specific online jobs. The explain plan can locate index inefficiency for specific batch jobs. Only then can you take the results from these two processes and determine whether you want to rebuild or drop any ineffective indexes present on your system.

At this point, you can evaluate your hard work to determine if you have in fact met your performance goals. If you have not, it is imperative to repeat this entire procedure until you have found the problems that are causing degradations in your performance. This can be a difficult process. Finding out where performance is lagging in a large enterprise system is akin to finding a needle in a haystack. This is why your performance-tuning team must be composed of dedicated individuals who will put in a great deal of extra time (usually during off-peak hours) to find out where system inefficiency lies.

Only then, after you have completed this extensive process can you ask yourself, your team, and your organization if your hard work has met your performance goals. If it has, you can finally say you are done, at least until the next software update or hardware trend is released, which would warrant another review of your entire integrated system's performance.

Conclusion

Simply put, dealing with the database is hard work. You must concentrate on your computing environment's integration, deal with security issues so that no one can steal your sensitive data, and refine your performance so that people can query the database and receive timely answers.

Knowing how to integrate the database is perhaps *the* most important integration tool that PeopleSoft offers. The next chapter will build on the integration methods you have learned in this chapter to take advantage of Forms API. This knowledge will help you specifically determine how electronic forms can become part of your integrated workflow business processes.

08

Forms API

Forms API enables PeopleSoft
applications to direct forms to an
electronic forms package as part of your
integrated workflow solution. This can
enhance your ERP environment and
allow you to utilize forms for a variety
of projects within any facet of your
business process.

253

Environmental Requirements

Whenever you use the Transaction Set Editor (TSE), you must remember to set up your environment by using the correct processes. These processes include copying code members in application edit programs, setting specific PeopleSoft parameters (that is, PTCTSEDT), and finally inspecting and killing any reserved TSE application fields that call up programs. TSE services are shown in Figure 8.1.

One important element occurs when you have to convert string values to dynamic SQL string format. In order to define the field value, type, and length variables, you must take the input field values and convert the embedded single quote to SQL/API double quotes for character field types. You can then use the zero padding and truncation of numeric fields based on specific defined field lengths. After that, you can enclose string-literal values inside single quotes and finally define the end of string with low-value bytes.

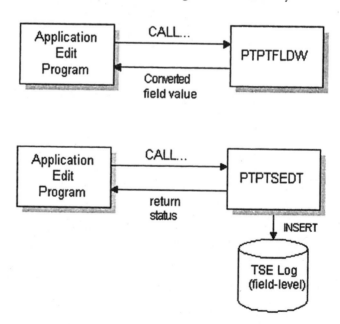

Figure 8.1 *TSE Services.*

The next tasks involve logging specific application errors, but this usually revolves around TSE application edit logs or API logs. Basically, the TSE/API functionality provides application edit processes along with a direct interface to the TSE field-level log tables.

When you use TSE log mode, all your application edit errors are logged to the TSE log table inside the same type of logical group as the TSE record edit errors are logged into. When the application's edit program finishes its own dynamic SQL call request, the complete SQL predicate string is transferred to the TSEDT-WHERE-CLAUSE and into the field-level TSE log table itself. If the application does not need the set edit request for a certain field/record edit, the single-row insert must be requested with the form of SQL-INSERT-ROW.

Outgoing Forms API

The PeopleSoft Application Designer enables application developers to use "routings" that allow them to transfer data from one business process step to another. Forms routing lets the system take data from a PeopleSoft panel that the user is working on and place it in a third-party form. When completed, this form is e-mailed to specific users.

Monitoring Tools

You can use several useful tracing tools to assist you in tuning and debugging your online applications, such as SQL Trace and PeopleCode Trace tools. You can also benefit from utilities that include DDDAUDIT, SYSAUDIT, and the Message Catalog.

SQL Trace stores information regarding the "connect router API" calls that the GUI tools and COBOL programs send to the database. This is an important tool that allows you to debug SQL. In addition, it can also help if you are unable to sign on to the database, because you can see the string that results from the failed logon attempt to the system.

SQL Trace's importance lies in its capability to trace several PeopleTool instances at the same time. Whenever you have a new PeopleTools instance initiated on the same machine, you will see several new line numbers defined by a unique trace instance number added to the trace file. SQL Trace can be activated in different ways, depending on the type of mode you are using and the type of operating system installed by your client.

In two-tier mode on a Windows 95/98/NT client and server, you can activate or deactivate SQL Trace by going though the Configuration Manager. Examine Figure 8.2 for the Configuration Manager Trace option. When dealing with Unix servers, you can changes parameter settings within the server configuration file. In addition, you can run a limited SQL Trace version from the Utilities window inside your PeopleTools applications.

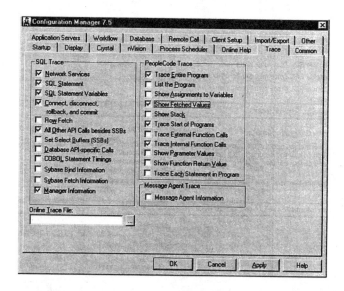

Figure 8.2 *Configuration Manager Trace.*

In three-tier mode, you can enable SQL Trace for the client in the same way as you would in two-tier mode. Be sure the Trace file is recorded only on the application server, instead of on any local client.

You will find you can control the specific client-tracing options authorized and established during a system-wide tracing level. All of these settings can be saved in the application server's APPSRV.CFG file.

TSE

PeopleSoft offers another type of integration tool, which has already been mentioned, called the Transaction Set Editor (TSE). It offers a batch-type approach to the high-volume editing of your application transaction tables. TSE can apply your PeopleSoft table edits to tables created through external applications. You can then use your PeopleSoft system to manage those tables.

TSE can support table edits that deal with data ranges, prompt tables, field requirements, table translations, and yes/no edits. TSE's record edit process is easily integrated into your COBOL batch edit programs and your applications can make calls to the TSE modules as they are required.

This section can help you define application batch edit processes for your standard database table editing functions. You will notice how they apply to record edits, log tables, and API services and edits. You can then determine how they apply to your machine.

TSE has two different types of program interfaces that include batch edit processes that must have the capability to apply record field edits. This type of record edit process is the most important function of the TSE and is very important to support tables that are not subject to internal online panel field validations. In addition, the record edit process must offer the capability to interface directly with the TSE record edit function while application-specific edit processes are taking place.

The TSE application program interface (TSE/API) function enables the calling of applications to acquire current edit requests. It offers a consistent level of error table logging functions throughout all the batch edit requests.

TSE's record edit process was created specially to be integrated into you COBOL batch edit programs via a call to the TSE modules for each user-defined transaction set. Every single set edit request will designate a group of specified transaction records that need to be edited by one SQL statement through the set process.

COBOL batch edit programs can ask for a certain TSE record edit function that applies to at least one PeopleSoft record field defined for field edits. This is based on the Application Designer's value for that edit table. You can also update all of your application edit table rows that do not have requested field-level edits. This establishes a column flag value that indicates the user-defined edit error status in tables that have error-checking columns. You can then log all of your field-level edit errors as well as your edit levels that are defined for each edit error type as well as each set-level that is defined for each transaction set, edit error, or user-defined log table for the TSE.

Application programs can ask for specific TSE/API functions that relate to acquiring Application Designer key fields and attributes. You can receive the SQL-WHERE clause that will designate your recurrent transaction set. This clause will finally create and run dynamic SQL statements that insert TSE log table entries based on a specific edit request from your applications.

Record Edits

When dealing with TSE, we must also consider how record edits play an important role. The TSE record edit process relies on the application edit request that is sent from the calling program. Once this request has been validated, the dynamic SQL statements are created based on edits and then defined through the Application Designer for the transaction record.

The entire process revolves around defining batch transaction records, referencing the "edit program" template, defining the application's TSE log records, and creating application edit request record definitions for record edit types, process modes, and environment requirements for the TSE.

In order to more fully illustrate the record edit process, we shall go through the entire procedure as it relates to TSE records. First, you must define batch transaction records. This means that if the requested edit table is defined in your application, you are pretty much done with this first step. But if your edit table definitions are not defined within the Application Designer, you must create or save the record structure and then create your database tables.

Secondly, you must reference the edit program template. Although the program shell will give you the foundation you need to define all your necessary tasks for creating your application set-edit request and calling the TSE edit process, you will still need the PSPAEDIT program to call the second program template. This template (PSPAAPPL) will help you determine your TSE/API call requirements for this step.

Third, you must define the application TSE log records. When the TSE log mode is requested, then edit error rows are inserted into the field-level TSE log table for each field edit error. You may notice that edit-level errors and set-level errors are always longer than their associated TSE log tables.

Fourth, you must create an application edit request record definition. You may choose to proceed by using the Application Designer to develop your application edit request record definition. The next step is to define the associated edit request panels. All of these definitions allow you to define several application edit requests so you can create several TSE transaction set edit requests. These requests will be processes within a single batch job cycle in your system.

Record Edit Types

When dealing with TSE records, the specific edit types will play an important role. The application edit program's call to request TSE record edits will offer specific edits from the application edit table that include the data range, prompt table, field required, and translate table edits.

Data range edits deal with each field that is designated to have a reasonable date edit. It must contain a value within a 30-day range and the requested as-of date.

Prompt tables edits are used for each edit table field that is defined with a prompt table edit, field value, and definition that is a required field. This means that it must exist within the defined prompt table, but if an edit field is not defined as needed, then the value would be blank or zero.

Field required edits mean that each defined field must not be blank, have a value other than zero, or be non-null if it is a date. All of the key fields and other fields that have any other edits defined cannot be re-edited as a required file.

Translate tables edits exist for each required field value that has a translate table reference that must locate a matching value.

Finally, yes/no edits deal with yes or no as the defined edit field value. These fields can only have valid response of Y or N.

Modes

The TSE has several process modes. The two primary modes can explain how TSE record edit errors can be processed. Table rows that have field edit errors can be flagged in the following ways:

- Error: Update mode

- Logged: Log mode

- TSE error log tables

None of the modes are mutually exclusive, which means you can implement them through the application edit process or application edit tables that can lead to error correction through the TSE update mode (shown in Figure 8.3).

As you work with record edit errors, note that they are processed by updating a specific requested error flag on the table that is being edited or the application edit table. They are edited with a user-determined default edit type value. The online acquisition of these flagged rolls will then work to re-edit all the panel data that has input fields through the activation of PeopleCode. The procedure goes from the application edit process through the insert command to the TSE log tables and finally results in batch log reports.

When dealing with the TSE log mode, note that record edit errors are processed through the insertion of rows into the specified TSE log tables. These specific tables can then be queried for batch error reporting and be joined to the application edit table for online error acquisition and modification. This operation starts with the application edit process and goes through the update command to the TSE log tables joined to the application edit tables to the batch log reports. Alternatively, the application edit processes are led through the insert command to the application edit tables to the join command with the TSE log tables for error correction.

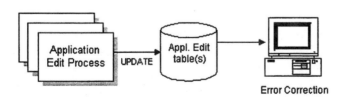

Figure 8.3 *TSE Update Mode.*

As you work with TSE record edits, you will realize that the application-editing process can only request an update mode against an edit table. This means it can only update all of the rows in error. The next event involves calling up the TSE/API function or API log to log only application-type edit errors in the TSE log table. Any flagged edit table errors and associated errors for PeopleCode can join the application edits. This enables you to acquire only the records that have edit errors, giving you the chance to display associated edit error messages in the panel scrolls. It is possible to request both update and log mode options when dealing with TSE record edits. If you do this, however, you will have to complete additional processing actions.

TSE Fields and Logging

Parameters set in the PTCTSEDT process are retained throughout the editing process for a specific edit request. However, the BUILD-WHERE-NO parameter is set to stop the rebuilding of the SQL-WHERE clause that is no longer needed.

When you deal with the SQL-WHERE clause that is requested for the PI log function, the existing set-edit definition that is used to create and append SQL-WHERE at the application edit result will return the whole clause string following the API call. Should a fieldname be needed in the message parameter field, application edits may also need a specific single-edit table record, as opposed to a group of records edited by each set-edit request.

Note that the application request from a single row can be inserted into the field-level TSE log tables, as opposed to the default row or set edit insert requests. Since there is at least one TSE log table field value achieved from the edit table SQL for each set-edit request, the single-row insert requests must offer specific values for each field prior to the API call. However, these values are given by moving the filename and field values.

When you deal with the WHERE clause, the TSE edit process creates dynamic SQL statements that are based on the requested record set request. This is the type of transaction set that is made for the SQL-WHERE clause.

One last interesting point involves the RSE/API that retrieves the Application Designer flag. When you send the USEEDIT value from the edit table definition to a program, the application has the capability to acquire the translated value for all Application Designer use-edit values. These values help in defining application keys and edit field attributes that you need for the application editing process.

API-Aware Process Requests

The Process Scheduler makes certain that all API-aware process requests include the following:

- COBOL programs
- Crystal reports
- SQR reports

Figure 8.4 shows process requests within your PeopleSoft environment.

All these elements must interface with the Process Scheduler as well as the Process Monitor, which correctly integrates calls to the given API modules. These steps are very important, as they tell the Process Monitor about the current statistics of your requests when they have been started by the Process Scheduler client or Process Server Agent (as shown in Figure 8.5). Two standard APIs are provided by PeopleTools for the Process Scheduler. One of these can support COBOL process, while the other can support SQR processes.

API interfaces for COBOL and SQR allow the process requests to update the following:

- Run status
- Completion code
- Message sets
- Message numbers

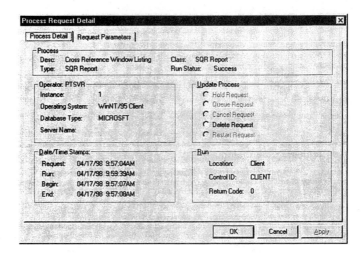

Figure 8.4 *Process Requests.*

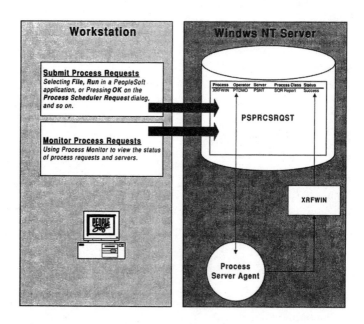

Figure 8.5 *Process Server Agent.*

Figure 8.6 shows the types of information represented within a given PeopleSoft process request.

In addition, these entities work together to enable you to go over several parameters that you can use with Message Get, Message Get Text, and PeopleCode. They all work to display messages that your processes are running and to make certain these requests are updated.

API-aware processes need to execute API calls prior to any COMMITs being processed. If any process should have an exception when it updates the database, it may need to be abnormally terminated and rolled back because any prior updates would be questionable. This means that your code should execute any rollback and use the API to update the run status and log an unsuccessful commit for an update in question, after which the process should quit. It is important that your information-specific processes be API-aware so that you can create effective process definitions.

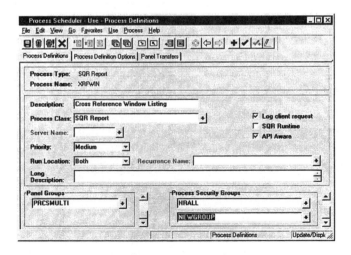

Figure 8.6 *Process Request Information.*

Any tasks you request to be chosen from the queue are updated via the Process Scheduler and the Process Server Agent. They must be start prior to sending the run request. If the requested task fails prior to loading successfully, then the run tasks would appear as if they are still on. You would then have to reset the operation by canceling it through the Process Monitor.

Any other tasks that stop for any other reason would have a run status of either being on or still processing. This automatically resets the Process Server Agent to an error status.

Whenever the Process Server Agent executes these types of functions, it needs to be actively looking for requests. When application development groups work together on PeopleSoft applications, you must make certain that the API is correctly included within the batch program code and is tested to make certain that all normal programs that have been stopped are coded into the application, which can then determine whether API run status updates are either successful or unsuccessful. This means that all program exceptions are forced within the program and the run status needs to be updated properly to reflect any errors before the program is stopped.

Awareness

It is important to distinguish between an API that is aware or unaware. The API-aware task is a process that can determine the status updates via the API of a specific type, such as:

- COBOL

- Crystal

- SQL

Should the application process fail to update in the Process Request table with status information, it is the application process that is responsible for doing all of the work.

Any tasks that are considered to be API-unaware include programs that have no defined program interface for the Process Scheduler. This can include WindWord.exe because API-unaware tasks do not update the Process Requests table because the system cannot determine whether the process has completed successfully. Furthermore, all API-unaware processes have a successful run status, meaning that the processes have been successfully started. However, success status in an API-unaware process does not mean that the process has in fact completed successfully. API-unaware processes that are either monitored or logged require manual fixes. This means you will need to cancel or delete specific failed requests yourself.

Conclusion

Understanding how records and edits can play a vital role in your ERP solution will help you discover how form APIs can assist you in refining your solution and dealing with enterprise data far more effectively. The next chapter builds on your ability to integrate various forms. Now that you can import data from a variety of sources, you need to know who to send it to. Understanding worklists can help your system function more smoothly by sending information to the proper person in your organization at the right time. This makes personnel an important resource that can be more fully exploited to bring greater worker productivity. In short, personnel is the most valuable integrated part of your PeopleSoft ERP solution.

09

Worklists

Worklists are ordered lists of work a person or department has to process. These worklists are sent to the proper person in a prioritized order, as defined using the PeopleSoft Business Process Designer.

Worklists

Workflow is helpful in managing worklists. Worklists help users document information regarding processes that could possibly hurt their job status. If PeopleSoft Human Resources uses Workflow to keep an eye on workers and job performance, it can place these descriptive items in the HR manager's worklist for a timely job evaluation review. Several benefits can be provided if you customize model processes for the purpose of creating your own business processes and integrating them with other applications.

Workflow Components

Workflow is composed of rules, roles, and routings. In explaining Workflow components, each of these primary concepts is integral to making Workflow function effectively.

Rules are important for achieving your organization's business practices through software. These rules are also essential in helping you realize exactly which activities are necessary to process your business data. In a typical Workflow environment, a rule can say that HR managers must approve all candidates for a specific position before an executive decision-maker interviews the candidate.

In many companies, rules are part of the policies and procedures that are not used as frequently as they should be. However, integrating these rules into your software implementation will ensure your personnel are following them without doing extra work to achieve their goals.

Roles explain exactly how your workers fit into the workflow of your organization. A role is a class of users who execute the same type of work. Business rules usually determine which user roles must be involved in order to complete a specific activity. A rule can say than an HR manager must approve a candidate for a job before he or she can be hired, for example. Figure 9.1 shows the "approve and deny" request requisition.

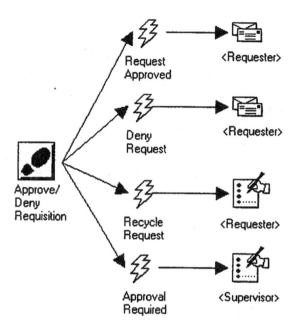

Figure 9.1 *Approve/Deny Request.*

Roles are directly responsible for the type of work a group of people does, as opposed to what an individual does. Determining what your roles are, instead of individual user tasks, can make your workflow easier to support. Roles are also constant, even when personnel change job positions.

Should a worker in a given department request a worker be added to their system, the PeopleSoft network will forward a request to the appropriate manager instead of another manager who may not be responsible for hiring people in the selected department. This workflow methodology is better for rules because they make it very clear why a specific person can approve certain requests. In short, the role fits the manager of a given task, no one else. The computer does not see which people have a unique relationship to the department; instead, it is more cut and dried and looks for the appropriate individual whose responsibility it is to hire a new worker.

The rules are given in a clear and defined format; they apply to several different situations in several different departments, as opposed to a worker who just manages that department on an occasional basis.

In addition, you do not need to change rules when another person takes the place of the HR manager. The computer identifies the right person to send information to by the job description, not the name of the person. Therefore, different managers can work in a position and the computer won't make mistakes sending information to the wrong person. In essence, the role of the person applies, not the person himself.

Routings are useful in linking together workflow activities. Routings are means by which your system can transfer information from one area to another. Routings work by determining exactly where information will go and whether that information will be:

- An e-mail

- An electronic form

- A worklist entry

Routings bring coherence and movement to your workflow environment. Routings can network together to establish a business process that is used to isolate specific activities within your system. Routings get the appropriate information to the proper people in an efficient manner. This enables users to function together as one group to achieve your business process objectives.

Routings help you deploy enterprise applications. They function at various levels and at various departments within your enterprise. They tie together all of the roles you need to finish complex tasks.

When dealing with a given system, you will find that you can also automate processing tasks by sending the electronic forms to each role via e-mail as the process progresses. Once the person on the proper role is approved, then the final order can become part of your process workflow. The information then moves its way through your system and can yield appropriate information that is sent out through your EDI system. When the information is processed and returned, it is triggered and approved on the receiving end and finally generates the final goal of your business process.

PeopleSoft Workflow

PeopleSoft Workflow consists of the Application Designer that incorporates several tools you need to both create and architect your business processes, such as Workflow rules and routing. It also consists of the Workflow Processor, which is a collection of online agents that operate and maintain the business process workflow in your organization. When you define business processes, you need to establish agents that can do specific tasks on your behalf.

When you deal with the Workflow processor, it is important to recognize several features that it consists of in order for you to achieve your business objectives. Worklists are the most common type of Workflow interface. They are not thought of as agents, but they are ordered lists of work that a workgroup has to do. When work is routed to a user, it is placed in that person's worklist. Workflow input is prioritized in the order you designate for the specific actions you are doing. Worklists can be sorted by criteria that include time, amount, or action class. If you wish to work on a specific item, the user will choose it from the worklist and then automatically proceed to the correct PeopleSoft system panel responsible for the action you need to perform.

Detecting when a business rule has been triggered is the responsibility of application agents. When users input data into an application, they must determine exactly who needs to act in this particular role or work instance. Then the data must be routed to that person through the routing command structure. Application agents are composed of several elements of PeopleCode and PeopleSoft Workflow panels to function correctly.

Message Agents (shown in Figure 9.2) are responsible for processing messages sent by external systems that include

- E-mail

- Interactive voice response

- Kiosks

- Workflow systems

- Internet (or other networked systems)

These elements provide the application programming interface (API) that permits external systems to integrate PeopleSoft applications effectively within their computing environment.

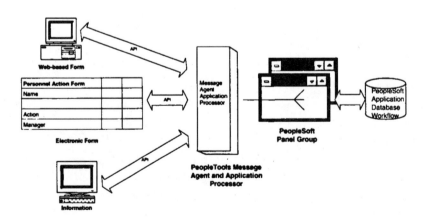

Figure 9.2 *Message Agent.*

Database agents are useful because they can monitor your database and determine if any elements must be entered into the workflow, including:

- Workflow

- Overdue requisitions

- Performance evaluations

- Departments in trouble

- Any problem area

Workflow and PeopleSoft Applications

Workflow can function efficiently as the catalyst that will enhance your applications. In the middle of your activities, you will find a panel group. Panels help you determine exactly what is going on in your database. Whenever you wish to execute employee information, an invoice, or a class registration, you can use any of these or other actions to access a specific panel and enter data in it. When you enter data and save your work, the Application Processor will come online to manage the system.

The Application Processor has several important functions that include:

- Verification of your data

- Displaying your prompt lists

- Translating values

- Running PeopleCode

- Updating database tables as needed

Workflow does not change these actions, but you can still communicate with your database through PeopleSoft panels. However, Workflow tools provide several options you can use to navigate through panels and input data.

Worklists are essentially execution lists of tasks that are listed in a specific priority. Choosing a work item from your worklist will automatically navigate you directly to the panel you need. Once complete, the system will route the work item to your next worklist.

You will find that the Message Agent is very useful for entering data directly into a panel as a reaction to your e-mail. Figure 9.3 shows the exact type of information the Message Agent uses, so instead of sourcing all your input from a user at a local workstation, you can use information from several different sources, including electronic forms and automated queries.

Your PeopleSoft system will still execute the same types of security verification checks and edits that it does under normal circumstances.

Data Query Automation

It is reasonably simple to acquire information from your system. You can access data through queries as well as

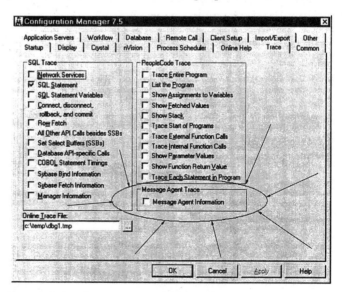

Figure 9.3 *Message Agent Information.*

execute queries in an attempt to create reports and review data records as needed. It is possible to execute queries at a predefined time. This can include queries that are created as a result of work that needs to be done. You could, for example, make a query for a list of all those who have not altered their passwords for a given time. You could then send them an e-mail telling them to change their passwords for security purposes. In addition, you can make the system run certain operations automatically on a regular basis as per your definitions.

Database agents have the power to run queries as background tasks. They can then send this information to the Message Agent, which then inputs the query results into a panel that can trigger an event to start a specific workflow.

The Process Scheduler can also perform the following tasks:

- Run queries

- Report queries

- Perform Database Agent queries

All these actions can take place at a predefined time or on a specific schedule. Scheduled Database Agents can check for certain conditions that can cause business events or trigger events to occur through the Message Agent itself.

Application Designer Background

It is possible for you to create applications through the Application Designer. You can use it to assemble various elements of your application, including:

- Panels

- Records

- Menus

All these elements function together seamlessly and without the user's knowledge. When you deal with Workflow, these elements use the Application Designer to put them into your application environment. You can also use the Application Designer to define the following:

- Message Agents

- Business processes

- Anything you need to automate

Application Processor Control

When working inside the PeopleSoft panel, note that whenever the Application Processor has control, you may see it running a PeopleCode application. If you select the text field for something you have updated, the Application Process examines the system edits for that particular field. It then performs both FieldEdit and FieldChange PeopleCode. When using the FieldChange PeopleCode, it is possible to exercise processing tasks based on the new field values.

Workflow routings work much the same way as they do when imitated by an Application Agent. Panels may have Workflow PeopleCode, but when you save the panel, the application agent performs the Workflow PeopleCode that can in turn trigger a routing through its associated business event.

Workflow tools enable you to choose from several different elements that normally exist within an open platform environment that includes:

- E-mail

- A database

- Electronic forms

- Workflow vendors

The Message Agent API (shown in Figure 9.4), on the other hand, permits the following applications to execute:

- Form packages
- Interactive voice response systems
- Electronic kiosks

Electronic kiosks are useful because they allow users to communicate with PeopleSoft applications. In addition, you can use the API to create links with various systems. The API employs the standard type of Microsoft Windows DLL or DDE (Dynamic Data Exchange) to communicate with the Message Agent for a variety of information transfers.

Specialized Processes

One of the most important benefits that PeopleSoft offers is the ease with which their products can be integrated into your organization. This is because the applications can be easily customized to fit your specific needs. You have total PeopleTool access that enables you to create:

- Database tables
- Applications
- Panels
- Reports

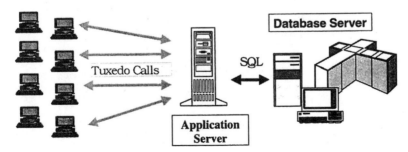

Figure 9.4 *Message Agent API.*

These capabilities provide enough flexibility to choose
the applications you need and customize them to fit your
organizational requirements. PeopleSoft's applications have
several common business processes that are Workflow-enabled
right out of the box. This means that their software can give
you a wide range of access to several standard business
processes that are achieved through the Application Designer.

You can use these customizable business processes
though specific panels that PeopleSoft has integrated into
the system. This integration appears in the form of preconfigured templates you can use to customize your
software. You can also develop your own business
processes and use your own rules, roles, and routings
to meet your individual business requirements.

Worklists in a Workflow-Enabled Application

Whenever you are using a Workflow-enabled application, it
is important to note that your daily operations always use
worklists to achieve their objectives. You must choose
specific items that will allow you to work on or from a
worklist. This means you must make your choices through
some automated means to access your panel group so you
can work on it. You need not navigate to a special window
and menu for a specific panel group. You can, however, use
the Application Designer to designate worklist routings
that will offer work items to other users who are also
executing the same types of activities. Note that worklists
are prioritized lists of work items that need the user's input
to achieve their objectives.

Worklists offer you the ability to prioritize work items.
This means that whenever you develop a worklist, you must
define the order in which work items will be displayed. Most
users will normally focus on items that occur in order;

therefore, this order will also be directly responsible for the priority of the worklist. In short, you can prioritize work on accounts to reflect high to low interest rates.

Assigned users for a specific role can work from a shared or pooled list of work items or assignments that can be specified for particular users within your organization. This means you can place specific items in a worklist so they can be processed from a high priority to a lower one. You can alternatively define invoices from a specific range of vendor IDs to a user, but that user will literally own the vendor relationship with those companies according to PeopleSoft's enterprise solution, so be careful!

Your system can also automatically define work items to other worklists if they have been dormant for a long period of time. This is referred to as timeout exception processing.

Application Agent Work Items

Getting more familiar worklists is an important concept now that you know a little about worklists and what they can do to help you. To recap, worklists are lists of work items that must be placed in a specific activity (invoices that must be seen, checks that have to be paid, and so on). Your PeopleSoft system will understand an activity order for each of your business processes and will add a work item to a given worklist whenever a user completes the former business process activity. This means that your system can add a work item to the worklist when a user enters a request for purchase, for example. The system will add the request to the worklist and wait for a purchasing manager to approve the request for the new item.

Within the Workflow definition, you will find a set of business events and routes that is connected with specific events. Business events essentially refer to a condition in which an activity is complete.

These types of activities can often include:

- Creating a new record
- Recording a specific value in a field
- The expiration of an overdue date for a given task

Routings are indicative of commands that make the system send information to the next level of your current business process. It is able to determine which information it needs to forward and where the information will be sent.

The Application Agent will check whenever a user saves a panel if a specific event has taken place. If it has occurred, then it can trigger the connected routings. In other words, if one of your workers inputs a new data field from an online panel, the agent can find out of the database has been updated. It can then choose to add the most recent item to the benefits administrator's worklist and notify any other pertinent people that the specified data field has been updated.

Database Agents

Business events can, at times, function only on the database status, as opposed to the user's actions. Should you wish to imitate a business process when a product becomes overdue and inventory falls below a certain level, you can use the Database Agent to observe these business events and trigger the appropriate routing.

The Database Agent can monitor the status of the database types in much the same way as the Application Agent does. However, the Database Agent can apply rules, determine specific business events that need to be triggered, and start any necessary routings that need to be run.

Database Agents can also execute queries and send those results to the Message Agent in much the same way as it does with data received from external programs. The Message Agent can send query results to a panel that in turn can trigger a certain business event. This means that the Database Agent can query for a manager to schedule a review at a certain time to perform employee work evaluations. The employee information can be sent to the Message Agent that in turn duplicates the employee data into a panel that triggers a certain event and e-mails the evaluation forms to the appropriate user's managers in each department.

It is important to have the database agent inspect the database status periodically. You may need to add database agents to the Process Scheduler in order to accomplish this goal in the background. The Process Scheduler will permit you to schedule recurrent database agents for any time duration that is needed.

Data Entry

You may find it necessary to input data using the Message Agent. Should you not offer every employee within your organization direct access to your PeopleSoft applications, you can send queries regarding these workers to an intermediate person who can can handle these actions.

Since the Message Agent can allow non-PeopleSoft applications to be used in your workflow, the Message Agent can perform many process requests with respect to the rules you designate. This means you can use a form from an electronic forms package, use its contents, and then add that data to your database. Since the Message Agent can be an automated user workstation and receive input from users, it can also function by getting data from other non-PeopleSoft applications too. The messages then inform the Message Agent to exercise many of the same actions that users can do, including:

- Navigating a panel group

- Inputting data into the panel fields

- Saving the panel

PeopleSoft applications can execute the same edits and security checks that include items running PeopleCode associated with the Panel. The data you enter can easily trigger a specified business event and start the workflow process. This means you can use information from various workers as if it was directly from PeopleSoft applications. This benefit can prove useful in any sized organization that does not have the PeopleSoft solution implemented in every geographically dispersed site.

Business Events and Routings

Inside your Workflow definition, you will find a collection of business events and routings that are connected with those events. Business events are conditions that inform your system of one of the following items has taken place:

- A system task has completed

- A new record has been created

- A record has a specified value

- The due date has passed on a particular item

Routings are essentially instructions that inform the system to send information to the next step of your business process. The routing is essentially the system's method of sending information around your network as well as from one activity to the next. Routings are directly responsible for creating your workflow. Routing can also determine where the information goes and if it will become:

- An e-mail

- A worklist

- An electronic form

Working with Activity Maps

Whenever you have to deal with an activity map within your Application Designer, you need to determine exactly what activities compose your business process and in what order each process must be completed. The activity map will give you a good idea of each process and make it simpler for users to navigate from one section to another. This map, however, does not actually give you a concrete link between one activity and the next.

If you want to create a good connection between workflow activities, you need to add routings to the equation. This will give you the chance to automate the information delivery to other users and their associated processes.

When you need to create a specific event, you must first develop an acceptable business event. Business events have a system of routing affiliated with them. This means that whenever you set a condition that becomes satisfied, you will want your system to execute a certain collection of routings. When you define conditions in PeopleCode in concert with the record definitions for each activity step, you will find that whenever a user saves the panel group (completes a given step) the system will run the PeopleCode program to test the condition and perform the associated routing functions.

Once you have defined a given event, you can determine exactly what routings you need to execute with respect to each event you have defined. Routing can transmit data through three forms:

1. Worklist entries

2. E-mail

3. Electronic forms

In order to create a given routing, you need to determine:

1. The routing you need

2. What type of routing you need

3. Who you want to send data to

4. What data you want to send

Routing data is almost always part of the information from the step that triggers the routing. In addition, you can create a mapping that designates how data moves from one panel and arrives at its final destination in your system.

You will notice that both events and routings will appear as icons on Navigator maps because of the activities that trigger them on your PeopleSoft system. Workflow icons are not interactive, which means users will not be able to select them to start a process.

When you use PeopleSoft Navigator activities, you will be able to determine exactly which events and routings a given action will put into motion. However, you cannot alter or trigger certain events in any manner except for the completion of the step. When you select a specific event or routings icon, you will see both the name and description of the event or routing within the Navigator Business Process display.

Worklist Records

Certain similarities can be found in all PeopleSoft data such that all work items are recorded within the database tables. You have the chance to specify the table architecture as well as the type of data your system will store for each item as it develops the worklist record definitions.

Worklist record definitions have the same architecture as worklists and can designate a specific database table that is used for holding work items in the worklists. You can also add a row to a table whenever a user completes a work item and the system updates the row appropriately.

The methodology behind creating the worklist record definition is the same as that of any given record definition. When you develop a worklist record definition, you specify each work item and how it will look in your worklist.

Worklist record definitions are used by the system to connect each work item with its workflow-tracking information recorded in the PSWORKLIST workflow system record. You can also use the worklist record definition to show information about each work item in the worklist dialog box so that your users can choose the one they need. You can define a specific order for work items within your worklist or acquire the record affiliated with the work item so that your users can work on them.

Other elements on a worklist record definition include fields that are specific to the application that creates the worklist in the first place. Application fields are what your users will see in the worklist dialog box. You will notice that PeopleSoft includes these fields for the purpose of acquiring specific records from the PeopleSoft database when users need them.

When you deal with application fields in your worklist definition, it is important to remember that the system will use these values from specified fields in order to search for a given database record. This means you will have to include all the key fields for the search record in order to accomplish your task. You must remember that the field ordering is very important, because your PeopleSoft system sorts your work items in a wordlist type of field and then performs sorts on all the key fields within your record definitions too.

Message Agent Input

The Message Agent functions as an application server Tuxedo service. This means it can take data that originated from an external application and input it directly into a PeopleSoft panel. This allows you to add several automated steps to your business processes through the Message Agent, instead of having the user do the actual data entry.

Message definitions inform the Message Agent exactly how to correctly use the data it acquires from an external application. Message definitions connect an electronic document within a PeopleSoft panel. This enables you to establish a connection between the electronic document forms and the record field of its associated panel.

The Message Agent resides on the application server. It receives messages from various Windows-type applications within your networked environment. These messages permit external applications to input data to and download data from your PeopleSoft applications.

The PeopleSoft software executes the same types of edits and security checks, runs PeopleCode, and can ultimately have the Message Agent trigger a specific business event for your system. The Message Agent can then function to enhance the business processes in your system to deal with both PeopleSoft and non-PeopleSoft application users. This means that instead of having to enter information into a given panel, users can input data using any software package they like. In fact, through the use of APIs, users can use an interactive voice response system, special forms, or even an information kiosk to send data to the Message Agent and the application processor, which then place the data into a PeopleSoft panel group, application, or even the database itself.

External Application Connections

One of the nicest benefits that PeopleSoft can provide is that it can integrate third-party applications effectively into your computing environment. This can definitely act as a cost-saving maneuver, but users will be happier because they can use whatever software packages they like to input data into your PeopleSoft system.

In order to permit other applications to input data into a PeopleSoft panel, you must create specific message definitions in the Application Designer. These definitions can establish a map between the fields sent to the Message Agent and the field it receives from the PeopleSoft panel. To accomplish this information exchange, you must have unique names for your business processes, because Windows applications send messages to the Message Agent informing it which message definition to use. If two names are the same, the application will become confused and choose one over the other.

Whenever the Message Agent begins implementing a message definition, it must move to the associated PeopleSoft panel. When it arrives, the user needs to choose a unique panel name from the supplied menu and then choose an action mode from the cascading menu. Only then can data be input into the search dialog box.

The Message Agent acquires values from certain input fields and sends that information into the associated panel fields. The Message Agent also functions by duplicating data from the panel and sending it to the external application. This enables that application to ensure the results are correct so that the user can review the information and use it accordingly.

You can also work with fields that have scroll bars. When you come across a panel that has scroll bars, it will have several rows of data taken from your PeopleSoft database. The message definitions can help you determine if the Message Agent has the power to add, update, or delete existing rows you see on your screen.

The Message Agent can actually receive data from a variety of applications, including:

- Electronic forms

- Interactive voice responses

- Web applications

Should you wish to develop your own message definition, you must choose the graphical icon that best illustrates the type of external application that will be sending information to the Application Designer. You can develop one message definition for every one of the following you need to process:

- Form

- Query

- Electronic document

Message Agent Functionality

The Message Agent does not have the capability to transfer a file attachment to a PeopleSoft panel. If an incoming form has a file attachment from an external application, the program sends it to the Message Agent to see how it can cope with this extra information.

If a program from another software program detaches any attached file, it can place it in the directory determined by the DetachDir setting that is appropriate in your operating system setting. This program will often receive a unique name using a consecutive number method if more than one file has the same name.

When a file attachment is detached, it writes the name and location of the file in the FileName and FilePath fields, so if you need to record the filename and location within the database map, you need to look for those record files.

If a level type of scroll is inside a panel for a specific message definition, then one transaction can offer you specific values for more than one row present within a scroll. If you want values for more than one row, you will need to map greater than one field to the same level 1 record file. If you have a form that determines high-level clientele, you could have field names Client1 and Client2. Each of these fields would map to the level 1 record field High-Clientele. When the Message Agent maps these fields, it creates two rows in the scroll for each value in the form provided. This means you can name values for several rows, but only if they are level 1 scrolls. If you deal with level 2 or 3 scrolls, you need to process only one row at any given time.

Linking Processes to Applications

Once you have compiled your needed business processes, you must find a method of connecting these entities to your applications. Once you have defined your processes, you must determine exactly how the application panel will trigger business events. It is important for you to establish panels that can start these events, but in order to accomplish this goal, you must add application agents to the PeopleSoft panels. Note that the Application Agent is actually an online agent that works with the memory in your panel. It can determine when a specific business rule is triggered and will result in taking the best course of action. The application agent is composed of both Workflow panels and PeopleCode programs. These two items can designate business rules that the agent can use, so it knows the best action to execute.

PeopleCode

Workflow PeopleCode is actually one of the events that is affiliated with a record definition. In order to trigger a business event from a given panel, you need to implement a PeopleCode program to the Workflow event on your record definition for at least one table to which the panel group can write. This means that in order to trigger events from a course request panel, you must use the Workflow PeopleCode on your specific record definition. This record definition would be the first item that your panel fields deal with.

When you trigger business events from a panel that has scrolls, you must make certain you can add the Workflow PeopleCode to the record definitions at the proper scroll level. Should you need to add an event to the record definition affiliated with a level 1 scroll, the application agent executes it once for each row at the level. This means that the Workflow PeopleCode program can reference specific record fields from the record definitions at the same scroll level or lower.

Workflow PeopleCode programs often examine the data from a saved record in order to determine exactly what business process event it needs to trigger. This can include using the TriggerBusinessEvent command function to execute a given event. It is also possible to add the Workflow PeopleCode to any field within your record definitions. However, you must remember to add it to a given field that the program can reference. This means you may have to add the Workflow PeopleCode that triggers an approval process in your approval status field in order to accomplish your objective.

Conclusion

Knowing how applications can send electronic forms into your PeopleSoft system is an enormous help. Integration doesn't just deal with PeopleSoft applications; now you can integrate e-mail packages and create forms from a plethora of other applications from non-PeopleSoft users. This useful feature can help you achieve greater productivity and integrate people both inside and outside your organization.

In the next chapter, you will see how the Workflow administrator can work with your data effectively and exercise greater control over your Workflow applications.

Workflow Administrator

Workflow Administrator provides the capability to access, monitor, analyze, and control Workflow applications.

10

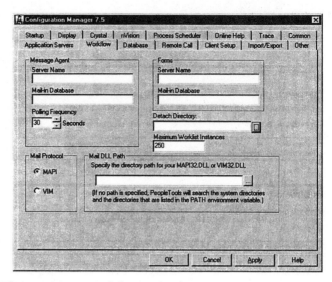

Figure 10.1 *Workflow Tab.*

Workflow Administrator

The PeopleSoft Workflow Administrator offers you the
ability to execute the following functions:

- Access

- Monitor

- Analyze

- Control Workflow applications

Figure 10.1 shows the Workflow tab within your
PeopleSoft environment.

Workflow Administrator Contents

The Workflow Administrator provides special tools that you
must have in order to ensure your Workflow runs well (see
Figure 10.2). This means that you must be able to define
roles, add roles, assign users' roles, set system Workflow
defaults, contact Workflow users, schedule Workflow agents

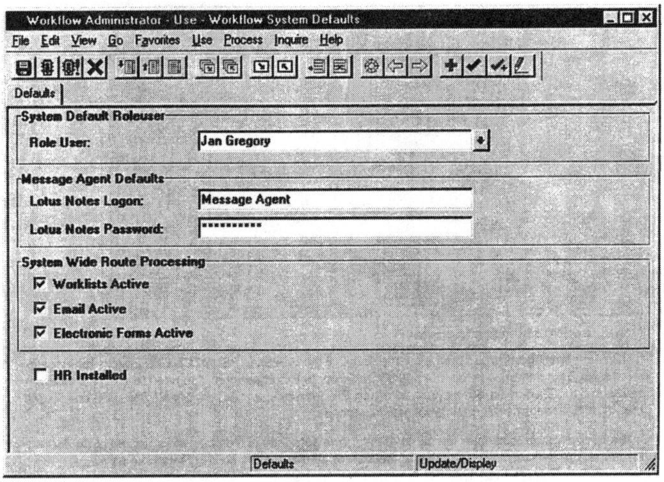

Figure 10.2 *Workflow Administrator.*

to run at specific times, and monitor the Workflow as it moves through your computing environment.

One of the most basic concepts is that you must know how to create a workflow. In order to do this, you must determine who is responsible for performing specific activities. You can then define users with respect to their role in your organization and in your workflow. This means that the manager must be responsible for approving requests from employees. Every hierarchical level in your organization deserves a different and unique role designation.

As your computer environment routes a work item from one activity to the next within your business process, the system will send that item to the user whose role fits the definition of that activity. In many cases, you can define a list of users who fit the role, while the system executes a query to determine who is the best user for a given work item.

Roles Defined

PeopleSoft workflow users are considered to be role users. This means that an employee's role user ID is analogous to having the same definition as their operator ID in many other sections of your computer environment. This definition allows the system to make a unique identification of specific users so it can tell which data a given user can access.

Role user IDs are used by Workflow, as opposed to operator IDs. This is because it needs a different level of information, as do the other elements of your system. Essentially, the system must know how to route work items to the user's e-mail account to contact him or her. In addition, the system must know exactly what the user's role is in the workflow. You can then integrate workflow users who are not PeopleSoft application users and don't have operator IDs. This is beneficial for any organization that does not wish to have PeopleSoft applications widely distributed among the personnel. Keeping tight access to PeopleSoft panels can enhance security and keep specified workers in responsible positions.

A group of users that perform the same type of work is a role. This can include analysts or managers, but the same business rules often depict users by roles, as opposed to names. If your organization experiences a great deal of problems, you will have to review what users are doing in specific roles; then you can determine why work is not getting done. However, this type of situation can also refer to a person's title, such as the executive manager of the HR department, which can be better than using that person's name. In this way, the right person in that position would always be responsible for approving a given task. This clarifies why the person's role is best suited for making an executive decision, as opposed to the name of a worker who may no longer work at the company. You can state rules in general terms so they apply to several departments, not just one. Finally, you need not change rules when a new person takes over the position, because the computer identifies a person's role, not a name. Therefore, you can designate specific business processes to determine which role performs a given activity. Workflow will define what roles a user can work in and what work items apply to that person.

A role can be as general or as specific as you want. You can assign a role to many people as managers, but only one role to the CEO. When you define business rules, you can make them more general so that a rule can apply in a variety of situations.

It is important to note that you can designate a role as one of two definitions:

- A fixed list of individual role users

- A query that selects one or more role users at runtime

Defining a role as a list of users can be achieved, but you don't need to worry about a specific person who can execute work assigned to a specific role. You can assign the management roles to be designated as a list of users. You don't need to worry about which person falls into that class and therefore the system can transmit the worklist of a specific concept to the first manager who chooses to handle the request, as shown in Figure 10.3.

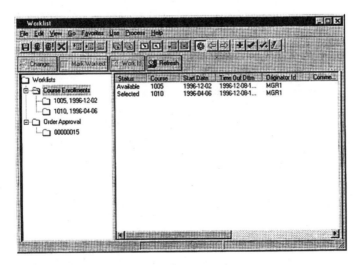

Figure 10.3 *Worklist.*

It is also possible to designate a role as a list of users who receive the same types of work items. If you have an automated worklist monitor, you can make the system send e-mail to several people from the worklist. This is especially useful so that every manager can get an idea of what the worklist entails.

In addition, you can designate roles as queries whenever you need to send specific work to different people at various times. The manager role can act as a query if you want to send specific requests to different managers. You can send this request to different people and different groups, however, especially if a different department manager made the request. When you define a role as a query, the system will try to determine who sent the work item. This determination is based on at least one of the fields from the panel group that triggered the routing. This means that the system will use information from its current context record to determine who will be the best users to work on it.

While we are discussing roles, it is important to explain that role users are people who are actively involved in your automated processes. These users may include people who do not have access to PeopleSoft applications but nevertheless need to send or receive data from the workflow processes in your system. If your processing workflow provides an electronic order form, then the person who receives those forms is a role user.

Some of the continuous tasks of the Workflow Administrator involve maintaining a list of role users. Role user maintenance means more than defining role user IDs; it means you make certain your users are assigned the proper roles for which they are best qualified. By doing so, you verify that you have each user doing the most appropriate work.

When you designate a person as a role user, you can inform the workflow system on how to contact that person. You can input various information on a user, such as:

- E-mail address

- User forms

- Work items routed through the system

Using this information, you can determine the following items:

- What roles the user is part of

- How to best use route controls

- Route control profiles

You can choose to designate a role user ID for anyone who wants to be involved in the workflow of a given process. This means you are not restricted to working just with PeopleSoft users within your organization. You can have customers, vendors, or users at other locations be assigned as role users; all they need is an active e-mail address to send and receive information to and from your PeopleSoft system. Figure 10.4 shows how an e-mail message can be entered into the workflow.

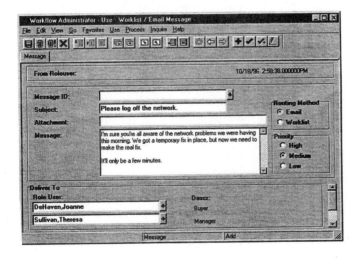

Figure 10.4 *Workflow E-Mail Message.*

When you use a route command, the PeopleSoft Application Agent can determine exactly which users to route work items to at any given time. This function provides a great deal of leeway so that users meet the qualifications for a certain role. The role user panel within the Workflow Administrator will allow you to search for role users based on certain qualifications, so you can use this role to determine which users are assigned work items for a given matter.

Role user searches are important when you need to use route controls. When you input different values for the route control parameters, you can determine how the right users can acquire the right work items; only then can you designate a user for a given case.

It is possible for you to archive role users even when the user will not be working with a work item for a certain time. However, you will want to make certain you can remove that type of information from your PeopleSoft system. Your system must maintain the role user ID that is connected with your data, but you don't want to route work items to a user. This means that when a user returns, you can reactivate the role user ID.

Whenever you archive a role user, you can choose to redefine the workload to another user if you need to. By doing so, you can determine how role user archiving takes place from the alternative role user option within the Role User Maintenance panel. You can then define an alternate role user so that the system can send new work items to another user, but existing items can be left alone. A role user can be archived so that the system can redefine your current work items and stop any other items from being forwarded to a user.

Workflow Messages

If you are an administrator who must often explain system information to users, you might need to send everyone on your list the background schedule or other messages every week to update them on the kinds of work their group must accomplish. Workflow Administrator can use a panel specifically for creating and sending this type of general message to your workers. This type of message can be sent through either e-mail or the user's worklists. When you are dealing with standard messages that must be sent out at regular intervals to all people, however, you may find it useful to avoid retyping the whole message each time. In order to assist your efforts, Workflow Administrator enables you to create default messages and routings for those messages as well.

When saving a specific version of a common message, this can become your default message that can be used many times any way you like. When you work with the Worklist or E-mail Message panel to send a message, you can choose from a variety of default messages that you can add or change in any way before you send it out to your workers.

You will find that default messages are a good means of defining the standard type of mailing lists. You can designate specific default messages that do not have default text. These messages can be addressed to a specific set of users that may include all of your managers or all of the people within a specific workgroup. When you wish to send the message to a group, you only have to choose the default message you want, add the text, and send it out to the chosen default group.

Workflow Agents

PeopleSoft provides several predefined workflow agents. These agents execute several types of monitoring tasks, including checking worklists for timed-out work items and finding remotely requested reports that need to be delivered.

The specific types of agents PeopleSoft uses depend on the applications in your software portfolio. As you create business processes, you will add your own types of database agents to the workflow as well. Just defining workflow agents in the Process Scheduler is enough to make them available, but this does start them running. You will have to send Process Scheduler requests that tell the system exactly when and where you will run each selected agent.

In order to schedule Workflow Agents, you need to make certain that your Database Agents are a part of your business process. This means that you must include Database Agents that have been designated in addition to several other predefined agents. You also must make certain you have an application that can monitor incoming forms, but you need only to schedule this type of application if you are permitted to submit forms created by other applications, such as Microsoft products.

The Database Agent must also inspect worklists for timeout items, which can be done by having your Database Agents look for worklist volumes. These agents are also referred to as worklist volume monitors. When you initiate your workflow, you must define these agents to run on a recurring time frame. Once you do this, you will not need to start the agents each time you want them to run; instead, you will only need to restart them if your schedule expires or you want to make some changes.

The Workflow Administrator must make certain that work items will flow correctly through your several business processes. Should any work item stop midway in your processing schedule, you will lose all of your automated workflow benefits, as shown in Figure 10.5.

In order to determine where worklist volumes can have trouble, the Workflow Administrator enables you to designate specific database agents that monitor for any overloaded worklists. These types of database agents are called worklist volume monitors. They look at your worklists that have more than a certain amount of work items. When it finds these items, it sends you a warning message. You must remember that each worklist volume

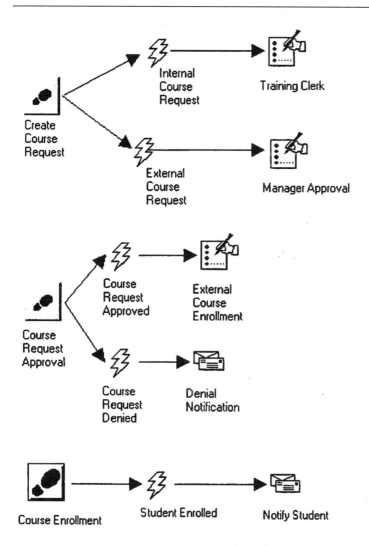

Figure 10.5 *Automated Workflow.*

monitor is meant for a specific worklist. This allows you to create at least one worklist for any item you need to keep track of at any given time.

Whenever you have defined a given worklist, you can choose to define a timeout condition. This type of timeout condition will determine how long an item is not worked on, prior to the system sending it to another worklist. Your system can use a database agent to examine each work item to determine if it has a timeout and the best way to forward that item within your organization.

Note that the timeout worklist is actually forwarded to the current user assigned to deal with it. Whenever a work item is late, it is added to the timeout worklist for the specified current user. This type of action can be seen within the Application Designer and is shown in the worklist attributes dialog section of the Workflow Administrator, as shown in Figure 10.6.

Working Online

You can examine the work items in your workflow with the Worklist Monitor. It doesn't matter where they are located, because it still gives you comprehensive status information regarding each item. In addition, it enables you to update individual work items and designate them to be worked on by criteria that involves:

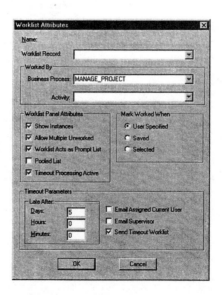

Figure 10.6 *Workflow Attributes.*

- Several different workers

- Changed status

- Editing of worklist entries

The Worklist Monitor can be accessed so you can search for specific work items. This access is founded on workflow properties that include operator systems so you can locate items wherever they are located in the worklist. In addition, you can also gain access with respect to certain worklist entry fields. You can even search for items inside a worklist too.

You will also find that the Worklist Entry Updates panel will allow you to reassign individual work items by modifying the operator assignment so you can reassign multiple work items. If you wish to redefine several items, this can be a very complicated procedure, but the Workflow Administrator gives you other methods for redefining work items:

- Use the Role User Archiving panel

- Reassign all work items from one role user to the next

- Reassign all the work of a role user you are presently archiving

The benefit of this last method is that you need not archive a user to benefit from this level of functionality.

The Workflow Administrator offers a set of standard reports that was created specially to offer status information about the work your users are doing. These types of reports involve worklist averages and provide an average processing time for completed work items. You can also use worklist totals reports that count work items by their status. When dealing with both of these reports, you can acquire information regarding all of your users for your business processes. You can also choose to concentrate your reports on specific users or certain business processes within your organization.

Routing Controls and Options

You can benefit from the following items by gaining increased usability when you deal with routing work items:

- Query roles

- Pooled worklists

- Non-Pooled worklists

The concept in using higher-level types of routing options is that the preceding commands do not always satisfy all of your needs for your PeopleSoft system.

Using additional routing options via the Workflow Administrator will give you several additional options that will enable you to designate complex specialized routing methods without having to know how to write PeopleCode.

The main idea behind route controls is that you can link application data with role users to advance your routing techniques. You can use this type of procedure whenever you need to customize several business processes in your PeopleSoft Financials software. In short, you can designate special route control types that are important in satisfying your individual business objectives.

You can specify query roles that allow you to return needed roles, but this is often difficult to accomplish. You can use the data from your panel group to trigger a routing, but only the proper list or role user ID can do it. In order to go from one item to another, you must know the architecture of your application data tables, but you need to write a few somewhat complex queries to achieve your goal. Even if you work with simpler queries, you will still have to locate a table that includes all the IDs you want to manage and join.

It important for you to make routing decisions based on detailed information. You may need to route items in various ways, according to the following types of criteria:

- Business unit

- Department

- Customer

- Vendor account

- Specific project

It is not an easy task, however, to locate the data you need in your database in order to connect role users to specific work items in great detail. Furthermore, these items are very unwieldy and difficult to use.

The Workflow Administrator allows you to specify certain route controls. These types of controls help you determine the specific aspects that you need to make your routing decision or they allow you to connect specific values with specific role users.

If you wish to route data to different buyers according to the specific vendor who gives you the ordered items, you need to determine the following:

- Which business unit has asked for these items

- Which department they are for

- How these different items interplay with one another

Only then can you specify a route control for items that include

- Vendors identification

- Business unit

- Departments

- Buyer range

- Buyer values

Route controls make the development of role queries easier and enable you to connect application data with role user information. You do not need to link several records together; you can just examine the role user table.

If you don't have route controls, it is next to impossible to determine if one person works with a specific vendor in your organization. When you use a router controller, you only need to inspect the role user definition to find out who is responsible for a certain vendor.

Route controls are also beneficial because they give you the option of controlling the routing that is stored on a database table instead of being pushed back in the query definition or within the complexity of PeopleCode. Should you need to alter the routing rules, only the user route control profiles need to be changed. This is helpful because you do not have to change the business process; you can only change the role queries or any PeopleCode that is involved.

Common Business Process

One of the most common forms of the business process is the approval process. Your workflow will give you a terrific means for supporting the approval flow. PeopleSoft has made the entire approval process much easier by offering the Virtual Approver tool.

Virtual Approver enables you to specify complex approval-processing rules. Thus, you can assign rules without having to write a great deal of PeopleCode. You can then specify your approval rules based on a series of panels within the Workflow Administrator. These rules are recorded on database tables that can be updated without having to refine all your business processes. This eliminates a great deal of trouble and helps you integrate information more effectively within your enterprise.

Finally, the workflow administrator gives you the opportunity to:

- monitor,

- access,

- analyze,

- and control workflow.

The Workflow Administrator can help you determine if a specific worklist has too many entries. If you discover a problem, you can define more staff and eliminate any backlogs that are present.

The Workflow Administrator can also speed the reporting efforts on your workflow. This can help you define where you need to focus your resources. In addition, you can determine exactly how much time each of your business processes will consume, which activities are the most time-consuming, and which worklists are overburdened. This helps you assign work so your organization does not suffer from a lack of human resources if a person is out sick or is taking a leave of absence.

Conclusion

Understanding how the Workflow Administrator plays a crucial role in your organization helps you more effectively deal with information flowing through your system. You can define roles, route information, and deal with business processes more easily.

The next chapter ties all of the previous chapters together and explains how you integrate third-party tools in specific applications. Understanding real-world situations is an important step in gaining an insight into the true nature of an integrated ERP solution.

11

Integrating Third-Party Tools

This chapter examines how PeopleSoft integrates tools with ERP applications including human resources and financials. We also look at the integration of Web interfaces for PeopleSoft applications and how they are integrated into their existing toolset.

What Are PeopleTools?

PeopleTools are an easy-to-learn and easy-to-use toolset
that can be used by:

- Systems analysts

- Business analysts

- Application users

All of these people can quickly execute the following
functions:

- Development

- Deployment

- Maintaining functionality

- Creating flexible business solutions

These solutions are designed to maintain functionality
and satisfy the individual requirements within your
business process environment.

PeopleSoft provides you with the ability to utilize
development tools to enhance specific functions or tools, such
as enhancing application customization or data management
tools. You can also use reporting and analysis tools to enhance
your information access and user productivity. Integration
tools are important in helping you support your workflow
and communicate with all your external systems.

Using Effective Interfaces

PeopleSoft offers Internet solutions that allow users who
only use your system occasionally to execute self-service
administrative tasks through simple Java applications that
were created for specific roles and user requirements. The
idea behind PeopleSoft's integration tools incorporates
functions that revolve around people. You can use role-
based Internet strategies so that your company can refine

both your business processes and enhance your level of customer service.

Automating Business Processes

You can automate business processes to enhance the limits of your PeopleSoft application. PeopleSoft offers several integration tools that can assist you in integrating third-party products into your workflow. The idea is that you can create an open network of:

- Applications

- Electronic forms

- Interactive voice responses

- Self-service kiosks

Several tools can be used in business processes. Both system analysts and application users can automate business processes in your organization.

Message Agent

The Message Agent can process messages that are sent to the PeopleSoft environment by external systems that include:

- Interactive Voice Responses

- E-mail

- Internet

- Intranet

- Extranet

- Kiosks

These systems also provide an Application Program Interface (API) that allows third-party systems to effectively integrate with your system in real-time.

EDI Manager

The EDI Manager is used to designate the data mapping for the electronic data interchange (EDI). In fact, EDI can be implemented as a general data migration tool that goes between the PeopleSoft system and your batches of data or files.

Workflow Processor

The Workflow Processor is a collection of online agents that both execute and support the workflow in your business processes. When business processes are defined, agents are created to execute business process tasks.

PeopleSoft Navigator

The PeopleSoft Navigator is the graphical browser that offers application users a graphical map of the business process they are working in. It provides users with navigation and selection options. Users can use these features to move through application panels by selecting the activities they need to do.

Database Agent

The Database Agent monitors your PeopleSoft database so it can identify any elements that need to be entered into the workflow to be processed.

Forms API

The Forms API allows PeopleSoft applications to send forms to an electronic forms package as part of a well-integrated workflow environment.

Worklists

A worklist is actually an ordered list of work that either a person or a departmental group can process. This list is transmitted to the appropriate person in a prioritized order.

This information is designated using the PeopleSoft Business Process Designer.

PeopleTools

PeopleTools defines the integration tools that PeopleSoft provides. These tools can create customizable solutions to manage information effectively. PeopleSoft provides highly effective interfaces that connect your system to the Internet to help you send information easily both internally and externally to other systems.

Internal and external users in your geographically diversified organization can use this one Internet solution to connect everyone seamlessly to your PeopleSoft environment. Administrative and upgrade tools make several tasks much easier, including:

- Workstations information

- New database platform migration

PeopleSoft offers security tools to control your access to certain applications and data. Developers can also access objects they can work with in your computing environment. Both information system managers and your support staff can use PeopleSoft's integration tools to increase your system efficiency and implement PeopleSoft applications.

Application Installer

PeopleSoft's Application Installer adds a significant level of automation to your application installation process throughout several client/server network environments. You can reduce your overall workstation maintenance and make navigation easier through:

- Hardware

- Database

- Connectivity

All these elements directly affect your PeopleSoft applications.

Data Mover

The Data Mover has the power to archive and retrieve data that is stored within your PeopleSoft application database. It is able to help you transfer data from one operating system or platform to another. The data mover is shown in Figure 11.1

Operator Security Controls

PeopleSoft Operator Security controls maintain and support your data accessibility levels that are provided to user classes throughout your entire company.

Import Manager

The Import Manager can load data into your system much faster than any other technique. When data is created by

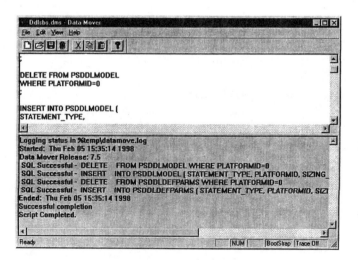

Figure 11.1 *Data Mover.*

external computing systems, it is imported into your relational database management system (RDBMS) server so that you will have information that can access your PeopleSoft applications.

Process Scheduler

The PeopleSoft Process Scheduler refines the performance of other routine tasks. It maintains time-based events that are received from distributed clients executed on either the client or the server.

You may also have to deal with specific batch processes or programs that the Process Scheduler deals with, including:

- Journal creation

- Payroll processing

- Voucher posting

- Reports that do not require user intervention

PeopleTool Advantages

PeopleTools has some important advantages. Programmers find it useful because PeopleTools reduces a great deal of problems present within old toolsets. PeopleSoft provides a computing environment that meets your organization's individual business needs. They offer an easy means of information access.

This technology platform and toolset comes with specific applications that are the cornerstone of your ERP (Enterprise Resource Planning) solutions. This simple toolset enables you to adapt your applications to satisfy your business needs.

Development Tools

PeopleSoft's development tools allow you to quickly create and deploy custom modifications to your system.

Administrative and Upgrade Tools

PeopleSoft's administrative and upgrade tools help refine several elements of your system:

- Implementation
- Operation
- Application upgrades

Reporting and Analysis Tools

PeopleSoft and Analysis tools help you perform essential tasks that include:

- Access
- Summarize
- Analyze

You can execute each of these tasks to manipulate information and promote an increased level of efficiency throughout your entire system.

Integration Tools

Integration tools are the heart and soul of this section. They illustrate exactly how you can tie together each PeopleSoft process for the purpose of automating business processes within your organization.

The primary PeopleSoft integration tools are listed as follows:

- OLAP integration
- Workflow
- Development tools
- Administration and upgrade tools
- Reporting and analysis tools

PeopleSoft-Supported Platforms

PeopleSoft and its associated applications can function on Windows 95/98/NT/2000 platforms. PeopleSoft applications also function with several Web clients.

You will find that PeopleSoft is working hard to provide functionality to its customers through nine of their business units. The most recent PeopleSoft release, 7.5, incorporates a higher level of functionality and more individualized solutions for specific industries that include:

- Communications

- Transportation

- Utilities

You can also use specific PeopleSoft projects to provide a high level of integration with Microsoft projects.

PeopleSoft Projects

PeopleSoft offers several applications that enable optimized resource planning and scheduling. PeopleSoft projects support an enhanced integration with PeopleSoft Asset Management for benefiting from asset-intensive projects. PeopleSoft Asset Management provides a good level of financial and tax accounting for fixed assets and operating leases.

Financial Services

PeopleSoft provides several financial services that satisfy specific requirements for:

- Global business practices

- Global procurement

- Business Event Manager

- Data integration tools from New Era of Networks (NEON)

Profitability Management

PeopleSoft also provides profitability management for financial services that offers a new application suite that provides functionality for:

- Banks

- Insurance companies

- Securities firms

Financial Products

Several financial products are provided from PeopleSoft that offer functionality including Activity-Based Management (ABM), Funds Transfer Pricing (FTP), and Risk-Weighted Capital (RWC).

Healthcare

PeopleSoft provides Materials Management for the healthcare industry to provide enhanced cost management functionality for:

- Stockless par inventories

- Procurement cards

- Electronic catalogs

- Bar code entry

Higher Education

PeopleSoft provides two applications for higher education. This concept is to provide support for

- Grants for research proposal development

- Award management

- Advancement to support fund raising

- Donor and alumni relationship management for universities

PeopleSoft manufacturing provides global manufacturing and supply-chain management solutions as well as demand-planning and quality applications. Several system enhancements to the remote configurator are also available as well as new embedded supply-chain order processing solutions for your computing environment. You will also find several integration solutions that can benefit financial and human resource operations in the retail industry.

You can achieve global functionality in all of your product lines to make it easier for a retailer to embrace new market structures. These types of solutions (or performance measurements) satisfy important retail requirements for activity-based management. Economic Value Add (EVA) elements fit very well into merchandise procurement and retail sell-through cycles. You will find treasury applications and stock administration applications that provide functions for retail application software suites.

Service Industries

PeopleSoft provides several functional enhancements to PeopleSoft projects that satisfy specific service needs from organizations that include:

- Complex project-billing and revenue recognition

- Optimized resource planning

- Deployment through integration with Primavera P3 and Microsoft desktop applications

One of the benefits you will find in PeopleSoft's Human Resources management that assists service organizations deals with

- Recruiting

- Deployment

- Compensating a multinational workforce

HR for Education and Government

PeopleSoft provides Human Resource management for both education and government. It enables you to keep records for all of the workers within your organization.

You can use PeopleSoft to create a global workforce profile that deals with your entire organization as a whole. You can benefit from your HR management for education and government through specializing in your decentralized office locations. You also benefit from cost-effective HR department centralization.

PeopleSoft HR offers a detailed application suite to deal with all of your HRMS (human resouces management system) operations so you can choose one application to institute a comprehensive solution. It can really allow your organization to grow by turning your employees into strategic advisors. These integration tools also help you automate routine tasks and allow your staff to concentrate on strategic planning.

PeopleSoft HR helps you provide several important services:

- Counseling

- Performance management

- Recruiting

- Compensation

- Skills tracking

- Successions planning

- Training

You can work on your HRMS to acquire a system that will grow with your company as time goes by. These solutions are scalable and work with your company to process complex HR demands in an open environment. This means you can have your choice of the following:

- Server hardware

- Operating system

- Database

The nicest part of this level of integration is your ability to work with standard graphical user interfaces. You can integrate standard desktop tools and switch from one platform to another. Other tools can also be supported to optimize your HR environment and your corporate information structure can be unified on a PeopleSoft technology platform.

PeopleTools gives you the chance to both effectively use tools and allow your enterprise workers to:

- Develop applications

- Implement applications

- Adapt applications

- Maintain applications

Development Tools

Development tools allow you to enhance your application customization. You can effectively use both administrative and upgrade tools for simple system administration. In addition, reporting and analysis tools allow application users to benefit from a growing number of integration tools to not only support internal workflow, but also to increase productivity on external systems that can be integrated into your system.

OLAP Integration

PeopleSoft integrates Online Analytical Processing (OLAP) tools that include:

- Cognos

- Powerplay

- Arbor Essbase

These tools assist you in reporting and analyzing important business information quickly and easily. OLAP enables you to report on various types of employee compensation. You have the option of integrating information within your HR database with external systems such as:

- Word processors

- Spreadsheets

- E-mail

- Fax

PeopleSoft has what they call a "cube manager" so that users can designate the data they need to extract into an OLAP cube. This enables you to quickly look at information from various angles so you can test your conclusions and initiate "what if" scenarios to compare alternative methods.

You can utilize multidimensional information in formats that can easily be read so that your managers can execute faster decisions and deal with competitive threats much more easily. You can also determine if any inefficiency exists within your system so you can make your business work smarter.

You will find that desktop OLAP is useful, as it can integrate Cognos's Powerplay OLAP tools with your applications. PeopleSoft has an integrated form of Powerplay that works together with PeopleSoft metadata trees so you can execute:

- Effective dating

- Translate values

- Work with security

You can use all of these features with PeopleSoft Query. PowerPlay also integrates with the Process Scheduler to automatically create cubes and can distribute them effectively.

PowerPlay templates work for areas that specify multi-dimensional analysis. This means that your HRMS can offer a PowerPlay template so you can analyze specific forms of data. You may choose to have accounting provide you with a form that enables you to analyze employee performance too.

The benefit of PowerPlay integration with PeopleSoft applications allows you to use applications to perform multidimensional analysis that is integrated within transactional applications. PowerPlay works as both the desktop OLAP tool as well as the presentation tool for use in data markets.

Data mart OLAP is also used to support multi-dimensional analysis on server database markets. The integration of Hyperion's solutions has provided an integrated Hyperion Essbase OLAP server with your applications. This level of integration lets you map data and metadata together into a Hyperion Essbase database so you can load data without the need to compile customer code.

OLAP templates tie all of these elements together because they help you benefit from everything discussed in this section. These templates use:

- PeopleSoft business models

- Industry sector knowledge

- Application knowledge

Multidimensional Analysis

Fraught with errors, multidimensional analysis is the most difficult task that you will ever use to maintain your database's synchronization with transactional data and metadata. PeopleSoft with Hyperion Essbase forms a unique integration to reduce the cost and number of errors found by changes in metadata as well as Essbase database updates. You can also automate the Hyperion Essbase load process by using the Process Scheduler.

Workflow

PeopleSoft has the power to integrate your workflow and refine organizational operations through:

- Refining business processes

- Automating administrative tasks

- Reducing paperwork

As you employ new people within HR management, you can start processes that deal with all of the employee activities that allow you to inform your workers about certain tasks that must be completed.

Workflow functions can be automated and can refine your business processes so you can accomplish the following tasks:

- Automate business processes

- Eliminate paperwork

- Reduce costs

- Increase operational efficiency

These PeopleSoft capabilities allow your system to completely support your workflow so you can enhance the range of tasks to be automated. You can allow your system to function with Workflow so that your applications can accomplish more work. Should you require a manager to sign off on a given report, your system can automatically forward the request to the proper person.

Value Workflow is important in eliminating time-intensive administrative tasks connected with paper flow in your company. This enables employees who execute specific functions to achieve more value-added work in your workgroups.

System workflow can also be optimized to improve your system power. It ties specific groups of information together so you can mine your data for new options and improve the business processes that form the foundation of your system's functionality.

Application Designer

The Process Navigation feature of PeopleSoft's Application Designer can establish graphical representations of your business processes. Maps can be viewed through the PeopleSoft Navigator to explain different activities you need to work on at any given time.

External users can be integrated into your system through non-PeopleSoft applications and can be added to the workflow process. These add-ons can be done using tools for gathering data from:

- Voice response systems

- Interactive kiosks

- E-mail

- The Internet

Web-Enabled Applications

The most prevalent theme within any enterprise is its capability to integrate Internet technology for assistance in distributing functionality across your entire enterprise. You can easily benefit from these applications and use their functionality within your intranet. Also, you need not install applications on every desktop workstation in your company. Figure 11.2 shows the PeopleSoft Web start page as the starting point in Web-enabled applications.

Instead of using various applications, you can use a Web browser to support operations that include:

- Human Resources research

- Benefits

- Payroll data

- Enrollment

- Training

- Job postings

- Online applications

- Update benefits

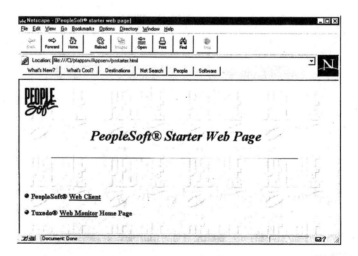

Figure 11.2 *PeopleSoft Web Start Page.*

You can also benefit from PeopleSoft's use of the Internet to enhance application functionality and information for several enterprise users. The Web-enabled applications are composed of two primary elements:

- Self-service applications

- A Web client

Self-service applications are created for users who only need to access the PeopleSoft system on an occasional basis, but that need to use Java Web clients to access enterprise data. These applications assist companies quickly and easily integrate cost-effective, distributed functionality in your enterprise for a diverse group of users through the Internet.

The intuitive interfaces that PeopleTools applications provide include the following:

- Employees

- Customers

- Suppliers

- Occasional users

These people can execute self-service administrative tasks that are unique to each person's role in your organization. This means that one worker can enroll in a specific program through the Web, while a vendor can update corporate information through your external Web server.

Self-service applications are not the same as applications created for function experts. These applications are used over the Web to offer simple applications created for the occasional users. They are good in that they do not require your personnel to have extensive training or documentation. These applications are connected to PeopleSoft's core business process solutions, including

- Human Resource management

- Accounting and control

- Supply-chain management

The benefit here is that they all use Workflow technology to complete their goals. They have been created using the same types of PeopleTools that form client/server technology, which means that all of the following processes are not duplicated through the use of individual tools:

- Edits

- Business logic

- Workflow processes

Self-service applications use the Web client, which is composed of Java applets that can be downloaded at will and executed on a standard Web browser (Netscape Navigator and Microsoft Explorer) since both of these platforms support Java. The Web browser supports an open system that offers a good foundation for enterprise solutions with the most diverse user community.

Using Web browsers eliminates the need to install specialized client software on every user's desktop. This means that applications are simply accessed through the Web browser. When changes occur, they occur for everyone involved instantaneously.

The Web client has been created specifically to give users functionality and information based on their individual roles within your organization. The Web client also incorporates Worklist and query interfaces. This means you can integrate any occasional users into the business process flow of your company while improving access to the information they need.

All data sent between the Web client and the application server is completely encrypted so that your security is heightened. Web clients can take advantage of PeopleTools server-service applications and can be used throughout the Internet or intranet with common elements that include:

- Business rules

- Workflow logic

- Security functions

The Web client was specially created to work with your corporate intranet so you can have the same type of look and feel as your GUI environment.

Open Systems

PeopleSoft provides an open platform that ensures you achieve a high level of performance on both local/wide area networks. They offer a three-tier transaction processing option that enables you to deal with several users as you support reliable network performance statistics on your corporate network.

You can also utilize powerful load-balancing and fail-over functions to make certain your Human Resource operations run well. You will also find in this chapter that PeopleSoft continues to provide two-tier functionality for any organization that has a local area network (LAN).

E-Commerce

Electronic commerce is an important tool for integrating your systems, as it provides you with the ability to refine your business processes and quickly respond to employee and business partner needs. It helps you reduce costs by using e-commerce strategies. These strategies integrate some important tools within your organization:

- Electronic Data Interchange (EDI)

- Intranets

- Interactive Voice Responses (IVR)

- Touch screens

- Interactive kiosks

- Electronic catalogs

- Workflow

E-commerce focuses on people and creating a reliable setting whereby users can combine content, business functionality, and convenience to create a powerful transaction processing environment that will take place across several tiers.

E-commerce strategies help create a user-centric solution that is intuitive enough to allow people to complete several business processes and commercial transactions over the Internet. The idea is that PeopleSoft creates e-commerce solutions based on the ERP e-business background that enhance their existing PeopleSoft application investment. PeopleSoft provides its PeopleSoft Business Network (PSBN) for electronic commerce. This is a business process that take place on the Internet. Therefore, centralized solutions function well for your network needs.

E-commerce refines your business processes enough that you can meet your organizational needs and keep costs down. The electronic benefits enable you to receive documents from the following sources:

- EDI

- Intelligent Bar Coding

- Intranets

- IVR

- Workflow

The beauty of this system is that you can electronically receive documents so you can:

- Refine quotes

- Confirm purchases

- Confirm receipts

- Confirm payments

You can use services like intelligent bar coding and do all of this with hand-held, wirelessly networked devices to automate data collections. When you do so, you effectively enhance count cycles and refine both the ordering and receiving processes. In addition, automating accounting helps increase your accuracy.

High-Power Integration

PeopleSoft's goal is to offer solutions that can provide a great deal of performance. This offers better processing across

- Systems

- Sites

- Components

This open system allows you to configure your enterprise so that you can best satisfy your company's processing needs, including:

- Distributed network computing

- Three-tier configurations for WAN

- Two-tier configurations for LAN

PeopleSoft provides you with details to create performance-tuning teams that can make certain all your performance goals are met. This section will provide you with increased details about how to assemble a performance-tuning team and how you can take advantage of their skills in making your system operations flow as smoothly as possible. Figure 11.3 shows how a performance team can assemble a checklist for refining your overall system performance.

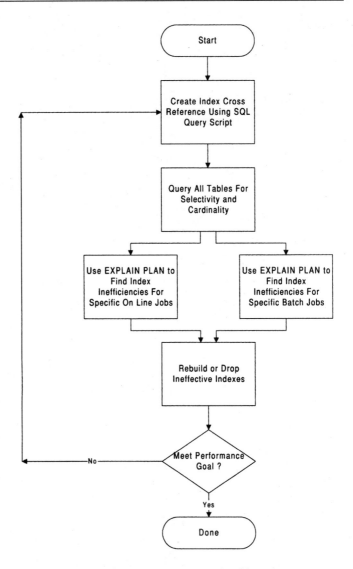

Figure 11.3 *Performance Tuning Checklist.*

Enterprise Management Applications

PeopleSoft's enterprise management applications enable you to view your organization as one entity. This means you can more effectively:

- Share information

- Collaborate on various projects

- Work together for agency goals

These solutions are useful in providing tools that you can use to respond quickly to change. In addition, your workers can exercise the following options:

- Sharing information between:

  - One project and the next

  - Departments

  - System processes

- Report information accurately

- Adapt to changes in business practices

- Institute emerging technologies

- Adapt and maintain applications

You have the power to convert information into a more productive environment so you can refine processes to

- Collect

- Process

- Monitor

These actions enable you to manipulate information in order to fully benefit from your client/server systems and from networks that provide useful information throughout the organization.

Workflow GUIs will help you create interfaces for self-service applications. You can also benefit from integrated financial applications in your enterprise just by managing:

- Core accounting processes

- Budgets

- Assets

- Projects

- Reporting

You can access important information and data to assist you in making effective decisions. You can standardize financial management so that you can accomplish the following tasks:

- Create accurate budgets

- Create accurate forecasts

- Manage analysis and reporting

- Record corporate information

- Access information regarding:

  - Purchasing

  - Depreciation

  - Insurance

  - Replacement

  - Disposal of Assets

You can customize programs to satisfy your corporate objectives and gain reliable statistics for strategic planning to provide data for all your departments.

Vendor Management

Automated vendor management allows you to use the Internet to make certain you can offer:

- A consistent environment

- Reduced redundancy

- A current status

- Increased accuracy

- Distributed requisition

You can increase management functions over the Internet and manage your enterprise so that you can deal with inventory and automatically renew any needs your company may have. Automation plays an important role in helping you take bids with enough flexibility to control workflow and deal with OLAP analysis.

Managing Workers

Management can process payrolls and provide accurate information regarding employee records at any given time. You can use "credentializing" to identify and analyze job skills throughout your organization.

Compensation for organization changes can be made across your entire organization. You can use this information to manage HR in the following ways:

- Hire employees

- Train employees

- Promote workers

- Allocate resources

- Retire personnel

- Track staff

- Update staff

- Report staff credentials

You can comply with the Joint Commission on Accreditation of Healthcare Organizations (JCAHO) and collect labor costs so you can perform detailed analysis and automate Fair Labor Standards Act (FLSA) calculations. You can also offer career-planning functions to help manage your workforce more effectively.

You can also minimize both the time and cost you need to manage your supply-chain or materials management processes. The Internet will help make certain all your information is current and will assist you in managing and planning for materials across your entire enterprise, regardless of whether or not you must supply several geographically dispersed sites.

Strategic Investment Model

The Strategic Investment model is helpful to your customers, so you can create more objective business cases that will allow you to support your technology. This tool is useful for increasing your return on investment (ROI) for several enterprise software options. It helps you satisfy the following conditions within your company:

- Improve inventory control

- Track assets from joint ventures

- Track certification, licenses, and credentials

- Connect with corporate goals

- Payback investments

- Deal with risks

This model is provided at no cost for 60 days of temporary licensing, so that your organization can see if this model is really going to help you.

Human Resources

PeopleSoft's Human Resources management lets you maintain where all of your people are within your company. It enables you to create a workforce profile that can be local or global, or even concentrate on one unit.

You can configure your Human Resources management so that your PeopleSoft HR implementations will redefine your HR approach. It doesn't matter whether or not you decentralize your environment or create a more cost-effective, centralized HR department, because PeopleSoft tools can support your entire workforce.

Your HR operations can be refined with PeopleSoft applications that are designed to work in an environment that can make workers into strategic advisors. These solutions help automate routines tasks so that you staff can concentrate on management functions that include:

- Counseling

- Performance management

- Recruiting

- Compensation

- Skills tracking

- Succession planning

- Training

HRMS enables you to form a system that can grow with your needs. The idea is to provide scalable facilities that deal with either a local or global agency with complex demands. The idea is that you can choose the best server hardware, operating system, and integration tools with your familiar desktop Windows environment. You can maintain all these things together and then upgrade to new releases.

HRMS solutions enable you to manage positions and momentary compensations. You can easily comply with regulatory requirements and process payrolls. You have the power to get accurate employee records as well as the information. The benefits from variable compensation allow you to be flexible in your organization so you can deal with workers and your network. You can view job lists and help provide career planning functions to manage your workforce effectively.

Public Sector

PeopleSoft works for the public sector by providing software that can tie together departments, people, and systems from across your entire geographically diversified organization. The idea is the public sector organization can maintain control over complex operations. Their solutions provide superior management of:

- Financial accounting

- Human resource processes

- Materials management

- Business performance measurements

You can also optimize resources and manage change in your enterprise applications. Your workers can exchange information, regardless of location. These enterprise solutions provide you with tools that allow you to respond to change on a moment's notice.

You can execute sound financial management decisions and help manage your core accounting processes at the same time. You can standardize processes as you create budgets and accounts to meet your needs.

PeopleSoft's asset management can protect your investment by processing and recording information for dealing with assets, including:

- Purchasing

- Maintaining

- Insuring

- Replacing

- Disposing

Effective dating is also important when dealing with public sector applications. This allows you to input transactions at any time before or after an effective date. It works by eliminating the need to input large volumes of data at peak times in your data cycle.

Materials Management

You can minimize the time and cost needed to manage materials as well as perform the following tasks:

- Increase efficiency

- Provide fast services

- Enhance vendor relations

- Manage inventory

- Track internal and external goods consumption

- Automate vendor management

- Use the Internet to enhance productivity

Healthcare

The benefit of PeopleSoft healthcare is that it can tie together all of your departments throughout your entire organization. PeopleSoft healthcare has better control over complex operations and provides superior management over processes such as:

- Financial accounting

- Supply-chain management

- HR management

PeopleSoft has tools that not only increase business performance but also optimize your resources. You can support changes through your organization and accomplish various objectives:

- Optimize resources

- Manage change

- Share information

- Collaborate on projects

- Work together for a common goal

These solutions include tools that allow you to rapidly respond and adapt to business changes.

Manufacturing

PeopleSoft provides a good way of unifying departments and systems in the manufacturing sector. This solution offers several methods and practices for both manufacturing and distribution that include:

- Made to order

- Assemble to order

- Make to stock

- Repetitive manufacturing

- Mixed mode operations

PeopleSoft creates applications that can grow with your business, optimize resources, and manage change. These applications allow your employees to both share information and collaborate on projects. PeopleSoft's solution offers goals based objectives that foster enhanced levels of performance.

Global solutions support manufacturing operations in several different ways:

- Geographically dispersed locations

- Different international currencies

- Different languages

You can access global functionality that supports operations in virtually any country. This integrates localized applications to provide country-specific functions necessary to expand your business process. They offer global capabilities that provides universal functionality for a multinational enterprise organization.

Production and Demand Planning

You can also balance supply and demand globally with demand planning, which offers accurate forecasting throughout your enterprise. You can use PeopleSoft production planning to schedule production so that you can optimize factory resources.

In combination, production and demand planning allocations can achieve the following goals:

- Enhanced forecasting activities with database and workflow technology

- Plan production and distribution using materials availability, capacity, and inventory

You can see how these plan modifications will affect your supply chain; therefore, you should avoid any unnecessary transportation, overtime, or delivery costs that may raise your prices in the long term.

Product Configurator

PeopleSoft Product Configurator makes it simple for you to gather the right customer order when it is first entered into your system, making your customers happy and reducing costs involved with reentering information.

Product Configurator allows you to

- Enable sales reps to prepare accurate orders

- Allow sales reps to create quotes right away

- Download complete quotes from a remote location

- Create production orders

- Route complete quotes directly to the ship floor

- Deliver products to the customer with his/her exact needs

- Use off-the-shelf costs

- Gain lead time

- Integrate into manufacturing and the supply chain

- Automatically create bills of materials

- Create component lists

- Route lists effectively

- Simplify production scheduling

- Refine order-to-cash cycles

- Quicken the distribution of new production information

- Accelerate execution engineering

- Executive price changes for configured orders

Deliveries can be made on time and you can also provide superior promise dates. PeopleSoft's order-promising capability satisfies demand by changing plans and allocating sufficient resources and capacity throughout the supply chain.

Order-promising applications allow you to:

- Establish customer order promise dates with respect to current supply-chain capacity and materials

- Reduce order-to-cash cycles by setting promise dates

- Evaluate inventory availability

- Evaluate raw materials availability

- Evaluate distribution constraints

- Evaluate transportation alternatives

Quality

PeopleSoft is excellent at improving quality and enabling your manufacturing groups to collect and share critical quality information.

PeopleSoft Quality includes several benefits that include:

- Automating labor-intensive tasks

- Improving communication with your enterprise

- Accelerating implementation

- Improving quality analysis

- Reporting by combining online data collections with your relational database

- Creating possible scenarios without effective information

- Identifying trends and addressing problems in manufacturing using real-time data

- Accessing information and creating reports on demand

- Identifying and controlling quality issues within your organization

When you implement a quality solution, you gain functionality for:

- Process configuration

- Statistical controls

- Process control

- Quality data analysis

Planning

You can plan more effectively in your supply-chain collaboration using PeopleSoft Quality. It coordinates planning and supports real-time communication with suppliers and customers. This tool plays an important role in your planning by allowing you to:

- Share forecasts with suppliers

- Request products

- Broadcast available inventory and capacity

- Reduce inventory through increased supply-chain coordination

- Provide customers with a reliable promise for a fast turn-around

- Deliver access to a Web-enabled system through embedded Web browsers

Transaction Management

You can also increase transaction management by providing transaction management capabilities that fit your enterprise needs.

These needs often include:

- Managing orders

- Supporting pricing promotions

- Purchasing (for better vendor management)

- Ensuring production is on schedule

Refining the Supply Chain

You can refine your supply-chain solutions by increasing the level of automation involved in:

- Order processing

- Purchasing

- Optimizing inventory levels

- Planning for resource utilization

All these factors can take place in real time. This means your supply chain can integrate effectively with financial management and manufacturing applications so that you can periodically allow for important financial updates. You can also benefit from adding the following components to your supply and distribution enterprise:

- Workflow

- EDI

- Internet/intranet interfaces

- Automation

PeopleSoft EPM

PeopleSoft's Enterprise Performance Management (EPM) analyzes transactional data from enterprise applications together with all of your other internal and external data sources.

In short, it will help you:

- Improve customer satisfaction

- Optimize ROI

- Reduce risks

- Maximize profitability at every level

You will find EPM includes components such as

- Enterprise warehouse

- Funds transfer pricing

- Risk-weighted capital

- Activity-based management

- Balanced scorecard

- Workbenches

- Performance measurements

The Integrated Analytical Application environment within PeopleSoft EPM offers a well-connected level of integration that ensures integrity is maintained throughout your entire enterprise. It has a modular design that increases the system value as time goes by, adding new applications as your needs change.

PeopleSoft EPM has an integrated set of PeopleTools that functions on one common platform. It has a main repository of enterprise information that forms the foundation for all EPM solutions in the enterprise warehouse.

The data warehouse gathers information within applications as well as other third-party information systems to be processed in the enterprise warehouse. Only then is it used for meaningful analysis and decision-making exercises.

You will find profitability to be important with EPM, as it will help you determine the cost of the requests a given customer will make each month and how it will affect your profit market.

EPM can analyze cost and profitability with respect to your:

- Products

- Product lines

- Customers

- Services

- Channels of distribution

- Geographic area

Strategic Cost Management

Strategic cost management systems in the PeopleSoft EPM can deal with several advanced cost management methods that include:

- Activity-based costing (ABC)

- Economic value added

- Target costing

  All of these methods assist you in determining

- Pricing

- Products or services

- Sourcing

- Product design

- Customer service

- Process reengineering

- The cost and efficiency of business processes

- Each department's role in a given process

  Balanced scorecards with relevant measures are important in PeopleSoft EPM. Companies can populate items with meaningful information to make better decisions that lead to greater profits. It is possible to track financial and operation data so that these balance measures will offer you a faster business view. You can determine how your customers view you and how internal politics affect your organization's ability to improve and create values.

Role-based information access, analysis, and reporting provide a great deal of information to a substantially large user base. You can use OLAP tools to execute desktop analysis so that users can stay ahead of operation performance.

You will find that PeopleSoft provides preconfigured reporting templates in a multiple reporting environment that includes:

- PS n/Vision

- Cognos

- Hyperion solutions

All these tools help for making better decisions.

Financial and Management Accounting

Financial and management accounting is viewed within the PeopleSoft EPM and is also integrated with several other financial applications that includes:

- The general ledger

- Payables

- Receivables

- Budgets

- Projects

- Asset management

These tools deal with both financial and management accounting processes. You will also find that financial statements and internal management reporting and performance measurement work together to create your financial management solution.

Planned/Simulated Activities

In PeopleSoft EPM, you can benefit from planning and simulation functions that are integrated into your system. This combination offers resource planning with respect to:

- Activities

- Business processes

- Products

- Customer portfolios

You can simulate business activities and help define the proper amount of resources you need to satisfy your business budget, performance issues, and business objectives.

Higher Education

PeopleSoft works very well in the field of higher education, as it has the capability to connect diverse departments, people, and systems in your organization. This software set assists you in managing the following:

- Student administration

- Financial accounting

- Human resources processes

- Access information

- Administrative tracks

- Optimizing resources

- Managing change

You have the flexibility to enable your employees to watch the organization function together and share information so that everyone can meet your objectives.

Student administration can be simplified with PeopleSoft integration tools that help campus management in the following applications:

- Campus community

- Student records

- Admissions

- Financial aid

- Student financials

- Academic advisors

The entire campus can work from one centralized data source for student administration. Students can collect and share data along with the staff. This eliminates duplicate records and creates checklists that monitor and automate activities in your organization.

Enrollment tasks are refined, as you can define enrollment restrictions and prerequisites. You can automatically enroll students from wait lists, managing them in several academic programs, and accelerate tasks that deal with records, including:

- Maintaining records

- Organizing records

- Automating records

This program can significantly help in the admissions process, as you can:

- Plan admissions

- Manage admissions

- Track admissions

- Handle recruitment activities

- Plan and coordinate different programs

- Specialize admissions requirements for individual academic programs

- Measure recruiting event success

- Measure admission decision success

Financial aid can also be effectively dealt with so that your programs can automatically match financial aid sources that are worthy of eligible students. You can automatically define budgets for students and even use Workflow for electronic data. You can deal with fund imbursement and integrate financial aid information with student financials. This program gives you several benefits that allow you to:

- Track student disbursements

- Charges

- Payments

- Provide access to account information

- Automatically create and track collection letters

- Automatically tag updates for student accounts

- Automatically create refunds

- Automatically generate processes for split or directed online payments

Academic Advisors

You can automate degree auditing and execute online comparisons of student programs. Thus, you can execute an analysis based on certain conditions, as opposed to academic programs. This means you can perform an analysis to customize academic programs for students in case exceptions to the rule are necessary.

Managing Finances for Education and Government

You can deal with financial information throughout your enterprise with respect to:

- Monitoring

- Administrating

- Analyzing

- Reporting financial information

- Collecting and accessing information

You can effectively deal with resources that have extensive analysis and reporting functions. This enables you to handle tasks that includes:

- Requisitions

- Vendor contracts

- Purchase orders

- Receivers online

- Integrating purchasing with other financial applications

- Integrating payable information with other business processes

- Creating a billing system that mimics your business operations

- Managing the flow of budget data with workflow technology

- Managing Assets

- Defining Calendars

- Determining depreciation periods

- Ensuring compliance with current tax laws

- Managing inventory

- Controlling stock movements

- Minimizing carrying costs

- Increasing service levels

The idea is that you have the ability to strengthen your advancement programs and refine business functions with PeopleSoft's advancement solution. This means you can service:

- Alumni

- Non-alumni

- Corporations

- Foundations

- Non-monetary contributions

- Functionality for all levels for users

- Records

- Dealing with commitments

- Analysis

- Searches

- Prospect information

- Planning events

- Implementing events

- Goals

- Fund-raising efforts

- Volunteer activities

- Organization membership programs

- Constituents' information

Grant Management

Comprehensive grant management allows you to grant accounting and research management solutions, such that grants are one-software solutions for large research entities that handle all sponsored management and accounting processes. You can benefit from e-commerce responses from the customer on demand. You can effectively reduce costs associated with e-commerce and integrate functionality from:

- EDI

- Intelligent bar coding

- Intranets

- IVR

- Touch screens

- Interactive kiosks

- Electronic catalogs

- Workflow

Federal Government

PeopleSoft offers a financial package for both the education and government fields that serves as the cornerstone for collecting and administrating financial data in your entire enterprise. This application is created as both an individual solution as well as a joint solution; both can work together to complete integrated business processes that include:

- The record to report function

- Plan and budget

- Manage employee expenses

- Asset lifecycles

This financial solution offers current information access and provides a solution that can support the financial management of one central unit for a multi-tiered governmental or educational computer environment. These financial packages provide your company with:

- Standard systems

- Equal metrics

- Multi-currency translations

- Common data sources

This main idea here is to collect information from different groups. If you have a geographically dispersed company, you can work together to produce current financial data.

By maintaining control and compliance, PeopleSoft's financial management package incorporates functionality to control how documents are handled with respect to:

- How records are changed

- How tasks are routed

- How requisitions are made

These solutions integrate compliance methods that include:

- Edit validations

- Approval routed by workflow

- Controller-defined exception parameters

Whenever you need to collect and record transactions and then report the findings, the Record to report option in the PeopleSoft general ledger can support:

- Transaction recording

- Management information

- Regulatory reporting

Multibooks are used to record transactions at the same time in multiple currencies. Multiple ledgers are used in the following areas:

- Budgets

- Forecasts

- Allocations

- Translations

- Revaluations

- Consolidation

Multi-currency support is offered that includes both translation and revaluation.

Conclusion

This chapter has brought together all of the concepts discussed in the previous sections of this book. You can see which roles each integration tool plays in your real-world environment so you can more effectively take advantage of each tool's features and functionality.

The next chapter completes this book by taking all of the concepts you have learned and applying them to sample implementations. You will understand how these integration tools not only work in real-world situations, but understand the future directions these tools are taking and how they will apply to your current and future organizational structure.

The Future of PeopleSoft Tool Integration

This chapter provides a nice overview of the specific tools highlighted within this book. We look at the future directions that PeopleSoft is taking in order to satisfy both its clients and end-users. We also examine what new tools are in development.

PeopleSoft Tools

PeopleSoft's PS/nVision reporting tool offers a detailed and accurate financial statement and report within a common spreadsheet format. PeopleSoft's tree manager gives you a visual hierarchy so you can organize and view financial information.

Asset Management

PeopleSoft's Asset Management allows you to administer the lifecycle of your assets. This tool integrates with other PeopleSoft enterprise solutions to manage and control your assets, including acquisitions, planning, and retirement. It provides you with several functions that include:

- Unlimited asset books

- Compliance with tax and regulatory requirements

- "What-if" scenarios for depreciation projection

- Asset capitalization upon invoice receipt of shipment

- Full asset leases

- Insurance

- Licensing

- Regulation

- Physical asset tracking

- Verification

You can deal with purchasing much more effectively with functions set aside for:

- Requisitions management

- Vendor contracts

- Purchase orders

- Receivers

- Online merchants

- Online purchasing solutions that provide a cost-effective procurement of goods and services

PeopleSoft also provides several integrated tools used for purchasing that includes:

- Sourcing decision support

- Reporting utilities

- Purchasing orders dispatched by fax

- Purchasing orders dispatched by EDI

PeopleSoft Expenses

You can effectively manage employee expenses with PeopleSoft's tools. You can automate your expense reimbursement process with global functionality that works with your personnel domestically and internationally.

Expenses can support several different functions such as:

- Support for several languages and currencies

- Detailed VAT processing

- Economic and Monetary Union Support (EMU)

- Accurate spending information that allows you to manage business travel costs

You have access to tools that can optimize your financial management packages so you can achieve better performance and more efficient working relationships.

Project Management

PeopleSoft's project management helps you satisfy management problems that engineering and maintenance organizations face. You need to have increased amounts of communication and coordination for any large-sized project, and doing so requires increased information access.

The secret is to optimize both production and delivery within your company. You need to communicate and coordinate tasks for all of your departments. The goal is to synchronize job requirements to your available resources. Then you can acquire cost approvals and establish actions for each worker within your enterprise organization.

Supply Chain

PeopleSoft offers supply-chain solutions for the enhanced management of assets from purchase to payment. You can use intelligent capital asset acquisitions and management so that your enterprise communications will give you sufficient tools to manage your assets more efficiently.

PeopleSoft's material management solution offers application modules for the following industries:

- Purchasing

- Payables

- Projects

- Budgets

These projects are literally a cost-staging area that reflects all of the costs pertinent to capital assets. You capitalize assets with respect to certain creation or completion stages.

Asset management supports information about your capital disposition and gives you grouped assessments that process retroactively for long-term projections. Asset management also provides the ability to track capital unitization for projects with rate recovery for processes that can be repeated. You can use joint ventures through mass group assets to deal with depreciation or other corporate assets.

General Ledger

The general ledger provides you with options for gathering information. This increases your analysis abilities by providing you with account applications that are integrated into your business tasks. They work to help you in the following ways:

- Manage cash disbursements

- Optimize your cash flow

- Deal with budgets

- Integrate data from other applications

- Plan budgets and forecasts

- Dealing with expenses

- Control reimbursement process

- Merge information from several financial applications

  Cash management can perform the following tasks:

- Analyze cash position

- Forecast future position

- Maintain bank relationships

- Execute automatic bank reconciliation

- Start payments and cash transfers

- Function as an in-house bank

Shared Services

Business workgroups work together to serve geographically dispersed users without having any networked flow of standard information. This means that PeopleSoft provides enterprise solutions that help you grow into multiple data centers that have different systems with formerly incompatible practices. All of your business units can concentrate on business without having to worry about working on routine administrative tasks. As a result, this software assists you in integrating shared services throughout your organization.

When you use the shared service model, you are taking your best purchasers and processes so that you can manage purchasing throughout your enterprise. This means you can acquire superior levels of performance that have better discounts pertaining to your organizational needs.

In an international company, shared services can be very important for intra-company operations that create major savings in all related business operations. This is an important model to integrate within your organization so you can be certain your PeopleSoft solution is working well for your needs.

Supply-Chain Planning

Supply-chain planning assists you in managing your complete supply chain through an informed decision-making process. You can use this integrated software selection to allow suppliers to satisfy customer demand, while you:

- Reduce inventory

- Improve throughput

- Provide on-time delivery

Supply-chain planning offers a detailed set of applications that helps you enhance several of your important services, such as:

- Production

- Distribution

- Implementation

- Information access

- Supply-chain information

- Forecasting

Demand Planning

Demand planning enables several users to work together as one unified group so that they can do some forecasting. These groups will use multidimensional databases as well as integrated workflow.

Demand planning moves the enterprise plan and assists your ERP system by forecasting demand with respect to:

- Order history

- Economic indicators

- Employee input

- Suppliers

- Customers

The goal is that you can produce and deliver products on time. This means you have some excellent information to determine exactly when and where you can produce and distribute products with respect to the availability of ingredients, such as:

- Raw materials

- Aggregate capacity

- Finished goods

The goal behind enterprise planning is that it effectively integrates with PeopleSoft production planning so that planning at the factory level meshes well with your standard enterprise plans.

Reliable Order Promising

It is possible to create reliable promise data for customer orders through your enterprise system. You can ensure that items are delivered on time by determining which available materials and capacity exist within your supply chain before setting a promise data for customer orders.

Order promising assists you in determining the factors that dictate your ability to supply products, including:

- Evaluate inventory

- Raw materials

- Disruption restrictions

- Transportation

- Alternatives in your supply chain

- Integrate customers directly into the planning process

Collaborative Forecasting

Collaborative forecasting is part of the PeopleSoft supply-chain collaborator. It allows cooperative planning as well as real-time communication with both suppliers and customers. This means you can share forecasts with:

- Suppliers

- Requested products when needed

- Broadcast-available inventory

- Broadcast-available capacity for customers

You can better coordinate your supply chain so you can effectively reduce inventory as you provide customers with reliable promise data and deliver items much more quickly.

Balanced Inventory

Balanced inventory helps establish the balance between inventory and replenishment. This is part of the PeopleSoft enterprise planning that enables you to figure out your product availability and create planned orders. This means you can effectively define your priorities and create optimal inventory allocation according your what your customers need.

The goal is to get the right material at the right price. You need to correctly determine all of your procurement requirements. Then you can interface with PeopleSoft's purchasing modules from its inventory and order management processes. This allows you to effectively achieve the following goals:

- Manage requisitions

- Manage vendor contacts

- Manage purchase orders

- Deal with receivers online

- Automate sourcing facilities

- Automate bulk purchasing through preferred vendors

Dealing with Inventory

You can deal with your inventory and control the variability of your products and services throughout your enterprise. The types of items you can control using PeopleSoft's integrated tools that:

- Control stock movements

- Reduce inventory costs

- Improve customer server levels

- Manage data collection (bar-code scanning and RF devices)

- Material movement

- Material tracking

- Material recording

You can use automatic material replenishment to ensure you have proper materials in stock and that they can be replenished quickly after you have consumed your current inventory.

Materials management enables you to create replenishment requisitions based on several factors, such as:

- Current stocking levels

- Economic order quantity

- Reorder points

In addition, you can receive and store good uses of the procedure in storing and processing your inventory. You can review and choose alternate storing plans with respect to several elements, including:

- Match

- Spatial match

- Empty locations

You can also efficiently track goods and collect real-time information on both the locating and status of material within your supply chain. In addition, you can get your enterprise system to accurately track usage patterns.

Automated purchase-order processing is also useful in this arena, as you can use it to approve purchase orders online. In addition, you can convert low-stock levels in purchase orders automatically and benefit from integrating tools that can optimize your materials management system.

Global Functionality

PeopleSoft integration tools work globally to support cash management throughout several financial accounting variations. It gives you functionality to deal with multiple entities and multibooks so that you can collect and manage various currencies and accept multiple payment methods too. The goal is that you can support several methods and international assignments for various languages.

PeopleSoft has provided international functions for its global financial accounting suite of applications. This level of support is used for counties that includes:

- Latin accounting models

- Germany

- Japan

- Brazil

You can also benefit from using the Economic and Monetary Union support (EMU) that is included in PeopleSoft version 7.x. This version can deal with several business processes that are directly affected by the euro currency, such as:

- Multibooks account functionality

- Parallel running

- Multi-currency capabilities

Automatic Integration

PeopleSoft provides you with automatic integration on multiple platforms and diversified applications. You can quickly integrate business applications with financial applications, such as:

- The general ledger

- Pre-format integration libraries

- Transforms and posts

- Business events

- Financial applications

You also can integrate legacy systems and scale all of your computing systems to grow with the needs of your company while meeting the needs of each department.

Business Logic

PeopleSoft's business logic allows you to:

- Define

- View

- Modify

All of the features work with your accounting and reporting rules within one centralized location to reduce continuous maintenance cost. You can simply use your business rules throughout your enterprise and execute changes to applications operating in various places. Thus, you can maintain business logic via GUI interfaces and provide control to those users who know your business information needs.

Financial Management

PeopleSoft provides you with smart financial management for your accounting and control integration procedures.

You can provide functions for elements within one software program:

- Report financial data
- Consolidate financial data
- Adapt accounting architectures for any corporate changes
- Refine the budget cycle
- Automate the budget cycle
- Distribute accurate data from one department to the next
- Utilize multiple ledgers
- Use an alternate account
- Administrate asset lifecycles
- Deal with acquisition planning
- Retirement

The goal is for PeopleSoft to provide a series of advanced reporting analysis tools. These tools assist you in implementing procedures for:

- Executive development
- Succession planning
- Evaluation competencies
- Maintaining your competitive edge

Project Management

PeopleSoft's project management provides you with several integrated tools that provide you with the ability to:

- Create assets
- Create project processes
- Access project information

The goal is to provide the power to integrate your project management throughout your entire enterprise. You can integrate several applications as well as third-party project management systems. This will establish a enterprise-wide solution that will be useful for your project management responsibilities.

Project management is actually a centralized storage facility for project-specific items that include:

- Financial information

- Distribution

- Labor information

Several modules are included within this category of PeopleSoft integration tools that includes:

- Projects

- Purchasing

- Payables

- Expenses

- Assets management

- Inventory

- Time and labor

- Payroll

- Budgets

You can use this information to support product information without experiencing much difficulty. Project management can reduce several time-intensive tasks:

- Data entry

- Refining the addition and maintenance of projects

- Continuous project status updates

- Project schedules

- Costs

Project management helps you make better decisions through its strategic analysis. It offers you financial tools with the roll-up function that enables you to analyze business projects through multiple dimensions that include:

- The customer

- The geography

- The industry-sector

- The business unit

You can look at possible what-if options that enable you to examine the financial impact of several business conditions that includes:

- Reorganization

- Mergers

- Acquisitions

- Divestitures

Project management helps you maintain accurate project budgets. You can refine your project budgeting process so that you can prepare detailed, multi-currency budgets that allow you to manage your budgets and control your financial operations. In addition, you can benefit from historical budgets and project data so that a more accurate budget can be created for your organization.

You can bill your project costs easily in this architecture. Billing is seen as one billing engine for your projects. You can also enhance cash flow by establishing more billed items. You can achieve greater speed through the acceleration of the billing process through automation that includes an electronic data interchange, so you can inform personnel about costs for your projects and explain your invoices more easily to customers.

Another benefit is that you can specify which personnel work on your projects. This helps you successfully balance the supply of and the demand for your labor costs. This is where human resources management components allow you to work with people in your projects.

Utilities

PeopleSoft offers a solution for utilities that deals with a globally diversified enterprise. You can even satisfy global competition and deregulation with enhanced services at a reduced price. The goal is to assist you in managing your enterprise as one integrated entity that connects:

- Employees

- Suppliers

- Customers

Basically, you are offered a global solution that can deal with operations regarding different locations, currencies, and languages. In fact, you can acquire global functionality that can support operations regardless of your country. You can use this framework to localize applications and provide functionality that is specific to the country with which you are working. In addition, you are provided with a global functionality that offers you the basis for your global organization.

Managing Customers

PeopleSoft offers a customer management information system for its utilities. Some of the features that this functionality offers include:

- High-volume billing

- Accounts payable

- Processing contracts

PeopleSoft integrates CIS Plus (a customer case solution from SPL WorldGroup) to accomplish the following:

- Add new products and services

- Modify existing products and services

- Automate time-consuming processes

- Increase speed

- Increase accuracy

You can also run what-if scenarios to optimize your business performance and effectively collect data. This gives you a better means of dealing with purchasing trends and patterns. You can also effectively work with new products using information collected from your customers.

Performance Measurement

PeopleSoft's performance measurement is an effective means of analyzing your profitability as it maintains important performance indicators. By using it, you can more effectively deal with cost and profitability based on several operation dimensions.

Transportation

PeopleSoft offers transportation functions for a global environment. You can use these solutions to deal with global competition and deregulation. These functions can help you expand services, lower prices, and assist you in managing your enterprise as one centrally integrated environment that globally connects employees, suppliers, and customers.

Global transportation solutions support your operations in several locations, currencies, and languages. These solutions provide functions that can support operations in any country. This structure allows you to localize your applications to offer country- and industry-specific functions and a centralized repository can deal with local functions in your enterprise.

Treasury Management

Treasury management can be integrated into your daily operations and is helpful in performing tasks that includes:

- Planning

- Processing

- Reporting requirements

- Refining and automating business processes

- Structuring user-defined trees

- Position analysis

- Providing template panels for financial tools

- Adapting the system to reduce costs

Treasury departments need tools so they can quickly deal with changing requirements in multiple locations. PeopleSoft's treasury management assists you in managing your core treasury operations at one central point. Thus, you can adapt your systems and grow over a period of time. The idea is that you will be able to use position analysis and cash position worksheets to deal with templates for financial elements. Your system changes so that you get more life and less ownership costs over the long term.

Service Industries

PeopleSoft offers a solution for service industries through a global software solution that connects:

- Diversified departments

- Personnel

- Geographically dispersed computing systems

PeopleSoft's solution has the power to integrate the following entities:

- Financial information

- Human resources

- Supply-chain management

- Support for your system

- Change management

The benefit here is that you can effectively optimize your resources and support global enterprise management changes that will permit your employees to view your company as one central unit. The goal here is to benefit from project information from various departments and systems. You'll be able to report on accurate information and adapt your system to changes present within the regulatory enrollment and business practices. PeopleTools will help you utilize emerging technologies and integrate them into your system.

Competency Management

Competency management can play an important role with your employees, as it works to optimize your organization's skills and performs the following tasks:

- Measures workforce performance

- Plans and executes training programs

- Refines employee skills

Competency management solutions assist you in determining how you can reward those workers who have helped your enterprise succeed. You can also deal with individual competencies with respect to:

- Position

- Project team

- Job requirements

Each worker's ability to meet certain requirements can be managed. You can also integrate training and administration applications so that you can hone your training efforts to merge skill sets with your corporate goals.

Recruitment

You can also manage recruitment by creating and maintaining job requisitions for qualified applicants and employees. When you deal with internal and external positions, you can schedule interviews and track results by managing recruiting expenses.

You can also manage compensation by retaining valuable workers and reducing the amount of employee turnover. This means you have the power to:

- Set salary guidelines

- Plan salary administration via:

  - Geographic location

  - Currency

  - Company

- Coordinate performance reviews

- Increase salary based on time with the company

- Track salary grades

- Maintain current salary plans

PeopleSoft Select

PeopleSoft Select was created specifically for medium-sized companies that must deal with end-to-end packaged solutions. Select offers you the ability to receive everything you need for purchasing and implementing your integrated solution. The Select software package incorporates application software for

- Human resources

- Financial informations

- Distribution management

- Hardware

- Operating systems

- Databases

Select offers comprehensive implementation service and support that deals with an implementation program called SelectPath. Select permits you to gain a faster rate of investment (ROI) by providing you with implementation services that deal with project management and support tasks.

SelectPath is a rapid implementation schedule that reduces the implementation cycle without eliminating system power. It includes several benefits:

- Reduced cost

- A fixed-bid approach

- Refines the implementation process

- Offers the least disruption to your business

SelectPath uses all the best practices that PeopleSoft has learned from its implementation experience. This experience resolves around individual customer needs. You can benefit from using transparent processes that define what you intend to deliver and reduce any expensive miscommunication.

SelectPath implementation centers are in existence to ensure you are provided with one-stop shopping and don't need to deal with third-party vendors. In fact, Select enables you to effectively deal with core business processes and work with both PeopleSoft and their select partners for your integrated enterprise solution.

Conclusion

This book has examined various integration tools. Many tools have been detailed so you can determine what kinds of benefits you can achieve.

PeopleSoft provides an effective ERP solution that is competitive in all industry sectors. The most important part is that it has an open architecture. You can integrate non-PeopleSoft applications, work with PeopleCode easily, and utilize a Java-based Web environment to work with your system in a friendly and intuitive manner.

It is my hope that this book has helped you understand how the PeopleSoft solution was formed, the importance of integration tools in your ERP environment, and not only what these tools do, but, most importantly, how to use them in your ERP environment more effectively and achieve a greater productivity for your company now and in the future.

Index

Boldface numbers indicate illustrations.

About the Author

Mr. Miller is a well-renowned analyst, consultant, and author. His work with many Fortune 500 companies has placed him in the top of his field. Stewart is the President and CEO of Executive Information Services, a research and consulting firm which has consistently demonstrated the ability to increase its clients investing power and provide a unique and fresh insight into all IT marketing trends. Mr. Miller's research and analysis strategy reports have become an invaluable resource for his clients. Best known as an "efficiency expert," Mr. Miller has ascertained success for his client's endeavors and is an integral part of any mission-critical IT decision-making process. Mr. Miller can be contacted via e-mail at: Miller@ITMaven.com

—